John Adrian Short

Bins, Benches & Broken Bikes

Published by

MELROSE BOOKS

An Imprint of Melrose Press Limited
St Thomas Place, Ely
Cambridgeshire
CB7 4GG, UK
www.melrosebooks.com

FIRST EDITION

Copyright © John Adrian Short 2010

The Author asserts his moral right to
be identified as the author of this work

Cover designed by Jeremy Kay

ISBN 978 1 907040 61 0

Printed and bound in Great Britain by:
CPI Antony Rowe. Chippenham, Wiltshire

Jamie • Danielle •

for

Ceridwen-Siân • Serên

&

Ashley

Contents

Prologue
Blood on the Pillow

I was lying in bed in a two-berth caravan built in the late sixties. The caravan was a bit younger than me but slightly more battered looking, with windows which never shut properly, and a door permanently bent out of shape. The only electric luxury I had was a lamp, well, a bust-up Renault 5 nearside head-lamp 'taxed' from one of the seventy or so old cars and vans which littered the scrap yard, or *ferro-velho*, as they are called in Portugal. My electric came from a couple of old car batteries, which I would charge up either weekly or when they lacked the power to operate the car radio and the two mismatched speakers roughly wired up together.

Today was different. I began waking from another alcohol-inspired kip and knew it must be Sunday because I couldn't hear Portuguese voices or engines outside of my 'hutch'.

Sundays in the Algarve are easy: nothing gets done except for family stuff and socialising, and this place was not any holiday destination people associate the Algarve with.

Dehydrated, I tried to lift my head to look for an immediate nicotine fix off the shelf nailed to the back of an old wardrobe next to the head of my bed, which straddled the front of the van. As I leaned over, I found the pillow stuck to the left side of my head!

Then last night's memories and the pain that the anaesthetic of alcohol had numbed began getting louder. I had gone to sleep in the blood all down the left side of my face, which had trickled down from my left eye socket and from the abrasions running down my left cheek. Slowly peeling the pillow from my face pulled the congealed blood away from my skin, allowing more blood to trickle across the first layer and onto the pillow and bed-sheets. This process took a few minutes before the pillow was off my face. I then got up off the bed and staggered across the cold floor of this little caravan for a pee outside, not before banging my head on the redundant lamp fixture stuck in the middle of the roof! This was a daily occurrence.

Still coming to terms with the previous night's events, I began to decide on a course of action at that moment which would take me on a journey across three southern European countries on stolen pushbikes, and with no money, decent food or any shelter. This journey was literally life changing and necessary. Back in the UK, I was facing jail for a couple of years at least for a Section 47 assault charge, several charges of criminal damage, and the theft of a truck, all on 1 January 2007.

I had built a sort of 'half-life' since arriving in the Algarve at Faro airport on 9 January 2007 with about thirty-five pence in my pocket and the clothes I stood up in. Behind me were bad memories and then nine days of roughing it around the docks of a cold, wind-and-rainswept Liverpool after driving from north Wales and dumping the lorry near Bramley Moor Dock; then finding a cash-in-hand job earning peanuts, to blow it all on beer and a one-way plane ticket. I ate with fellow homeless in the Sisters of Mercy on Seal Street, where I had spent many good nights out in recent, better times.

Not even realising the reason why everything had gone so pear-shaped up to that point, I was going to realise just how drink and recreational drug use creep up on you and wreck your judgement so much that one day you sit and total up the wreckage of your life and the damage you have done to others as well as to your own life.

Despite what had recently happened, I was still escaping into alcohol and dope to numb the memories. I hadn't yet the 'bottle' to deal with them. I hadn't suffered enough. That was going to change.

Chapter One
Julio's Scrap Yard

Julio's scrap yard was on the outskirts of a town called Almancil. I loved it because it was devoid of mobile phones, bills, supermarket food, tax returns, laptops, hire purchase payments, mortgage payments and stress – in fact, any of the modern-day things that we are forced into thinking we need today. It was similar to returning to the complete lack of responsibilities I once had as a working teenager in the eighties, shortly after leaving school. Yet though this was 2007, even the surroundings looked circa 1975.

I could dissolve into anonymity here forever if I wished to, no questions asked. For a start, it was difficult to find and if you did manage to find it, no one spoke English

"Well, where's it by then?" asked Dangerous Brian. "Is it near the carting place?"

I turned and grimaced at him.

"Why do you want to know where it is?"

"Because Jilly wants a strut for her Jeep."

"Well, it's just past Pequino Mundo, then turn right and look over to your left into the olive grove field," I explained. "Anyway, why are you after bits for Jilly's motor? She's already asked me to get a strut for her."

"That's just a dead end, isn't it, or—"

I cut him off, explaining that it would be easier if I got the strut for Jilly because he would never find the yard or the strut, but didn't explain to him that I knew he had enough work as an ad hoc builder and I needed the mechanical

1

jobs more than he did. Besides, Jilly had invited me out for dinner if I did it, and food was more of a draw than money at this time, especially when an attractive lady with a villa invites you.

The yard which was about fifty metres across, was in a field about two metres beyond the back road towards Quarteira. It occupied about a third of Senhor Morano's rough stone-strewn farmland and had metal fencing surrounding its borders – the kind of cladding that comes from dismantled factory buildings. Senhor Morano was Julio's father-in-law and lived in a house across the field to the east, next to the road. If you drove past and blinked, you would miss the scrap yard and buildings unless you had local knowledge.

The scrap yard contained the cars and vans that the larger, more organised scrap yards would otherwise have crushed up and sent to Faro docks to feed the demand for scrap metal, largely coming from China. Apart from a few classics – a couple of VW splitties, some old left-hand-drive Minis and an old Peugeot 403 in black – the motors were really junk mainly: not quite old enough to be classics and not new enough to fetch in a roaring trade unless you loved old Ford Sierras or Audi 100s and suchlike.

My job was to strip one car per day and do the occasional repair on old motors that belonged to Julio's friends and acquaintances, or on the skint local farmers' bangers. Great fun, but one motor per day was asking a lot on a hot day. OK when the motors were small like a Fiat Punto but a bigger motor could make me sweat, especially when trying to remove the underside stuff. Mostly I would tip the motors on their side, using steel bars and jacks. If I was short of work I had to strip a huge pile of gearboxes and engines after dragging them about half the length of the gravel-covered yard on a slight uphill to the roughly tamped concrete outside the workshop, which was an oversized garage with a corrugated canopy long enough to enable work on a motor in the rain. The rain is regular in the winter and the mound of engines and gearboxes next to the nearby fence never seemed to diminish, even when two or three of us were stripping them for their respective alloy steel and brass parts. Rain-and-oil-soaked metal ain't a nice environment to work in, and rain is all it seemed to do for the first fortnight or so here.

In return for this work, I got free board and lodgings, meals and beer (within reason) from the ramshackle bar, built out of scrap, next to the garage. Onto this bar the kitchen and scrap-covered patio was thrown up, mainly from breezeblocks and anything which was to hand at the time. Next to the corrugated-sheet-covered patio was Julio's 'house', which was an old Portuguese coach, where he and his wife Maria and daughter Retina lived and slept. Next to the bus were three old caravans, and behind them, a wooden shed. Three other fellas lived in the caravans but never in the same caravan for more than two nights in a row. They were Shiko, whose real name was Francisco, and Jacques and Silfostheen. Julio and Shiko looked like Spanish revolutionaries from the old days. All they needed were criss-cross bullet belts draped across their chests. They had those 'Hey, Gringo!' moustaches and the matching gravelly voices and well-lived-in skins. Julio always stood with his hands in the pockets of his lumberjack coat, his wise brown eyes almost hidden under his thick dark hair. Maria was his busy wife, always talking faster than I could cope with despite my steep Portuguese learning curve, which I was acquiring as a result of the fact that nobody spoke English, and very rarely would I meet anyone who could. Maria was a petite fifty-something with hardly any teeth, and one white eye and long bushy dark blonde hair. She was slim and always on the go. I called her Mai (Mam) when I got to know her better. At first I thought she was a pain in the arse. You could hear her voice from fifty metres away – she was that high pitched and noisy – but it was just her way and just reflected most local busy family mams.

Shiko always wore an old-fashioned black leather jacket. His eyes were almost hidden under the peak of a chequered brown flat cap. He seemed to be permanently on duty behind the bar, and served from a stainless steel discoloured serving hatch about six foot across and propped up by an old brush handle which I only saw knocked out and the large serving hatch bang shut, without injury, once. A stainless steel ledge, a foot wide and with four cast-iron bar stools, formed the bar. Almost any drink could be bought cheaper at this place than in the local bars. A bottle of 'Sagres' or 'Super Bock' was twenty-eight cents. Pride of place was the big stainless steel coffee machine. Disputably the Portuguese make the best coffee and despite how ramshackle this place was – with cobwebs, dust, oil and concrete – the coffee and food pots and pans were spotless because they were always in use. Tiny cups of strong thick coffee on a matching plate with two little bags of sugar neatly placed with a clean spoon seemed to contrast with the make-do-and-mend surroundings. Dinners were great usually, with about eight or nine of us sitting around a giant electric cable drum lying on its side and covered with a plastic tablecloth. Then Maria would shout everyone for dinner at about 2.00 p.m. On the 'table' she would put a huge well-used aluminium pot, with either some kind of meat, fish or veg with rice, or soup or stew, all with a unique taste. A large round loaf was passed around and there was red wine with every meal, day or night, which was dispensed in order of hierarchy, so Julio always got his first. The wine, with proper wine glasses and a little paper napkin with every meal, and those little coffees afterwards, seemed out of place amongst the working surroundings and the people there. When would you ever see this in the UK?

At the end of a working day, which could have been whenever the sun set, I would get a large bucket of warm water from the toilet and have an outdoor scrub next to my van. The water would only be warm if there was any gas in the gas bottle that supplied the kitchen and the shower – a standpipe with no showerhead and limited water supply. After work, a scrub and a change of bucket-washed clothes, drip-dried on the scrap aluminium outside the vans; one of the jobs I inherited was to chop wood small enough to fit into the bath with metal legs welded onto it, and fire it up. This was great because just as it got dark I got to know many of Julio's *amigos* and customers. They would come and stand around the fire after work and 'shoot the breeze' about their working day, and have a bottle of beer and a smoke. It was a meeting place where I learned my basic Portuguese – you know: the slang, the swearwords, the everyday working banter and chat. After about two hours, the fire would have died down enough to put the metal grating across the bath, full of hot embers, to cook the meat or fish; a task which Shiko took over. Forever studying exactly until he judged the food to be perfect, having only the light of the embers to work by, and being 'advised' by at least eight or nine extra cooks. Shiko would always cook the huge steaks or giant ribs or fish to perfection. The southern Portuguese – the 'Algarves', pronounced with an accent on the 'e', as they proudly referred to themselves (the Algarve was its own territory historically) spoke with an accent and shortened their words, in contrast to the northerners, say, from Lisbon. After about four months, even the Portuguese people I spoke to noticed my Algarve accent, which shows that even accents are picked up by speakers of other languages. Like with the Lithuanians I worked with in Ireland, and the Poles I worked with in Scotland, accents can place you.

Every night, three hundred and sixty-five days a year, they cooked like this, and many other families and farmers I met did too. Even the more well-off householders had an old barbeque out the back somewhere. The real people I met were so social and almost communistic, and well-chilled people – characters – nothing like the UK, where people disappear into their homes to microwave their supermarket scram.

I had built up a good rapport with most people. I would write down the more complicated parts of conversations I was trying to learn, exactly as I heard them, as I sat around and got involved in the banter after the lengthy evening meal

With usually a dozen bodies around the table and lining the bar, all conversations here seemed to blend in and very rarely would two or three people be having a quiet yap on their own. Everyone was involved in every conversation. One big moustachioed construction bloke, Eduardo, gave me an A4 pad and a pen and Vitalina – Julio's niece – gave me a Portuguese dictionary. That was it: the fastest way to learn another language was to work and live where almost no English is ever spoken. I would write about stuff I had done every day and what I had heard, in Portuguese, and then I gradually slipped into conversations, speaking faster and eventually thinking in Portuguese. When it comes to learning foreign languages, if you have your own language to cop out with, you will never learn fast. Many of the expats I met had lived in Portugal for over ten years. They would freely admit they only spoke a few words of Portuguese.

Once you have sussed the verbs and a few conjunctives you just add the everyday words and string 'em together, and you find yourself thinking in the other language. However, I got the context wrong a few times, like when I fell out with Julio for him calling me what I thought was 'monkey' every day. *Usar estas mechanicos equipamentos…* came out to me as 'You mechano-es you-s are mecacoes', and *mecaco*, I thought, was a type of monkey. Things like this gave 'em a laugh months later when I was able to explain myself. I also found the mongrel language of English back to front when describing certain things when compared to the older languages like Espagnol, Portuguese, and Cymraeg. For example, 'hot water' would be said as 'water hot' if spoken in the latter three languages. I regularly trip up over these differences; I guess that whatever you learn first stays with you the longest.

On Fridays, Julio usually gave me fifty euros – more of an 'allowance' than a wage. I could go and have a few in The Poachers: an English pub near Almancil run by Gary, a self-made businessman from the south of England; and Adriana, his Romanian girlfriend. He was an easy fella to get on with and always gave me a couple of free bottles and sometimes food. He was 'seducing' me with freebies to the point where I ended up doing more work for him than for Julio over time, but the deal with Julio had always been for work, food and bed until I could get back on my feet. Things were getting better but my enemy alcohol was looming, as was trouble in the form of another character called Senhor Mendoza. He was one of Julio's acquaintances – a lifelong 'friend' of Julio's family ever since Julio had fallen into a well near Senhor Mendoza's home at the age of five. Senhor Mendoza was a *usaiario*, or moneylender. Whenever he visited the bar, I sensed an uneasy attitude amongst the various people and I was soon to find out why.

Mendoza could speak English just a bit better than I could speak Portuguese at this point. After I repaired his Frontera Jeep diesel, which had a knackered starter motor, and built one good one out of two motors. The first attempt had the engine rotating backwards and I couldn't find the words for "the magnets in this one have opposite poles" – hard enough to explain in English – Mendoza asked me to come and visit his 'garages' and maybe do a little work for him, but he spoke in English, which appeared to annoy Julio a little. It turned out Mendoza had about twenty-five cars, most in showroom condition, ranging from a tiny restored Vespa and a mint silver Riley Elf, to Mercs, Rollers and a few Yankee motors including a 1956 Elvis Presley open-top Cadillac in brilliant red, just like the one in Stephen King's *Christine*. It was almost seven metres long. This collection was kept in his 'village', as Julio referred to it. He was right: twenty-five cars housed in marquees, about a hundred metres apart and with another fifty-metre-square marquee between them, separated by cobbled and small tarmac roads lined with exotic plants and various palm trees and neatly kept grass areas and a pond half as big as Julio's scrap yard, as well as enclosures for ostriches and peacocks, a paddock for horses, a burrow and free-range fowl by the three dozen. The whole complex was called Monte Val de Guas – The Hill of the Horse. It covered about a dozen acres and you made your way around on motorised golf carts, of which there were three. One of them even had three rows of seats. The place had its own chapel for weddings, an art gallery, and an enormous semi-covered kitchen and dining area, built in stone, as big as most people's homes. Well extravagant! Everywhere was kept spotless and well maintained by various labourers, stone-faced apart from a cool dude called Lami. He was about mid-twenties and had a spotless souped-up bright yellow Fiat Punto with a 'boss' sound system. I called him Senhor Lami and he called me Senhor Johnny. He told me a lot about the gap between the up-and-coming youth culture, which is a world apart from the older traditional generations.

We would laugh at Mendoza and his penny-pinching ways. Lami disappeared one day from the employ of Senhor Mendoza, for the same reason I eventually would.

Mendoza had just bought a Ford Model T – the first mass-production car ever made. Henry Ford pioneered mass production. It was a 1917 model in black, "Any colour you want as long as it's black." And this black I would get sick of!

As Mendoza showed off this old motor to me he pointed out that it needed a 'bit' of work doing. Not wanting to miss an opportunity, I offered to do the gold coach painting on the running boards, which Mendoza requested to be extended to each panel, then the bonnet (hood), then the radiator, then the engine and compartment, then the back valance (rear panel), and wheels. In fact, most of the restoration. This was my ticket to at least a month of decent money.

"I'll pay you whatever you want."

Whatever he wants to pay me, he meant. He wasn't shy with any equipment I needed but shy of putting his hand in his pockets for wages. Right: twenty Euros every day, no pressure, and a final payment which I would work on. Big mistake. I remember a Portuguese lady telling me, "Watch those who have the most money; they are the ones who pay the least." She was right.

Because of the amount of time I was spending away from the scrap yard, Julio and Maria had taken on another mechanic, called Fernando. He looked like an oven-ready parrot, with glasses as thick as coke bottle bottoms, which also made him look like a crazy anorexic scientist. I don't think he weighed seven stone wet. He didn't smoke or drink, and worked like a Tasmanian Devil at a hundred miles an hour, and had a habit of slinging spanners anywhere once he had finished with 'em. He also worked for board and lodgings but was relegated to a double bed in the back of the garage. He never spoke to me much, his excuse being that he was from the north of Spain, where no English is spoken, except I was rarely using English by now. As I had arrived a few weeks before him, he probably saw me as more of an obstacle to the caravan I slept in, as the vans were dished out as first come, first served.

Me, him and Silfostheen were stripping a pile of gearboxes – about forty or so – into separate metals, at a rate of about seven to ten per day, for about a week. This created an oil slick and a sea of nuts, bolts, gears, springs and alloy casings chopped up with a ten-inch angle grinder. During this time, Fernando would be on the job earlier than me and Silfostheen, and finish later than us, but he gave up after a week after realising that the wage was not up to much: it was more of a live-in allowance. It suited me to find work in other places.

When it rained in Portugal, like in Spain, it rained. One night, me and Silfostheen were suitably 'mellow' and on the wrong side of the limit for driving. At about 11.30 p.m. the rain was battering the corrugated tin sheeting above us in the bar, We had just watched Benfica on the bar's little telly when a guy burst in, wet as a drowned rat and plastered in blood from strips of torn skin from his head – lacerations everywhere, staggering and bleeding all over the place. We calmed him and gave him a coffee, and he told us he had smashed his van into a wall up the road somewhere and needed it recovering. "*Nao police faz favor, Senhors,* please," he insisted. Worse for drink and clearly in shock, he was sobbing. I was 'volunteered' to drive the recovery truck because Silfostheen valued his driving licence. He was too wrecked anyway. Off we went through the rain in the dark for a couple of kilometres until we came to a wall-lined straight containing an orange grove about half a kilometre long. A VW Transporter bus blocking the road at the point, the fella had lost control and hit a concrete wall end about a metre square, totalling his van and putting his head almost through the windscreen in the process. The driver's side wheel was almost a metre back from where it should have been. With the rain coming down in buckets, the dark, the state of the van and the state of me and Silfostheen– it took us a lot longer than it should have done to winch the wreck up onto the bed of the truck.

The bloke was some sort of painter, so by the time we got back to the yard we were about four different shades of household gloss paint, making it a 'colourful' experience.

Mendoza's Ford Model T was looking good by now, with six-millimetre gold coach lines on the full-length mudguards from front to back, and then on every panel as well as the rear valance and the wheels. All that was left to do were the number plates, the bonnet, the engine and other bits and bobs. Another week later, just the bonnet to finish, but the gold reacted with the black paint so I ended up stripping the bonnet back to the bare metal. Then the primer I used reacted with the black paint I sprayed on it, which Mendoza had provided. I should have checked out 'compatible' in the Portuguese dictionary. Another day lost and another paint session and the same process. Mendoza began getting impatient by now, translated to 'You ain't getting twenty Euros per day until it's finished!' Fair enough, except that when I re-sprayed the bonnet for the third time, the temperature had dropped, so the finish was like black orange peel. Then to top it all the ninety-year-old windscreen, which I had leaned against an old oil drum in order to be able to paint the window frame more easily, had fallen over and shattered into a thousand ninety-year-old pieces! Largely due to haste. Mmm! That's gonna affect my last payment! And it did so. When he eventually paid me, it worked out about two Euros an hour for a month's work on this motor and other stuff. The motor did look good though – shiny black with its gold pin striping, gleaming engine and wheels. I did other jobs mechanically for Mendoza but he never forgot the fucking windscreen and it reflected in his payments! So I became less available for him and more available for Gary as a result.

This eventually led to Gary offering me the position of heading up a gardening business for him after he became happy with my work rate. No problem getting cash off him, but the only snag was Gary usually paid me from the takings out of his pub! So I became used to nipping in for a few swift ones after work rather than going to the Portuguese bars and cafes which I preferred, 'cos aside from the more interesting company Portuguese bars were about a third cheaper all round. Result was another Brit on the beer habit, food either late at night or not at all, as well as finding a plentiful supply of 'philosopher's blend'. Across four months I had learned another language, began earning money from a couple of sources, was pleasing myself when I worked, met a lot of colourful and interesting bodies, but then began to fall into the trap of hiding behind beer and ganja to again cover the memories. But at least I wasn't doing speed in the daytime whilst repairing or driving lorries in the cold and wet.

The beautiful sunsets and chilled lifestyle couldn't cover up the pain of missing my kids, and then all the things which make up a worthwhile life. They had disappeared in less than six months, but I chose to cover 'em in an incoherent blur of all sorts of alcohol and drugs. Busy people don't do unhappy, do they? They appear to get on with it.

The memory of my girl bent over a sink top with her stoat of a brother-in-law 'engaged' with her from behind was just the catalyst. New Year's Eve 2006 was the final straw in a long line of tragedies towards the end of one shite year. I just wish I had found what I found a little earlier than on this soon-to-happen journey. But then that didn't seem to be the plan.

Chapter Two
Time to Go

Around this time, I would go to a place called Cafe Bol o Rei. It means 'King of Cakes'. It is on the corner of the main junction in Almancil. The locals called it 'Red Square' because of the amount of Romanians who hung out there to meet their mates and pick up work etc. I sat outside on the aluminium chairs next to a table in the sun, with a cake and my tranny radio, to relax and read my Portuguese dictionary and keep away from anywhere which served alcohol. Cafe Bol o Rei was well chilled. You sat watching all shapes and sizes of motors, opposite the three-way traffic lights on the rough, well-worn and sun-bleached tarmac. Three-wheel Vespa pick-ups, full of the local families, complete with animals in the back; black Hummers with blacked-out windows; busy clunking and hissing arctic trucks straining to a stop, always fully loaded and well over fifteen years old; to boy racers on full-power quad bikes; 'boom boom' boys in their maxed-out wrecks; and everything in between. The waitresses used to come and chat so I got to know 'em quite well, Eduardo, my Portuguese-speaking mate from Guinea Besal, would introduce them to me when we were out but they already knew me. A great social life but my conscience was beginning to stir.

I overheard a conversation nearby in English. The old fella chattering away looked like Lee Marvin, with a white sailor's beard. He was talking to another bloke in his late forties about the fact that he needed an old-style caravan tow hitch. One from a scrap yard would do. I knew where there was one!

Turned out 'Yorkie' was an old, hard-as-nails oil rig worker, marine engineer and fitter, who had worked on just about every type of engineering job that took him far and wide but too near a bloke needs to be to bars when you possess plenty of disposable income and have an alcohol problem. As a result, he had had a stroke in his late fifties. Yorkie had the patience of a two-year-old but the experience of any mechanic worth his salt when he could control his flailing right arm, which would point to the sky when he was in a rush or when he got upset. I ended up fitting a tow hitch to his tiny caravan, which he towed behind his nineteen ninety Saab. He brought it to the scrap yard and Julio charged him fifty Euros for the tow hitch. I set about removing the tow hitch off the caravan I slept in and, after an hour of drilling, cutting and welding, Yorkie had his 'new' tow hitch coupled up. While Yorkie had to wait an hour, he began cursing and swearing, then throwing his stick and muttering to himself, which he later told me was mainly because of frustration that he couldn't do the things he used to be able to do. It was quite funny to watch sometimes but I kind of felt sorry for him too. He was obviously a proud fella at one time but had fucked himself up with ale. I also thought 'What if I end up like that?'

I went with Yorkie, together with one of the bikes in the back of his van, to the site. He asked me to help him pitch his van, with the ulterior motive of plying me with whiskey and other booze and then proposing that I accompany him back to Southampton, where he lived. Somewhere, I must have given him the impression I was thinking about it. He wanted a steady month's ride back across Spain and France and needed some help with driving etc and that he had to leave because he had told the site manager he was "A fucking wanker!" – A standard Yorkie expletive.

As far as I could see Yorkie had been on the site near Quarteira for almost two years and had fallen out with everyone he came across, especially "Them that don't speak English!" as he put it, which was about eighty per cent of the people there.

"Well, I'll think about it, Yorkie. It sounds good, but I've got some loose ends to tie up first and I need to think about that job Gary offered me," I explained.

I agreed to do some work on his caravan and check the brakes and transmission on his car, plus about a dozen other jobs he needed doing.

I rode back from Quarteira – about six kilometres – on the dark back roads to the scrap yard at about ten at night, slightly drunk and with no lights. I came to one place, which ran parallel but about fifty feet higher than Almancil town, approximately three or four miles away to my right. The lights of the town reminded me of the view of Wrexham from Brynhyfryd (Summerhill), where I lived for most of my teen years. Now in a nostalgic trance, I rode on and only realised I had missed the turning past the orange grove to the right when I rode over a pothole in the dark – which woke me up! When I got back to the scrap yard Julio and a few *amigos* were chatting around the table, with bottles of beer on the go whilst playing cards, and a few were watching the telly up in the far corner of the bar. Julio wasn't too happy with my mate Yorkie – apparently the fifty Euros only covered the purchase of the tow hitch and not the welding, wiring and fitting of it. Why the fuck didn't he tell me that when I was doing the job then! Next day as I explained this to Yorkie he voiced out loud what I had thought and said, "Fuck 'em. They should have told me that while I was there."

"Fair point," I said, but thought, 'You don't have to live with 'em, Yorkie'.

Whilst I was doing the work on his car, then caravan, and about four or five other jobs which he would change his mind about two or three times in an hour, I witnessed why Yorkie had fallen out with everyone. First, there was the visit from the long-suffering site manager, who Yorkie goose stepped towards and shouted, "*Jawohl, mein Fuhrer!*" in direct sight of his German neighbour!

Then he insulted the next-door-neighbours, who were Spanish, and some Portuguese campers across the way. Funny to watch but he was completely alienating himself to anyone around. Yorkie was a right cantankerous old git. I tried my best to explain to the site manager that he had suffered from a stroke etc – in Portuguese – but his reply was, "I don't care. Your 'father' just causes trouble with everyone and is very abusive. He must go!"

The manager explained this to me as I leaned on the roof of his little van. I turned my head to look towards Yorkie, who was about fifty feet away and standing in the door of his caravan shouting expletives to the manager and at the same time 'flagging' him with the V sign, with a grin like a bad schoolboy on his dribbling lips. I did my best not to laugh but couldn't help a smile at the situation, which the manager noticed and then drove off with a grimace on his face and slightly putting me off balance.

That afternoon I had agreed to help out Dangerous Brian. His landlady had just evicted a family who had left a mess, and another bunch of holidaymakers were moving in next day. I was to get a free roast dinner out of it and a night's drinking paid for. Done! So after about six hectic hours of cleaning, painting, and sweeping most of her villa, Brian cooked me a roast dinner in his American motor home parked in his landlady's back yard. This was to half make up for a fall out me and Brian had whilst we were plastering one of Gary's villas. He wasn't happy with Gary giving me plenty of work so he 'accidentally' gave me the wrong materials to complete a job, which got me a bollocking. Then he 'accidentally' ran over my radio with Gary's minibus. Dangerous made no secret of the fact he hated music while he worked and so I made no secret of the fact that I definitely was not impressed with him! Happy days! Good food in my belly and now for a night of fun.

Dangerous was a right shark! He could trick punters out of their money as soon as look at 'em. Anyone who came into the bar was subjected to his endless card and coin tricks, which always cost the punter fifty cents or a euro, which never got returned. He became a right pain in the arse when he had too much beer inside himself. Another lad, from south Wales, in his fifties, called Richard, was exactly the same. He was Brian's nemesis. When sober, Richard was dead straight to the point of being 'anal', but after a few he was a total dick. Dangerous had only gotten his name from the dodgy wiring and various jobs which needed doing twice before they were considered safe. These lads and various others were colourful characters who made up the twenty or so regular lads and girls that were always up for a laugh – not the tourists and holidaymakers: we didn't bother much with that lot. It was like a form of snobbery amongst the Brits' typical mentality. The Portuguese bars were even better: not even the expats would go in, so no Brit bullshit at all, especially not in the black clubs, which seemed to stay open most of the night. One night a beautiful Brazilian girl began speaking to me. At the same time, someone kept shouting "Shortie" over the mike system. It was Lami, the dude who disappeared from his job at Mendoza's. I went up to his DJ box and had a chat with him

"*Com estas, Amigo.* How did you spot me amongst this crowd?" I shouted to him above the bass boom.

"Oh! – Easy! You de only white guy here!"

With a huge grin I replied, "Oh right, I see. Ha!"

Just then, Eduardo told me not to return to the Brazilian girl, who was standing and smiling an inviting smile in my direction, because "she costs money and you will have to pay!"

A little later, me and Ed returned to The Poachers for a 'nightcap' at Ed's invite. He and Sonia – his girl and Gary's ex sister-in-law – were having a sort of house-warming for the first night they were taking over the management. Here was the start of the decision. Eduardo and Dangerous insisted that we had a few Super Bocks and '51s' and then some. I mentioned that I was thinking of going home 'for a bit' so Eduardo plied me with a few more 51s, which I returned the favour to him. Way, way after midnight, I called it a day and said *Adios*, put my tool-filled workbag I had left in the bar earlier over my shoulder, and tried to mount my bike. I wobbled up the road on the half-size bike – not the full-size one I salvaged from the scrap. I was not safe to walk, let alone ride. I rode off in the opposite direction to the scrap yard, which I only realised when I was halfway down Almancil hill and gathering too much speed. The heavy bag slung across my back fell to one side and I veered towards the kerb. Then I overcorrected and went the other way, gathering more speed. I couldn't get straight, as my co-ordination was well gone. I had done this lots of times before but not quite when this drunk. Just then, a boy racer with his 'boom boom' car flew past me and pulled over about fifty feet in front of me – easy enough to avoid. I swerved, mounted the kerb at a rate of drunken knots without losing control of the bike on the gravel, and tried to shoot between the parked car and the wall. However I couldn't quite make it through the four-foot gap, largely due to my inability to focus at this point. Just then, my toolbag dropped around my waist and I veered off to the right, smack into a set of stone steps which went about four up. These stopped the bike dead from about twenty miles an hour. I personally didn't stop until a fraction of a second later as I slammed into a thick cast-iron gate at the top of the steps, half sort of shoulder on, half face on. Bang! The left side of my head felt numb and wet all at the same time. My legs were lying behind me, with one thigh throbbing because it had struck one of the stone steps. My left shoulder was also throbbing. I tried moving these all bit by bit. It hurt but I could just about move 'em! Slowly I turned over and almost sat upright. I felt the warm blood dripping down my front. Dazed, I sat there for a bit and even tried to roll a ciggy but gave up because the blood was soaking my efforts. Then I started feeling sick, you know, that too-sick-to-move feeling, so I sat there for ages. I just didn't want to get up. Must have been there a while because blood was starting to congeal on my left cheek and chin until a fresh spring would pop open and drip warm and then cold down my face and onto my coat and jeans.

After an eternity, I stood up and almost blacked out. I then picked up the remains of the bike. It was in three separate pieces: the forks and front wheel had sheared off just below where it joins the frame, and the handlebars were now only connected by the brake cables. Even the frame headstock was bent back about forty degrees. This was not the first time I had wrecked some sort of bike. Eventually I started back up the hill, staggering towards The Poachers, which was about half a kilometre away. This was a long journey, dragging the three-piece bike with me. I stopped twice, almost falling over. Then I gave up and tried another rolly, successfully lighting it this time but throwing it after dry-heaving a couple of times. I got to The Poachers and slung the remains of the bike behind the back, then plodded on the long walk in the coldness of the dark night for about a couple of kilometres, towards the scrap yard. The lane's hill and the blackness made me well cold. By the time I had reached the high, corrugated double gates, they were locked, as they usually were by the time I got back of a weekend. I had to climb them very slowly and carefully, and drop off the top – about eight feet – which always woke the collection of six noisy dogs of varying shapes and sizes, some 'free range', with the two biggest chained either side of the gates. The resulting barking would usually wake everyone up. But, being this late, the dogs all remained asleep. Even Baros, who looked like a giant Yorkshire terrier on steroids, never uttered a sound as I part fell off the lee side of the gates to a crunch and slam as my back hit the back of the doors. I didn't wake anyone up. I didn't care anyway. I was too tired and sore to care; I just wanted my 'pit'. I negotiated the junk and scrap fridges and aluminium extrusions parked in front of the van entrance, and paused to look at the bright full moon – for a moment it looked so close and huge that night – before climbing into the van and finally bed, but not before banging my head on the lamp in the middle of the roof. This was a daily occurrence!

Chapter Three
Off with Yorkie

The blood which had glued my face to the pillow, had also matted my hair, which was almost shoulder length by now. I had dyed it black because when I arrived in the Algarve it was white, and I mean white. My ex was a hairdresser, so another stupid drunken decision resulted in me getting her to dye my hair white. A mechanic in a scrappy with white hair? Wrong!

I chanced a look in the small mirror towards the end of the van. What a sight! I looked as if I had self-inflicted injuries by a ballpeen hammer. For the next few weeks, strangers were giving me double takes.

I had more work to do on Yorkie's van and car and as he also had Nescafe, which would give me a short sharp hit of caffeine, I decided I couldn't be bothered explaining in Portuguese what had happened to me whilst waiting for the water to heat for a decent coffee in the bar. After a quick swig of *agua* I bypassed the bar before everyone was up. There was no way I could get out of the gates without waking everyone up though: the dogs went crazy all at once whenever anyone approached the exit. Whatever, after getting through the gates I slowly pedalled towards Quarteira on the one remaining bike via the cool lanes around the orange groves and ramshackle farms: the one with one brake and bad gears. By the time I reached Yorkie's site he was already pottering around with his tape measure and off cuts of wood, and saw me. Swearing to himself, he stopped for a minute to ask, "Who's given you a pasting?"

"What?"

I'd forgotten what I looked like as the cold morn air had numbed my face a bit.

"Tell you later," I muttered.

As he limped around the side of his van, he asked, "You gonna come to England with me then?"

Decision almost made.

"I'll give you an answer by the end of the day."

I 'necked' a brew and did a bowlful of his washing up in the nearby sinks. Thinking about this decision got me too deep. I started thinking about my kids and what I had heard a few weeks previously after calling in at a chapel service which a bunch of Brits had held in the town's social services hall. One of the Portuguese ladies who worked there told me to visit the chapel for job contacts etc. It was the first time I had been near a chapel since I was about eight or nine. It was well comforting and the people were really nice, welcoming and unassuming. The leader was talking about our kids and how forgiving they are, with trusting, unconditional love. I was realising how much I'd let mine down, not just because of this situation, but in life in general. I had put work first too many times. My children – one son and three daughters – are four different personalities from four different mothers. The first two children – one now a young man – were older and living further away. The two youngest needed their dad but their mothers didn't think so. In 2005, I married a woman – a children's social worker – that both the youngest girls' mothers decided they disliked, even though they didn't even know her. One mother decided she didn't want her daughter around this woman and kept to her promise: "Marry her and you won't see your daughter!"

The next mam followed suit because it was the excuse she needed to concentrate on her new family.

All the mams now had fellas, who obviously treated them a lot better than I did or could. This one and only marriage was a total mistake. The things we had in common were recreational drug and alcohol use, and plenty of disposable income with no idea how to use it wisely. The good money I was earning arrived after a decade of graft and promises of money to come I had made to the respective mams. If you lose the loyalty of a partner, you lose a solid base.

As a result, I ended up with partners that were 'good time girls' – quite glam but as shallow as puddles and just as dirty. I spent money freely on 'em – this is what women want, isn't it? Another flawed thinking pattern. What good is it for a man to profit but to lose his life?

Stupidly, I even began referring to the mams by 'number' rather than addressing them by name (not to their faces though) because it was far worse getting their names wrong when facing them on the doorstep on a Sunday morning. I can only now understand how they resented me so much. But it was my children I felt sad for eventually and many times over twenty years, Sundays were the only days I felt part of my own family. I hated dropping off my kids at their mams on a Sunday evening. I was so desensitised to everyone else's problems. The pain of seeing a little 'un's eyes well up hits you like nowt else.

Their mams never saw this and didn't care. Sunday nights for me became a total incoherent blur. The mothers of my kids seemed as insipid as the wife whom I had recently married.

My wife had taken to shagging one of her colleagues by now while I was babysitting her son of eleven, "because I could", whilst wearing the various bits of gold and jewellery I had bought her.

I always wondered if this dick of a colleague would have the same feelings of lust after seeing her in one of her many slobbering fits, with me nursing her around afterwards because of love and not just lust... but in reality, I later found that she had done half the village, most of 'em barely legal. It makes me laugh now. What was I thinking?!

I ended up living in a 33-year-old camper van in a waste transfer yard for a short time. The whole mess crashed. In the space of two months I lost two family members, access to three daughters, left a marriage, and lost my driving licence and my two businesses but then, at a low ebb, I thought I had met 'the one'. Nah! What a wanker I was! What followed was the shit hitting the fan...

About midday Yorkie brewed up, and leaving a few jobs half done, we sat in the sun and I told him I was coming with him, which he was quietly chuffed with.

"What about this gardening business with Gary?" asked Yorkie.

"It don't even figure in my plans. Besides, he ain't gonna be short of workers!"

Yorkie planned to make a long trip of it across Spain, then slowly across France. That was it; a month maybe was enough to get my head around a stint in jail. Yorkie must have been expecting a yes because he invited me to crash in his van until midweek, and then off we would go.

"Right, I've got a few loose ends and my stuff to get from the other van at the scrappy first." Yorkie offered to pick me up near the scrappy whilst he said a few goodbyes to his drinking buddies in the Quarteira beach bars, where they hung out on a daily basis, sitting in the sun – the same group of southern old boys and their wives, drinking away their retirement funds in the sun. Lucky bastards.

I paused at The Poachers to collect what was left of the bike. As I loaded the bits into the boot of Yorkie's old Saab, Sonia appeared outside the door and looked shocked to see me. I kept forgetting about the state of my face. No time for explanations: we were on a mission.

After a couple of days of messing about, we loaded up and hit the road. Within thirty kilometres, Yorkie decided to park up in a campsite on the outskirts of Olhao.

"Is that it?"

"Yeah. We're staying here for a few weeks. Yer can get yerself a job for a few weeks."

This wasn't part of the plan – or was it? Right. Start again. After a few days of doing jobs twice, and the cooking, washing and biking around Olhao on Yorkie's small-wheeled bike, which had a slow puncture, I was getting a bit fed up with the stagnant 'trip' so I decided to disappear. Into the early-afternoon sun I went, along the road towards the dock, and then turned down a trail which led to a sun-baked dirt path around the tidal lagoons which faced the Ilha de Culatra: an island largely populated by old hippies, and which can be visited by a boat that passes the point at the edge of the lagoons. This place was one of the most peaceful places I have ever spent time at. The lagoons were a huge collection of rectangular and large misshapen dead flat, calm, shallow pools with tiny entrances with sluice gates or just five or six-foot gaps in the embank-ments separating the lagoons from the sea, where the gentle and clear Atlantic would flow in and out. These would have powered grinding mills to make flour. There were one or two restored mills but most are now ruined, just a few bare inlets like most around towns and cities on the coasts of Portugal. The machines were used for grinding corn before power became cheap enough to make them all redundant. Along the causeways that made up the edges of the lagoons – the gaps where the sluice gates were – massive fat fish could be seen circling in the big eddies and currents washing in or out from the pools, looking for smaller fish, maybe. The only sounds you could hear would be a quiet gurgle from the current as it exited the lagoons, and the odd seabird warbling in the distance. Huge storks nestled nearby up giant trees or specially constructed poles. You could walk for miles around the nearby nature reserve along the shores and into the wooded area and not see a soul, but just absorb the dead flat calm of the little beaches and woods. The whole place just took you a million miles away from your troubles.

Upon returning, this revelation was wasted on Yorkie. He was still complaining to himself about the Portuguese, then about the other site users, and then about people in general. He was a right Victor Meldrew. I had come with Yorkie to get back and make a steady journey back to the UK. Yorkie wanted company and a helper – that was the deal – but I began doubting me sticking with that plan.

After about a week of me doing the washing and cooking, Yorkie had fallen out with his neighbours just like he had on the previous site. He then got drunk and fell out with a few couples in the campsite bar, and would return and have a moan about whatever. I began to think about returning to Almancil and Gary's offer. So, the next day, with one of Yorkie's books, I went off to the point at the edge of the lagoons to think the situation through, and read. Never previously having had the time to read a book or having the peace of a place like this one, I tried to make a decision. The book I took, he reckoned was 'shit'. I didn't bother explaining or discussing anything with him by now: it was better if you stayed quiet around him or he would just walk through your words and mutter to himself about nothing. The poor fella's mind just didn't mix with alcohol anymore. It was putting me off long-term drinking.

The book was called *The One That Got Away* – about that SAS fella, Chris Ryan, who had walked hundreds of kilometres behind enemy lines at night to evade capture, without food and very little water. It told me that with the right mental conditioning, you can push a human body way beyond what you think it can do. After that, I began weighing up how long it would take me to ride to Gibraltar on Yorkie's bike. It was only a couple of hundred kilometres away and I could easily rough it for a few days… hmmm!

Two days later, on 9th April 2007, it was early evening. I had cooked the stew and we were sitting down outside – me on the van step; and Yorkie next to his ramshackle tent that we used for cooking in, eating his stew out of a bowl on the two-foot-square folding table while sitting on one of those camping chairs. He began moaning about a south Wales couple whom I had met. They had complained to me about him abusing them in the bar. Like a lot of people, he couldn't understand the Welsh mentality for banter. Often we will talk just to prevent silence and like most of the people I grew up around and worked and played and eventually drank with and then married into, we would start a random story or a conversation which would always have a funny anecdote, sometimes add a piss-take to it. For example, and this is true:

"Where I come from there's a dyslexic tattooist 'cos a bloke who came into the pub still wearing them seventies denims with 'Status Quo' on the back had 'Hell's Angles' tattooed on his arms. But mainly I laughed at his black mullet and German porn moustache."

Like the Scots, the Irish, the Scousers, Geordies and other folk from the north, the Welsh would banter, and Yorkie was a typical southerner – reserved. Not strictly true nowadays maybe but back in Yorkie's day. When it came to various business and work dealings, the ones I had met were straight and decent – great clients – but boring as fuck on a piss-up and they would always say "what" with a correct pronunciation of the Queen's English. I realise now they just couldn't immediately 'tune' themselves in to my bastardised accent, which is predominantly north-east Welsh with a smattering of Scouse thrown in. I guess the Scots and the Irish and the northerners are divided from the southerners by this. This method of humour, the banter I was used to, was lost on Yorkie. He would just get well nasty. This time he ranted on about how "we let you lot stay in 'our' country", then what "bastards" we all were.

"WHOAA! Hold on there, Pal. If it wasn't for a Welshman, your van would be un-roadworthy by a long way and your car would have no working front windows or brakes, as well as your cooking, cleaning and repairs I seemed to 'ave inherited. Don't slag off my country people!"

"I could have taken it to a garage."

"Yeah, and it would have cost you well over a thousand Euros as well. If you don't want me around tell me now 'cos I've got enough on me mind as it is, Pal!"

As you can guess, my sympathy was waning at this point. Also, the words that a couple of his southern mates had said started echoing through my head:

"You're not going with that moaning old twat, are you?" to which I'd defended him up till now. So whilst Yorkie staggered off to the bar, what clothes I had went into my rucksack. I loaded up his small-wheeled shopper bike and nicked a small sack of his oranges, and I was off! The bike was a crock but it was for services rendered. I half thought of going back to Almancil but that would take about two hours. Nah, I reckon I can make Gib in two days... can't be that far...?

Chapter Four

The Border

Olhao to Villa Real de Santo Antonio 45 Kilometres,
Villa Real de Santo Antonio – Alcoutim – Isla Christina 122
 Kilometres,
6th April 2007 to 7th April 2007

It must have gone seven because the shadows were getting longer. I left the site on the eastern side of Olhao. Before heading out of town I called in at a 'Plus' – similar to an 'Aldi' or a 'Lidl' but even cheaper. This was to pick up some 'provisions', which comprised four bottles of fifty-cent vino and the same amount in litre cartons, together with a few bars of cheap chocolate and a giant pack of 'Marie' biscuits. I piled all this into a plastic bread tray I made my carrying rack, and I was off!

As I rode on along the flat straight road I thought about the book I had read at that spot next to the flat calm Atlantic, and the peacefulness of the lagoons, and realised that that was the first time I had been alone for more than a couple of hours, for about five months, or maybe a decade. Looking back, I thought about a few of the events leading up to my departure from north Wales. I thought of my Nain (grandmother) dying and nobody would tell me what was wrong with her. I had heard she was riddled with cancer but I only heard it off a stranger who knew a friend – who knew another. She died with the added stress of my nephew Ashley, killed at nineteen in a car crash after my sister Lianne, his mam, saying to me, "Take him Ashley under your wing."

I could have but I didn't. I needed an extra hand at the time in a growing hands-on repair business, and taking him on might have stopped him going off the rails. I should have, could have, would have, but didn't!

He was killed after he lost control of a car he had took... for kicks.

Just prior to the moment I was presented with the news that I had a daughter of sixteen – well confusing for the emotions.

In my haste to explain this great news to my biological mother, who I had hardly talked to since my teens, I dialled her number, then cancelled it nervously, then dialled her number again; before I became connected my phone began to ring! It was my mam and she had just rung me! So, precisely at that moment I had received the grim news of Ashley's death from her, I mistakenly tried to explain to my mother about her third granddaughter, news which she was in no mood to listen to, understandably. She had looked upon 'Ash' as her son and had brought him up as her own, much as her mother did to me.

This was not exactly a positive time for anyone, let alone Danielle, my eldest daughter. Already one mixed-up girl because her mam had disappeared at an early age. Danielle must have thought no one had any time for her, especially her father, whose weekend spare time at that moment seemed to revolve around beer and problems.

After being told not to get drunk at Ashley's wake by my sister and my mam, I did. Worse still, I went and met some of Ashley's mates in Rhyl town that night for a kind of 'goodbye' drink and slept it off in my van in a side street, where the local constabulary arrested me, after waking me, to finish my sleep in the local police cells at about 5.00 a.m. Never leave your keys in the ignition in a drunken slumber!

I remember the duty officer saying to me as he let me out next day, "Not a good time for your family, is it, Son?"

All this finished my Nain off in her hospital bed. Then my mam didn't attend her own mother's funeral!

My Nain was my mam, my friend and my remaining close family member. Apart from my Taid (grandfather), who died several years before, she was the only person who would never lie to me. She had met Danielle the same week as she was grieving for the great-grandson she adored and also grieving over the suddenly curtailed access to my youngest girls, Ceri-Sian and Seren. Because of the marriage to my ex-wife they (Mam Three and Mam Four) stuck to their vows of denying the girls seeing their dad. This didn't help my Nain as she so much looked forward to my little girls' smiles, and now they were gone. She wasn't to see 'em again.

This sort of stuff, which is everyday life, just seemed to happen all at once. These sorts of things and other more mundane complications were clogging up my thought processes and instead of dealing with 'em bit by bit then solving whatever I could with a bag of cash, I had also lost a healthy income, so the bag of cash was gone too. Things were rapidly going down shit creek. Beer, bottles of Vodka and endless 'toking' became the norm – escape! But it wasn't escape – just a dead end.

The early-evening ride towards the border of Spain gave me the same feeling of escape but without the short-term memory loss as with the previous method. Before I started running my businesses, if I got bored in jobs I would just load up and leave without explaining. Picking up a fitting job or truck-driving job took less than a day, so why prolong the agony? Often I didn't even lose a week's pay as I would have 'cultivated' another job a couple of weeks previous to leaving the latest one. I think I had almost thirty jobs before finally cracking business.

The evening was beginning to darken slightly. As I was heading east, the setting-sun was casting my shadow a few feet in front of me. Legs plodding away to the rhythmical chink-chink of glass bottles banging against each other behind me. The road was mainly flat but occasionally rose and fell when crossing a *rio* or river valley. There were increasing stretches of flat straight road passing roadside *tavernas* or restaurants, then little houses and fields, then the odd village or two, then a small town with dusty road edges and poor tarmac. I even stopped next to a circus that had a lot of white lorries and tents to ask for a possible job as a lorry mechanic, but didn't put much effort into the conversation. As a result, a worker told me, "You cannot go here!"

I was a bit tired now and it was well dark with no stars. Only the lights of following cars would light the way. In the distance, I could see the orange glow of street lighting along a straight. Very long, it was too. It felt like it went on for a while. The air around me had cooled but I was sweating. I saw signs for Villa Real. I thought that was north somewhere. This place up ahead in the distance was Villa Real de Santo Antonia, the last town before crossing into Spain. The road ran as straight through the middle as a sharp knife, right up to the main square, which was cobbled and about fifty metres square, with traditional Portuguese stone buildings all around. For that late time of night there were many sightseers wandering around the place and chilling in the cool cafe bars; and everyone looked cool and well-dressed, from youngsters with their mams 'n' dads to older. Folk and fellas with their girls, all looking a lot better off than the native Algarves I had been used to.

I decided to have a 'reward' – a cafe 'duplo' – and sat at one of the little outdoor tables at one of the cafes with what little money I had left 'cos it might be a long time before the next one. On with my little 'Palito' transistor radio, and bliss – sounds and a brew after some effort to arrive at these surroundings, totally unaware of the distances and the events to come. Time to look at the beauty of this place, which had a 'posh' European feel, with hanging baskets of flowers draped off lampposts and smart stone buildings with thin, tall windows. I checked the time – it was almost midnight. I had barely come forty-five kilometres from Olhao and already it was time to find a 'hidey-hole' to kip. I rode out of the square, losing my orientation for a minute. Then after going down one of the narrow side streets, I came across a wide road. On the other side of the road, I discovered I couldn't get any nearer to Spain unless I could swim!

Almost at the border, I just had to find the bridge now. Heading north, I now found myself in the rougher-looking industrial area, and crossed train tracks set into the cobbled and concrete roads, eventually turning left after running out of the industrial area. This took me along railway sidings, with lines of coupled-up train tanker trucks outside a huge factory of sorts behind a distant fence separating the train tracks from it. The wide sweeping road I was on seemed to be turning round towards town, but it wasn't. I came across a lonely junction and, once again, my instincts directed me north. Another couple of dark kilometres along a straight, then up a rise past a castle on my left up on a hillside, which looked like the one in the middle of Faro which I had slept next to in a doorway on my first night 'on my toes' months ago. The tasteless powers-that-be had built new dwellings around the castle. About a kilometre further on I spied the *autovia* bridge, which I assumed must be the one heading to the river crossing. By now, I was sweating again and pretty tired. I decided to sleep under one of these *autovia* bridges.

After a slight uphill, I could see the main *autovia* passing over the road downhill ahead of me, about five hundred metres away. I stopped underneath it and climbed, to look towards the bridge and Spain. I checked the time and it was well after midnight so I decided to bed down on the shelf under the top of the bridge. Still quite warm from the ride, I laid out my lumberjack jacket, put an old towel around my feet, laid the bike down, necked a bottle of cheap red vino to the sounds of Algarve FM, and drifted off into a deep sleep.

About 4.00 a.m. a Portuguese roadside mechanic in a transit stopped his van after noticing my bike on the edge of the top of the bridge, and woke me up to tell me I "can't go on the *autovia*", which I already knew, and "cannot sleep here". A week later I would have told him to fuck off but in case he phoned the GNR (Portuguese traffic cops and dead bureaucratic) I told him I would only be here till 6.00 a.m. – which is the time the cold would wake me up anyway. As I couldn't go over the border without hassle from the GNR I decided to head further inland and upstream of the river. I cycled through small villages in the morning darkness but it got harder to stay in sight of the river, made more difficult by the hills, and vast and long recently-built concrete viaducts crossing valleys of empty mountainous scrubland. After a couple of hours, I got the impression I was losing the battle to find another crossing upstream. Every time I caught sight of the river, it seemed a lot further away. After cresting some well-steep hills just past a village called Odeliete, which sat on the eastern side of a modern dam, I was sure the road was taking me slowly further away and not nearer to the river valley. The day became warm and there were another couple of l-o-n-g climbs, with no traffic or civilisation around. I had used up a litre of UHT and a bar of cheap choc and a pack of biccies, and at the next opportunity I would head east towards the river or wherever it would take me. About an hour later, I found a lonely 'on' ramp up to a minor road so up I went. It looked so unused and remote it almost gave me the impression it was built just for my benefit, to enable me to get off the neverending rollercoaster of thirty kilometres per hour downhills and two kilometres per hour uphills to nowhere.

It had a small sign saying Alcoutim. I followed this single-track road for at least five kilometres uphill and down twisty narrow deserted lanes with un-farmable terrain of thick deep grass and hawthorn trees, dry winding streams and rocks, and rough pasture with one or two forgotten cattle, avoiding the odd three or four-foot-long green snake basking in the sun. Then the road started steepening down towards a tiny village of terracotta-roof tiled white villas, of which there were about thirty. Across the valley, I caught sight of a huge part of the river but kept losing sight of it because by now I was flying down this very steep hill, which made the frame shake and the brakes shudder and squeal. In the village, which had a tiny roundabout, I veered off to the right and found myself alongside the river, which looked about two hundred metres across – a lot smaller than the expanse of water that I had seen at the top of the hill, which, I learned much later, was part of a dam on the Spanish side.

Well, it was either more unfamiliar territory following the river, or heading back to the *autovia* up those big hills back to the main bridge and going across it. At least I would be in Spain. I had wasted a morning by now and I wasn't even out of Portugal yet! Decide now. Mmmm, get on with it and get back to the bridge ASAP… pillock!

At least the road was scenic and quite flat. I passed a couple of Brit-registration cars parked outside of lonely dwellings but, apart from the odd few houses, it was quiet. I had to climb away from the river at one point and onto a steep lane that eventually came out on a hilltop with a cafe and a couple of houses nearby. Time for a cafe duplo. The usual collection of local Portuguese old boys sat around inside. They noticed I had on a Benfica *casico* (tracksuit top) so I got into some Portuguese banter about footy with 'em about Benfica, Sporting Lisbon, Porto and Liverpool. I loved having the craic with the old fellas. They asked me where I was from and where was I going to, I told 'em: Pais de Gales (Wales) and where was I going to – Wales!

"What? On that cycle?"

"Yup."

At that point it dawned on me, 'It's gonna be a long journey!'

Over the hills for another ten or more kilometres, down small lanes, twists and turns; and the road flattened, then dropped. I caught a glimpse of the bridge in the distance for the first time in daylight, and it was still miles away. Maybe I had ridden further than I thought, or did those hills magnify the distance? It was 2.00 p.m. I had wasted half a day and some of my 'fuel', and was still in Portugal – not a good omen for a trip across two more countries. Anyway, I might find work in Gibraltar and stay! Another hour or so later I was on the *autovia*, where bikes are banned. About half a kilometre before the bridge there was a GNR station on the westbound side. From my experience, the GNR got on your case for any infringements, and I just wanted to get over the bridge without any hassle. As I drew near the station two fellas were looking out of a window so I crossed two sets of carriageways over to the eastbound pull-in, and went over a barbed-wire fence into a marked nature reserve that stretched under the bridge. After crossing two marshy areas separated by barbed-wire fences, I came across a dirt track and was almost run over by a flyin' quad bike. I made my way to the bridge supports, which had steep steps set into the concrete. I stopped to have a rolly in the shade, removed my shades and placed them on a ledge on one of the bridge supports – a decision I was later to regret!

I then climbed up onto the bridge via the steps available for maintenance workers. Looking back west, I could see the cops wouldn't get to me before I got over. There were no cops on the Spanish side so I struggled with the bike, box, bottles, oranges and clothes up the steps after forgetting my shades; then lifted the lot over the safety rail; and in less than a minute I was in Spain. Why didn't I do that in the first place?!

I could now follow the coast to Gibraltar, or so I thought. Spain seemed a little more commercialised than Portugal. The cars were newer and the tourists plentiful. I turned right off the main road and headed toward a coastal resort – the last bit of the bottom south-western tip of Spain before the Rio Guadiana, which separates the two countries. Typical of Spanish coastal areas, I found it was packed with holiday homes, villas, apartments, and clone supermarkets and speed bumps, and the sad disease of 'Fonestuktoearism' (say it out loud to yourself) everywhere. I wanted to cycle as near to the coast as possible and get some baccy with the dwindling cents in my pocket, and it was definitely more expensive than Portugal. Ayamonte caters for tourists.

Warm and sunny, it looked more tropical than the last week, with far more palm trees and sand. I went up a few hills past deciduous trees and holiday camps and hotels that were near the beaches. I was on the N431 and took a right turn, going southerly towards a little fishing port called Isla Christina. I rode across a dirty causeway that had salt-sea marshes on either side, with suspect-looking 45-gallon drums and various bits of debris marooned in the silt between the marsh vegetation. The small docks had a selection of fishing boats complicating the scene, with masts, GPS pods, and nets draped across white-and-blue deck machinery. I thought of asking around for work on the boats, thinking of a Spanish-style 'deadliest catch' but a lot warmer, then thought of meeting another Julio and Maria and drinking and eating around a fire, cooking fish and learning Spanish with months of yet another learning curve. Nah, I was enjoying this 'adventure' too much. I rode on along the beaches and even found a long wood boardwalk. It was later than I thought and the shadows were getting longer, mainly because I'd spent too much time at a locked-up beach cafe next to the boardwalk, which had the tables and chairs still out. I ate a couple of oranges on the comfort of a bench, with a table to lean on, and looked out to sea. I then decided to open a carton of *vino branca* (white wine), then a carton of *vino tint* (red wine), and wallowed in the total warmth and euphoria, looking across the sands. I just sat quietly, jealous of the nearby local kids kicking around a footy ball in the sand without a care in the world. Going off into a trance, I snapped out of it because I needed to find somewhere quiet to kip before I lost any more time. Back on the boardwalk I rode, well tipsy, finding a concrete seafront area with various hotels with their strings of multi-coloured lights. I had thoughts of sleeping in the sand-dunes behind a hotel which had parking spots for camper vans and suchlike. Too busy. Going faster than my co-ordination could cope with, and the fact that it was getting hard to see, combined with the vino I had drunk, I missed a corner on a downhill bend and ploughed into a sand-dune, losing the wide tray of assorted junk and wine off the back of the bike. I was too tired for this now, and had to find somewhere to kip. Eventually I came back out onto the tarmac, now lit by the orange glow of tungsten streetlamps. On a quiet stretch between two fields, I noticed two caravans behind a wooden fence. They looked deserted. No traffic around. I dumped the bike in the field and had a closer look. This will do for tonight! I thought. I then spent ten minutes trying to force the door of one of the caravans before venturing around the back to answer a call of nature, and noticed the back window wedged open for ventilation. In I went, then out through the front door to get the box off the back of the bike. A proper couch to kip on in this empty basic van, out of the coolness of this night. Radio on and a rolly, and zeds.

I was up at 7.45 a.m., which became a regular trend; don't know why. I gathered my things and cautiously left this 'borrowed' caravan. The bike was over a barbed-wire fence, where I had stashed it out of sight. Shit! The tyres were flat. Did kids do it? Had someone seen me climb through the window the night before? No, but there were loads of prickles where I had dumped the bike the previous night. No problem though. I hauled the bike over the fence and took it over the road. Nothing to repair it with though, you donkey! I set off along the fir-tree-lined straight, pushing my 'shed'. I came across a posh-looking seaside town with a roundabout, then a long boulevard with benches along it. Another kilometre or so of pushing that bike with two punctures, I found the main shopping area next to the beach, and a cheap Chinese shop, which had a one-euro puncture outfit. Sorted – or so I thought. I had both wheels off right in the shopping street, with tourists almost tripping over me. I inflated one tyre and then the other went down again. I put this down to the haste; I double-checked both tubes again and found two microscopic holes. Once again I was mobile – for about two kilometres – and then a repeat of the process again. Then another couple of kilometres and both were flat again. Every time I found the punctures, they were so tiny you could barely see 'em.

This went on all the way to a town called Lepe and then most of the way to the next town – Cartaya – which was a sort of big market town with a bullfighting ring near the centre, surrounded by a huge car parking area. I then went over a bridge-type structure and into the town's central area after riding down a wide boulevard with a truck stop at its top end and industrial buildings on the same side, facing the town homes. Barely over the border, the back tyre – once again – went down. I was getting pissed off with my decision to ride into a field of prickles the night before. I must have fixed the tubes at least half a dozen times each and had travelled nowhere today, and now the light was going. Getting a bit fed up, I headed into town to find a cafe bar: when in doubt get a cafe duplo and everything works out. I found a Spanish bar full of workers enjoying a beer after work. Here I spent half an hour planning my next move. Feeling more perked up, I returned to the industrial buildings next to the boulevard and looked behind them to find a hidey-hole for the night. On my way through the town I headed up a couple of streets which all looked the same – lined with white-walled homes all joined together, giving me the impression that Cartaya was a sea of little white streets and terraces. Along one of these streets, I came across a lad wearing an England top. I asked him if there was any work locally. He was Spanish and had just returned from the UK. He told me of a nearby city called Huelva and that there may be opportunities there. Right: tomorrow's goal sorted. Now, just find a place to kip.

Behind the industrial units, there was an access road from one end to the other, about half a kilometre long. Near the top were two brand-new wooden offices on concrete bases. I walked the length of the access road. Nowhere suitable to kip there, only a couple of skips. And steel shutters everywhere. After about thirty minutes, I returned to the wooden offices and sat out of view. It began to rain gently. Sitting on the concrete base at the rear, I rolled a cig and pieced together the day's underachievement with a disappointing end and no shelter. I looked up at the rear of the offices and then noticed one of the wooden shutters slightly ajar. I found it was open. I peered inside and lit my lighter. The office was empty and warm and out of the elements. Right: another 'hotel' for the night. I nipped back into town and bought a candle – same word as in Portuguese – *vela*. Returning to the sheds, I threw my stuff inside, clambered in and shut the windows, and cracked a bottle of wine as a nightcap.

I did have a drink problem but any addiction can creep up on you just as recreational drug usage does – first for laughs, then to numb personal problems, and then it becomes a way of life. A slippery slope with the small-time peddler on your speed dial. Let's not forget the socially acceptable and only legal drug of them all – alcohol – is as bad as any class A substance over time with heavy use. It was 10 April 2007 and I was lying in a shed in the bottom corner of Spain thinking, 'Everything will be OK. I've somewhere to stay, radio on, candlelight, and am warm and dry. I'll get through somehow!?'

Chapter Five

Cartaya to Huelva

Dozens of Punctures – Back on my Feet Again!

Next day, up at 7.45 a.m. I peered out into the daylight, which hurt my eyes. I climbed out of the shed window, leaving two bottles of cheap wine behind. They were not only heavy but alcohol was just slowing me down. Off I went, trying to find the road to Huelva. First, I'd better fix the punctures again. I found a petrol station about a kilometre away, near a recently-built spacious factory, where I blew up the tyres rock hard and chatted to a Spanish cyclist who was dressed like Miguel Indurain, the legendary Tour de France multiple winner. The bikey left without taking his yellow Sphinx shades. Cheers, Pal! These stopped me squinting in the strong midday sun, and replaced the pair I had left under the bridge over the border.

Back on the road, I managed another half a dozen or so kilometres before the rear tyre slowly deflated along a lonely straight. Usual process: unload all, strip, fix, and inflate with the crap Chinese pump. Another five kilometres, same again! I was down to my last patch now so I used fabric and superglue, bits of paper, bits of plastic and anything else to hand. I'd ride on the rim to Huelva if I had to... I did have to! The punished back tube just tore eventually. I rode less than five or six kilometres before encountering a very long and hot straight near an industrial unit next to a roundabout. The rim just collapsed in a heap. I was sure I could make it on my feet to Huelva: it couldn't be more than ten kilometres away. I abandoned the 'circus' bike and left it standing upright in the sun on the dusty white roadside, looking like the skeleton of a dog that had died sitting on its arse.

On I walked, and then realised how heavy the junk I was carrying in my battered rucksack was. A hot hour later and another long flat straight with bare and dry fields either side, I came across another little roundabout with a few trees around it, with posh-looking homes perched on a hillside to my right, and a really old, tiny wooden cafe cum shop. I paused to light a half-smoked rolly and realised my lighter, which I had owned for months, had finally just expired. I went into the place purely to cadge a light, gaspin' for a smoke and well thirsty. I wasted fifty cents on the best can of coke I had had in ages. The people in the place looked like they were in a time warp from General Franco's days in the forties, but they were kind because they gave me a half-used lighter after I asked the direction for Huelva. It was across the *autovia*, across the bridge, about an hour's walk across the nature reserve. Great! A city. I was bound to find work there. But Spain isn't like Portugal.

It was midday and at least eighty degrees Fahrenheit and I was sweating, partly from the heat and partly from the weight of the rucksack and the pace I was trying to keep. I reached the bridge over the *autovia* towards Sevilla. Over the bridge was a cycle path leading to Huelva. I couldn't see the city yet because of about half a kilometre of trees, mainly fir. After emerging from the woods, I could see the place in the distance across the flatness of the marshland nature reserve. It looked huge on the horizon, with rough marshland, pools, grasses and rivulets which were at least four or five kilometres across. The nearer I got, the more detail I could see stretching right across the horizon as though there was a distinct line preventing building anywhere nearer than the marshes. Nearer still, I realised why. The side I was on comprised of huge salt marshes and lagoons. There was a huge river crossed by two concrete bridges: one carrying the main Autovia and an older two-laner, both not worth a glimpse. There were also old-fashioned, Victorian looking cast iron piers further down the river estuary. These were a clue to Huelva's history. The piers appeared to snake from either side of the riverbank, giving the impression they were at one time connected.

I could now make out stainless steel chimneystacks, docks, boats, buildings and many houses. It looked like a small Liverpool from the Birkenhead side of the Mersey, with its old buildings surrounded by docks and industry. Near the end of where the bridges met the city, I could make out a shipbuilding yard, which had a couple of unfinished half-built ferry ships, one of which was still orange, rusty and unpainted. No problem getting a job in this place, I thought. I got quite excited about the prospect.

The walk seemed like hours but was probably only an hour or so; and the city seemed massive, but it was only a fraction of the size of Liverpool. Eventually I got across. The first place on my right was the shipbuilding yard, which looked a lot smaller than I expected. Around the corner, to the right, were small industrial units and little businesses. I tramped along the dock road past the fish markets. To my left the city looked a smart place. I stopped at a small park which faced the sea, and sat to rest my feet. Students and suchlike wandered around, looking podgy and well off. No one gave me a second glance and no one needed to.

Further up, I later discovered that Huelva was where Christopher Columbus sailed from, four hundred years after Prince Madog had sailed across the Atlantic from north Wales, allegedly.

In Huelva's marina apparently there are replica ships, and many streets bear Columbus's name in some form or another. The longer I walked, the less built up and more industrial it became along this tidal shoreline. After the docks came rough deteriorating concrete which separated the busy road from the beach. This was undermined by the tidal estuary.

To my right, with its back to the river estuary, was the city's footy stadium. The club is called Recreativo Huelva. Another kilometre or so further on were the big factories, which I planned to visit. Opposite these factories, the beach was sandier. Workers were busy erecting wooden walkways and footbridges. These connected the beachside walk, enabling people to avoid having to nego-tiate the road, thus avoiding various gantries carrying water from the river to the factories. The workers had left behind little piles of round off-cuts of timber about ten centimetres long – ideal firewood. Bed sorted on the beach tonight, I went for a small tour of the city. A long walk into the centre, which was well historic and cool, with the trendy and smart Spanish going about their business.

I got one of those free tourist guides from a fella giving them out in a little booth, and sat on a nearby bench to study the basic map of this city. Gasping for the poison nicotine, I lit a long dog-end. I had already begun to keep my eyes open for these after running out of baccy. Sitting in the centre of this city in a large leafy square with huge buildings all around, where everyone was busy but at a slightly slower pace than in British cities, I realised after a while that no one was giving me a second glance. I was anonymous. No one knew anything about the scruffy stranger watching 'em. Only I knew I had a total lack of cash, home and immediate future.

I walked around, intrigued by the place, until my feet got sore, and then decided to retire to the beach as it was getting well past five now. There I could plan my next move. On my way out I found that the footy car park was full of cars and people were drifting up the massive steps to see their team in action. I picked up discarded fags and fries and suchlike, which were still in the boxes. This stuff was my supper at bedtime.

The light was beginning to fade across the marshes. I sat with my back against one of the wooden pilings driven into the beach and supporting the newly-built walkways. Looking out west to the fading sun, I 'necked' my 'scram' and smoked one of the half-cigs I had found. The marshes were getting dark and peaceful. This was in contrast to the sodium orange streetlights waking up the dual carriageway behind me, and the distant hum of factories disappearing into the eastern distance along the shoreline. As the evening wore on I lit a fire with driftwood off the beach and the off-cuts from the wooden bridge. Soon roaring, it lit up my surroundings with a comforting glow and by now it was fully dark. I put my radio on and listened to the sound of a Spanish radio station. After an hour or so a fleet of fishing boats and trawlers passed by, lit up like Blackpool trams against the blackness of the other side, where the salt marshes were. As they headed out to sea, one by one at regular intervals, the vessels of varying sizes and shapes would leave a gentle wake, which would lap against the shoreline about fifteen foot away. There were no other sounds apart from the odd solitary birdcall far away. Warm and comfy on the sand with my fire, I lit another half-cig and drifted away, thinking of next day's plans. A beautiful estuary with the moon and stars seemed as good as it got at the time. I was thinking of how God may be looking after me despite my being skint and outside in a country far from my own. A bit of bliss – warm and peaceful.

The next day I woke at 7.45 a.m., left my dead beach fire ashes, shivering, and wandered the streets of Huelva, looking for food. I found the odd long hard stick of bread; and then at a McDonald's I found a burger with one bite out of it, some cold fries and about twenty red sauces. I even found about ten half-used ciggies and stored them in an old packet together with another old lighter. I was unshaven, scruffy and basically a tramp, wearing a red 'Coval Facil' back-to-front baseball cap with yellow wraparound shades and a heavy rucksack with my leather flying jacket stuffed into the sack seeing as the morning had got warm quickly and the sun was lifting the day's mood.

I proceeded to visit every garage, factory and industrial unit until my feet cried from fresh blisters. Like any city, Huelva was big, especially on foot. I found the Spanish well ruled by the European red tape. They understood my abilities well; I had practised my lines during a visit to the university's *bibloteca* (library). The words weren't much different to Portuguese except pronounced a little differently. Most of the people seemed genuine and wished they could help but the penalties for hiring someone without a permit are strict – no permit, no job. I could apply to the UK for a permit but seeing as I was actually 'on the run', I wasn't a candidate for a permit at that time! Time to hit the road again? Well, there was the last chance of a few informal conversations at the employment centres in the hope of finding someone who would let me 'slip through' the net.

Tramping around the city, I stopped and studied the tourist guide. I wished I had looked at earlier, for this showed a *bureau de employ*. There were actually two, the nearest being in the centre, next to the abandoned Columbino footy stadium, which was going to rack and ruin. When I found it, it seemed bang in the centre of the city, near streets full of hundred-year-old buildings all a couple of stories tall and blackened with pollution. Finding the centre, I queued and eventually spent a fruitless half-hour with a *senora* who looked at the paper-work I carried, explaining what I could do and showing my passport to give me some cred. She listened to my spiel, then handed me to a colleague, who sent me on a trip to the other bureau, where apparently someone spoke English. In other words, my Spanish was shit! Shame! I thought I sounded good. The place was along the boulevard out of town, near the university. Feet now barking with fresh blisters, I spent the next half-hour or so with a fella who dispatched me to a place that could use me and would give me some food as well. Also the place had a fella who could speak English. So after another enthusiastic trip back to the opposite side of the city, almost to the bridge, I struggled to find this place, which sounded vaguely familiar. It was on the second floor of a corner building, up a steep hill. The *Cruz Rouge* – Red Cross! It did have an English-speaking fella, who directly told me: no possibility of work without a permit, which I must obtain from the UK.... Hmmm… this ain't like Portugal. Disappointed, I made my way to the dock area, looking for food on the way. I also kept my eyes peeled for a bike. If I could find one 'left' against a wall or somewhere, this would help me get around quickly for jobs, food, maybe even another city. On another circuit I noticed a large pile of boxes, probably from new furniture, next to some apartment buildings. One was at least six feet in length and had large bubble wrap inside. If it got too cold, that would be my bed.

The trudge back to the beach seemed a lot further than before, and slower, because I was limping on both feet. There was a roadside cafe almost opposite the sand where I'd slept. I had kept my last euro for a cafe duplo in the event of a good or bad day dictating the use of it. And to get totally brassic in style. Sitting on one of those chrome-and-red stools at the bar, it was like being in an American diner. There were a few fellas drifting home, it seemed. I stopped one to ask if he knew of anyone who could use a labourer. By now, I had had another hot day sweating and trudging around the city, and became distracted by my rough reflection in the chrome and glass behind the counter, and tailed off with my conversation, which the bloke picked up on and with a polite *Nao Senhor*, almost walked through my words and made for home. There is genuine respect for European Union rules in Spain but, by now, I certainly didn't look very employable.

It was late afternoon by now and the wind had strengthened a bit. The sun hid itself away and the temperature dropped. I was gonna make an early fire. Rain began to spit so the fire took a bit of effort but it did catch. Sitting down on the soft damp sand was well therapeutic after walking back and forth across this small city. The fire was a fair size after half an hour but with the wind coming straight off the water across the marshes, it was hard to get as warm as I had been the previous night. The darker it became, the heavier the rain fell. I grew accustomed to the cold, but wet and cold ain't recommended. I thought of that large box and pictured myself warm and snug inside, away out of the wind. Someone at that moment walked right over my grave and I shivered. If it got too cold, that box would be my destination tonight.

Just after dark and a little snooze to get the best from the fire I had struggled to make, and after a visit from the police, who probably thought I'd set fire to the boardwalk, it was box time. So, late evening I set off across the city again. Getting there was cold and far longer than any of the last couple of the trips across. But the box was dry, warm and soft. It was also windless inside. I dropped off into a deep sleep in no time, only to be woken up at about 4.00 a.m. by Spanish binmen as they tried in vain to lift me into a compactor truck. I'm glad I wasn't any lighter! Night's sleep disturbed, I wandered around, shivering and half asleep. Around the rear of the apartment blocks was another block of flats being built, but the security was too good to penetrate without effort, so I settled for a small steel cage with plastic wrapped around it, in deep grass on the edge of the site. The cage was no more than a metre square, and there was the possibility of insects, but I was too tired to care. I was back to sleep for a few uncomfortable hours.

Next day, feeling negative, tired and hungry, I found an out-of-date road map of Spain near to the bridge where I arrived. Gibraltar didn't look that far on the map. Neither did France, but the map only showed the main roads. I kept the map – you never know! I was tired and disheartened. At that point, it pissed down with rain. I wandered around the dock area and the nearby suburbs, wondering whether God had this as part of a plan, or if bad luck existed. I briefly considered giving myself up to the police, then immediately discounted the idea, thinking, I've been through worse and survived. There must be a way out! With these thoughts, I growled out loud against the drizzle dripping down my face, "No way is this gonna beat me!"

Trudging, hunger-driven, in a roundabout way from the dockside suburbs towards town, I noticed a couple sending furniture up to the balcony of their third or fourth-floor flat using a huge ladder and a little engine which climbed up the ladder, using a sort of rack-and-pinion system. I had never seen one of those before. I got out and tried to light a half-smoked half-damp fag under the shelter of a giant weeping willow tree. Jealously watching people moving into a comfy pad, I turned around to shelter the lighter from a gentle damp breeze and spotted a couple of shanty huts built out of corrugated sheets and bits of wood. These dwellings were directly behind the dockside cop shop, which faced the fish warehouses next to the water. I went for a closer look. Maybe they would let me stay until I found a job. There were three loosely knocked together dwellings with old curtain doors and rough beds, and old bits and bobs. And a rusty and battered mountain bike leaning against one of 'em. It had one back brake; a choice of two, maybe three gears; no paint on the well-worn frame; but solid and good-nick tyres. Looking around, there was not a soul. Didn't need asking twice...

Off I went in no time, heading straight down that dock road for the last time, totally elated, back across the bridge which connected to the cycle path on to the old cast-iron bridge that led towards the salt marshes, well on a high. I remembered the signs for Sevilla I'd seen on the other side of the city. I stopped for a quick gander at the map. No bother though: I had a distance machine!

Chapter Six
Cold, Rain and Nightmares

Huelva to Sevilla 100 Kilometres,
Sevilla to Los Palacios 46 Kilometres,
10th April 2007 to 12th April 2007

After about ten kilometres of riding on the circular road that led to the *autovia* and Sevilla, motorists would blow their horns at this madman with no lights, but I didn't care. As far as I was concerned this was the most direct route according to my crap map, which showed only major roads. The traffic cops pulled me a few kilometres further up. They insisted I use the minor road that ran roughly parallel to the *autovia*. So after a quick passport check I left up an off ramp and turned right down a darker road through nowhere. Well late by now and, a bit sweaty and tired, I came across a lonesome lorry park. Opposite the lorry park was a Volvo truck garage. I headed into the lorry-park, which was puddled and gravel rough. Looking around, I wanted a flat deck trailer to kip on. A suitable flat-back timber trailer did the job for an hour or so until it rained again. I got off the trailer, bike and all, into a nearby box body, which was minus its chassis and had no sides. There was no wind so the middle of the body kept dry – just about – and I was able to lie almost flat, not absorbing the soaking timber floor either side of where I was lying. I managed a couple of hours' kip before aches and a bit of cramp woke me up at about four or five in the morning, with the odd trucker starting his engine, followed by others. These were Scanias. Briefly, useless thoughts went through my mind of how comfy and quiet to drive and easy to service these vehicles are, but that knowledge was of no use to me at this moment. Beginning to shiver a little, I needed to get some blood flowing. Loading up, I headed off along the road, which was part of the N-431, until I came across a junction and did a left in the dark. The road I was now on was pretty straight, with some gradual rises. I made some progress travelling through an industrial area with agricultural dealerships and truck repair garages next to several factories and processing buildings, which had the odd vehicle parked for the night in the dark spots of sleeping industry. I thought of nicking a car or a lorry or maybe a van to drive for a day or so, then dump it. Near what seemed like a power station and a garage along this straight I noticed a Renault Extra van parked on the right, next to a shop of sorts. I turned around to investigate. The front doors were locked but the back doors were open and stocked with next day's deliveries. There were about thirty fresh flat breads in plastic wrapping – sort of soft naan type breads – jackpot! A full stomach for a day or so. Wolfing a couple down, I was full of food, and feeling fit on a 'decent' bike. Let's go!

Some factories were working, whining and humming with faraway processes, disturbing the immediate surroundings. These places were soon left behind as I edged towards dawn on the A472 out of San Juan del Puerto. It became a little warmer. I cycled on along a straight, where I could see the main *autovia* far away to my left, which became nearer as the two highways crossed over each other as it became light, but not before I stopped next to a solitary scrap yard, with nothing else around but vast fields. Here I stopped for a pee. There was an abandoned Corsa parked outside the scrap yard, which seemed deserted. It had an inviting back seat and I was a little tired and in need of a 'warm' sleep. In I went for a much-needed cosy hour or so, undisturbed by rain, wind and cold. This did me the world of good because I rode the ninety-five kilometres to Sevilla almost without stopping but for water.

Like most cities, Sevilla's suburbs were huge. The map I had was not detailed enough to show me exactly where I was going, and like any huge place with its suburban sprawl, acres of housing, shops, businesses, cars, trucks, boy racers and Fonestuktoearism, had things which I didn't miss but which most folk consider essential today. For the stress and troubles I associated with mobile phones, and motors large or small, I realised that however rough things might have gotten recently; it was still so healthy to be free of the ridiculous graft of running a business whilst burning candles at both ends. I had left that life, glad to be free of it.

The deeper into the city I went the more I got lost and the more it rained. All the time I kept thinking how big Sevilla is. I dropped down big hills into the city's rough arse and up more steep hills, trying to look for signs that might have words that meant 'coast' or 'south' but ended up pretty hot and pretty lost, resorting to looking at bus stop maps, which were squarely drawn to represent routes around. Lost, I could have just done with a cig and a think, especially as I had developed a slow puncture, which was hampering decent progress up and down big hills. I had used up the last of the puncture outfit up on that last series of flats on bike two, which had collapsed on me a few days ago – problem! Then it rained harder. I found a garage and blew up my tyre. After another hour, I found a Lidl with two full bins outside, which I checked out. I found six in-date choc yoghurts with one damaged, a pile of biscuits, and some apples and oranges – great 'cos on this journey my appetite became huge so whenever I had the chance to eat I ate until I almost burst. Where would the next meal come from?

Moving on, I rode around Sevilla, getting disoriented, wet and fed up in the process of constantly pumping a rapidly deflating back tyre and searching for garages with convenient air lines. I studied another bus timetable map and almost figured out where I should head just as it rained again. Pissed off that I couldn't get clear of this city, at that moment I suddenly began recognising my surroundings! – I had just spent a couple of hours riding around in a big circle! Deflated, I leaned against the Lidl bin I had had a feed from earlier. Wet through but resigned, I stared into space for a few moments thinking, God, I've definitely upset you along the line. So I admit to having had a crafty prayer, just in case. Then I managed to light a half-smoked cig and drew the dirty but ever so relieving nicotine deep into my lungs, which temporarily made me forget my small problems. I looked in the bin to see if there was anything I had missed earlier. I'm so glad I did – I found a plastic blister pack with a chrome box spanner and a puncture outfit minus the pump someone had bought it for! Who would have guessed...? Maybe God was listening to my crafty prayer? Nah, just a coincidence...

I rode on after fixing the puncture and finding an air line, making the tyre rock hard. I had to get on the *autovia* towards the south coast before evening, but without familiar names or sights I was riding more or less by instinct, until I met a couple of bodies who eventually understood me enough to send me across the huge river and along the docks towards the outskirts. I found myself in more suburbs but this time more high-rise and rougher looking. In the rush hour with piles of traffic as it began to go dark, there were fields ahead. Yes, I was finally almost free of Sevilla. I had wasted hours going in circles but wouldn't have found that puncture outfit if I hadn't! The journey from Huelva, which was kind of overnight and most of this day, in circles with slow punctures, meant it was now sundown and I was only now finally out of the place. What a day! But it certainly wasn't over yet. I was not going to forget the next few hours in a hurry.

The A-376 going south from Sevilla was the right direction but because of the traffic and hassle from the traffic cops, I rode up a few roads, which I thought ran parallel to the main *autovia*. They didn't. So after a false road or two, I rode back again and went over the main road. Trying to make sense of my very undetailed map under a tungsten streetlamp, lighting a road leading up to an estate of two or three-million-euro homes, built next to 'Golf Sevilla', where a security chap in a car dispatched me out of the place – politely enough. A taxi driver was parked up at the top of the road next to the *autovia*, where, after a brief conversation, he reckoned there was a rough track next to the orange grove which ran next to the *autovia* for some miles until it became a two-laner – or that's what I thought he said. All I could see was a muddy track leading into the dark distance next to a used-car sales place, only accessible by climbing off the loop that connected to the main *autovia*. Off I went just as it began to drizzle; making sticky progress along the half mud and half gravel track, past a large farm-type house surrounded by high metal fencing and poplar trees. After this, there was nothing but a distant orange grove. After a while two lads in a long wheelbase Pajero Estate coming out of the distant dark told me to sling my hook, to which I agreed until they went out of sight. I found a track which led off up to a higher part of the orange grove, in case they returned. It rained heavier and stopped as quickly as it started. I noticed a building in the dark-ness of the trees further into the grove. I went to investigate. Sweating again, I thought this might be a hidey-hole for the night as progress was almost dead for today. It was a sort of concrete pump house, about two metres high, with a flat roof. There was plastic piping all around, looking like coiled-up black snakes in the dark. It was reasonably warm so I decided to make the roof of this pump house my bed. Throwing my now heavy rucksack up, I stood on the crossbar of the bike and pulled myself onto the roof, taking with me a bungee cord I had picked up off the road earlier that day, thinking that it might come in useful. With the bungee, I pulled up the bike onto the roof, as though I might have the bike nicked whilst I was asleep, even though I was a kilometre from any lights, people or civilisation!

About eight to ten kilometres away in the distance, I could see planes going into land. They passed me directly overhead, about five hundred metres away, en route to Sevilla airport. The wind died off and I had a couple of oranges and biscuits, laid my stuff out and decided that you can't make a good day out of a bad 'un, and within ten minutes or less I was asleep. I had taken hours to cross Sevilla and still couldn't quite get clear of the place. I thought to myself as I dropped off, that must be the worst of this day.

No it wasn't! It was about to get far worse. It was quite warm so I must have been asleep for a couple of hours then I heard this almighty scream of a jet engine – it must have been lower than normal for some reason and I woke up with a start. Lying on my back, I was looking straight up at a thick cloud momentarily lit up by the aeroplane's lights. Virtually as soon as my eyes opened this passenger jet seemed to burst through the underbelly of the cloud with the sound of a huge marshmallow being sucked up a powerful vacuum pipe with a loud 'schtump!' Before I came to my senses, at that precise moment the cloud ruptured above me and emptied its load on me as though the jet had broken its skin. Soaked through before becoming fully conscious, I had to find shelter or head to the *autovia*. I threw the bike down off the concrete house roof and in the soaking wet blackness, stumbling and still half-asleep, I strapped stuff to the bike and trudged towards the distant lights of the *autovia* through the thick dark orange grove. This was dangerous in itself, as I couldn't see the branches, which were almost gouging my eyes out. The rain got heavier and louder. I could hardly see. The bike became difficult to push because the muddy soil was a quagmire underfoot, eventually actually stopping the wheels from turning, so I had to drag and carry its heavy, awkward bulk.

What a situation: lost in the dark, torrential rain, no roads, no shelter. The orange grove thinned and I could make out a high dark wall of sorts. I couldn't see what it was made of or why it was there so I leaned the bike against a knobbed old orange tree and found the fence to be metal. I walked most of its length and found that the only way to get over and see what shelter there may be inside was to climb a tree growing next to it. With my heavy rucksack and being drenched to the skin, I carefully climbed up the tree and edged along a branch to the edge of the metal fence. I was able to clamber onto the corrugated metal roof of a building, making a lot of noise, which was being masked by the ear-shattering noise of rain battering the top of the building. Towards one edge there was a gap where the roof didn't quite cover its length, and there was a light on inside. It was a metal-fabricating workshop for skips, with familiar tools and equipment all about. I climbed down into this shelter, away from the battering rain, and dropped my heavy bag onto the concrete floor, chuffed to be out of the dark and wet as I dripped heavily wherever I stood. I walked to the metal front doors, which were slightly ajar. There was a very large yard, at least a hundred metres square, with dark rectangular shapes near and distant. Some were lorries and some were machinery and materials. To the far left was another entrance to this yard. It was a huge entrance but had no lights, just vague silhouettes. Seeing as I was soaked through I thought about finding a lorry to get into and get warmed up out of the rain. Carefully I made my way from truck to truck, trying the doors. Lots of trucks here. The rain seemed to get heavier, more so than anything we have in the UK, even Wales. This by now was like a waterfall, hard to see through. Most of the way across the yard I had tried the doors and then found a Jeep which was unlocked – aah! Except!! There was a fella reclining in the seat, asleep. He wasn't too happy about being woken up by a wet shape climbing into his space and it gave me a shock finding there was actually a body in that seat at all! At this point all hell broke loose. I went "Whoa!" and he did the Spanish equivalent. Then his noisy black dog bounded out at me but made more noise than bite. The fella quickly started his Jeep and before I could do anything he reversed back sharpish, putting his lights on, and tried to 'herd' me towards the entrance of the other yard.

"OK! I'M FUCKING GOING!!"

I shouted to him, out of frustration at not being able to explain why I was there. As I was walking with the lights behind me all I could see were piles of building materials, piles of sand, and to the right a row of skip lorries and a high heavy-duty chicken-wire fence, with what looked like barbed-wire on top. I trudged through ten feet across puddles, slowly, in defiance, and not knowing where I was going, rain still lashing down, pitch black. I upped my pace after I heard the first BOOM! The psycho was firing off a gun!! Now I definitely didn't need this! I had a moment of realisation of the worst possible scenario. It was well after midnight, there were torrents of rain on my head, I was thousands of miles from home, tired, and now being shot at. I quickly dropped out of sight behind some of the sand piles, losing 'Psycho' in his Jeep and his headlights. I could make out the corner posts of this yard about fifty metres away from the shelter of pallets of ceramic pipes and bricks. I plodded across more huge muddy puddles and climbed over the fence and barbed-wire. I didn't run. I didn't feel I needed to. I just wandered through the puddles in and out of the shield of materials thinking, He ain't gonna murder me, is he…? Almost resigned and saying, "Come on then, shoot me. It can't get any worse. My life is fucked anyway…" Well, I thought, I am glad I wasn't drunk because I would have been stupid enough to 'front' him. Not recommended: fronting a man firing off his gun!

Fuck me! The whole scene was like one of those nightmare films, but real and happening to me! I dropped off the top of the fence – about two and a half metres – thump! I then fell over for good measure. As I got up, Psycho shot off his gun again, but now it was at least a hundred metres away and the rain was dimming the sound. I took stock of things. First, I was alive, and not shot! That was a start. Drenched in the early hours in a storm. Oh shit! My bag, with anything of any use in it, was way over the other side of those two yards – about a quarter of a kilometre away in that workshop, and the bike was still leaning against the tree I had climbed to get into the yard. I needed them both.

Alongside this yard was a ploughed field that ran all the way up to the orange grove. I couldn't actually see through the darkness and heavy rain, but this was the only route to retrieve them. I started my way up along the outside of the barbed-wire fence, trying to remain upright as I kept a wide-eyed look out for Psycho. I fell over several times along the length of this rapidly filling muddy ditch, almost up to my knees and becoming deeper. I became brave enough to climb out of the ditch and trudge along the edge of the ploughed field. No gunshots for a bit. About halfway between the builders' yard and the wall surrounding the inside yard, I heard the sound of a diesel engine start, about fifty metres distant. Good! Psycho was busy with something else to do – except he had just started up a generator which powered floodlights! Instead of being inconspicuous in the gloom I must have stood out like a rabbit caught in the glare of headlights, smack bang in the middle of a ploughed field. I tried to run for the cover of the wall but the gloopy mud was heavy and sticking to my boots, causing me to fall over once again. Psycho began letting off more shots. Whether he had spotted me or not I didn't really care – let's get gone! I became sheltered from his view by the beginnings of the wall, which put me back in the shadows again. Getting to this wall took longer than it should have because of the thick mud – like having a pair of sticky dumb-bells attached to my feet. I had to catch my breath and I had to slog with every other step, making the guttural sound of a boot being pulled from wet clay mud. Getting around the corner of the wall to the tree where the bike was, I could hear Psycho still shooting off his gun but well away in the distance, and after every two shots there was a gap, so he must have been loading up sporadically. That would give me time to get over and collect my bag, which I did as quickly and quietly as I could although the noise of the rain was still like a million ball-bearings hitting a greenhouse.

Hurling the bag over the fence and quickly following it over, I made my way back to the field, which was going to be fun. I took a very wide track out from the glare of the floodlights, which lit the mud up for at least a hundred metres out across the wet furrows. This trip, way across the sloppy, thick, muddy ploughed field took it out of me. There was no way but to carry the bike whilst I slipped and slid all over, going over more than once and getting my feet stuck a couple of times. It was heavy and awkward carrying the bike in my haste to reach the *autovia*, the wheels being totally caked with thick topsoil mixed with sandy clay. I got well out of breath in this process. The journey probably only took fifteen minutes or so but it felt like a lot longer. I finally crossed a busy stream that didn't exist an hour ago, right where the field joins with its boundary, and then went up an embankment which separated the *autovia* from the field. A distant boom told me the well-rattled security bloke was pretty harmless by now and costing himself a lot in spent gun cartridges. I had ruined his night and mine.

I crossed the carriageway and finally began to pedal. Mud fell off in massive clumps, with me and the bike thickly caked in glutinous crap, and the mud slowly being dissolved by the torrent.

I cycled for a couple of kilometres until I found a lay-by with some kind of a bus stop next to a footbridge going over to a factory. I stopped and sat in the shelter, then kind of organised myself. I was hungry again so I pulled out some sodden biscuits and some fruit, and wolfed them down. Being shot at in the rain and mud is hungry work. I was wet but relatively warm at my core, and despite the rain I could see, with the light of occasional passing traffic, that I was steaming from my hands and wet jeans. I sat with my feet up and rested for a bit, actually nodding off, so I must have been tired from the day's, and the night's, adventures. Cooling down, I was woken up by the spray from the bow waves of early lorries flying past about four metres away. Though I was still half-asleep, it was time to get moving up and off before I started shivering.

The *autovia* was quiet but for lorries. It was straight and I cycled for at least a couple more hours before hitting an exit for civilisation over to the right. I would have loved to have found some shelter for a while. This was a small town called Utrera. I stopped and shivered at a roundabout near the centre, watching the Spaniards going off to work, lorries of all shapes and sizes, gangs being picked up in vans and minibuses, and the odd schoolkid waiting for buses. It was still dark and damp, and drizzling a little. I looked to see if my little radio was working and showing the time. It was 6.30 a.m. I checked my damp dog-eared map and, to get warm and move on, decided to take an unsigned road which looked like it was headed south-ish, only it was east, in my haste to inspire some blood to flow to my feet.

The miserable wet dawn broke. Daylight came and it did brighten up a little. I rode on along a windswept endless straight, eventually reaching a place called Los Palacios, which looked a bit of a one-horse town affair. I stopped to give my bum and legs a rest and checked out a map on a road sign. I then realised I had just ridden in the wrong direction for fifteen kilometres or more. I wolfed down some frankfurters and some more biscuits, and tried to figure the way back to the N-IV, which is the road towards the coast. Just at that time I had a severe attack of the 'squits' and there was no way of stopping it!

What a day – and night – I had just had, and to top it all I now had jeans full of shit! Well, I thought to myself, things have got to get better than this!

I slowly made my way to a roadside stream, which was a little lower than the road – one of many which drain the surrounding huge fields. I climbed down into the stream and removed the wet top pair of black jeans, then removed a skinny second set underneath and discarded them in the undergrowth. Inside the pocket of those shitty jeans was a last reminder of my last girl – a gold ear stud. This was a shitty watershed, literally! I then sat up to my stomach in this stream, next to the road, giving the passing motorists and truckers an interesting sight – a half-naked tramp sitting up to his belly, having a bath in a reasonably warm roadside stream. But the tramp didn't care as they blew their horns as they drove by. He wasn't likely to see those people again and didn't care what they thought at this point either.

Chapter Seven

To the Coast

12th April 2007 Los Palacios to Puerto de Santa Maria – 110 Kilometres,
13th April 2007 Santa Maria to Tarifa – 131 Kilometres

Movin' on, I rode along another endless straight, cycling across a dead straight, poplar-tree-lined flat area with a huge sky above and through enormous fields which would make fields back in the UK look like window boxes. In the fields were those strange field-watering apparatuses over a hundred metres long and looking like massive stick insects, motionless in the distance – the longest I'd ever seen.

I cycled along this flat-fielded area for so long that my jeans were almost dry by the time I got a change of scenery. When I came across reasonably flat-tish road I covered good distance, almost going into a trance, until I would start nodding off! The road intersected with the N-IV road, which headed towards Cadiz and the south coast. I stopped in the middle of nowhere, near the main road forking off back to Sevilla, and had about an hour's kip on a wooden picnic table.

Refreshed, for the next few hours of riding I rose and fell through deserted Spanish lowlands of grassy hills, with the odd silhouette of a black bull with horns, the first of many I kept spotting. I thought they were real, having nothing around them to give me a sense of scale, until I realised they were about twenty feet high.

Artic truck after artic truck, in both directions, would either briefly pull me or slow me down for a moment with the bow wave of the wind they pushed aside. As I climbed the hills, the chain would jump the cogs because of the knackered derailleur. I stopped to use another roadside-discarded, tattered bungee chord to tension the chain, and this helped a bit. Being stuck permanently in sixth gear I could only change the front crank wheel up or down two positions, because that was all this old bike had, so the hills were hard work.

I covered a few more rises, miles long, till the road began to flatten. The sun came out. I put on those yellow shades, to stop me squinting, on the way to Jerez de la Frontera. I felt I was shifting now that the natural endorphins were taking over. Pumping away at the pedals in top gear I began to 'scream' a couple of old rock songs: 'Livin' on a Prayer' and 'Summer of '69' and then thinking out loud, Yeah, it seems about right, doesn't it, the living on a prayer bit?

Along these long stretches of road, good memories flooded into my head, which were previously buried for years with graft, business and unending personal shit, supporting ready-made families as well as trying to keep – fading – contact with my own. Memories from my early twenties, with disposable income, motocross, going to rock gigs such as 'Monsters of Rock', 'Cumbria Rock Fest', 'Mildenhall Rock and Blues Festival', 'Stairways' and 'The Tiv', usually with sixteen lads and girls, in an old transit or suchlike. I then learned to paraglide and scuba dive in order to get away from the pub and to replace motocross 'cos it was costing me too many broken bones. Over a decade full of adventures and colourful people, good and bad. Mates that are no longer alive or around to recall the memories. And some girls that would return to haunt me years later. I thought that unless I learned something new every year I would get stuck in a rut with a telly guide – not my sort of life. My life was far from boring but far from peaceful or comfortable either. And ending up crazy by trying to please too many people and juggle too many things at once. The bottle and the drugs I took, eventually crashed it all in one go. The result: riding across the middle of nowhere on a stolen bike with no money, food and shelter. Hmmm!

Skirting the scattered outskirts of Jerez, still on the N-IV, I eventually rode into the busy town of El Puerto de Santa Maria. I was there only because my crap map showed one red line, which I had followed to the nearest part of the coast. I must have been well late arriving in this place because along the well-lit busy streets the music from clubs and bars was giving the place an alive feel, especially near the centre where the bridge crossed the river. Being late and feeling myself getting tired by now, I decided to stop on the southern end of the large well-built bridge carrying a wide and busy road across this river. On the right-hand-side was a triangular paved area away from the busy folks enjoying themselves on the streets with their bars and restaurants. I leaned against the stone wall and looked across the wide dark river with its muddy edges looking black in contrast to the yonder lights and music. Booming away, it sounded inviting, but I felt a million miles away from enjoying that scene!

It was warm and no one seemed to notice me. Nobody crossed this bridge much on foot. There were no benches here but the old stone bridge had well-built walls with wide stone plinths, wide enough for me to lie on under the orange tungsten lighting. I hadn't looked at my dog-eared map to suss out next day's journey or to gauge how far I'd travelled. Too tired, I soon drifted off on my back, trying subconsciously not to roll off the edge of the ledge.

The date was 12 April. I had travelled about a hundred and thirty kilometres (eighty miles) plus a few more to account for detours and getting lost without a decent map. A bit disappointing, but not bad considering the terrain. I remember waking up early on the concrete ledge and it was still dark. It was just after 5.00 a.m. I saddled up and got on the road immediately to get warm. My hands and feet were well cold, as a result of my deciding to sleep next to a major river. I followed the road towards the main *autovia*, the E-05. This became long, flat and straight, with the added advantage that I could dispense with using the map, or so I thought. Covering plenty of straight miles of good nick road – mainly *autovia* – I stopped only to eat some of my diminishing scraps of dried-out biscuits and oranges, and once to retrieve a back rack from the back of a discarded bike that was lying in a ditch between Chiclana de la Frontera and Conil. I fitted the rack to the back of my bike, using bits of electrical wire from the roadside, and lashed my heavy bag to it. That made things easier on the back and a lot less sweaty.

I found the N-340, which was to be the road I would become very familiar with. This began to take me inland for long hot periods throughout the day. I began to appreciate the green of Spain as I rode up and down vast tracts of rolling slopes between steep rocky mountains and cliffs which rose straight up as though they had punctured through the well-kept farmland. At one point,

I dropped through a river valley and found a junction next to a river bridge surrounded by trees. I stopped next to it and lit half a dog-end I had found, to give myself some temporary respite from my aching legs and back. I necked some water and thought of my now rumbling belly. I had to find the coast again but also didn't want to go on a detour and use up valuable energy and daylight. I got out the satnav map, which was no help at this point. It only showed one unmarked red arterial road, which I presumed was the N-340.

At this junction I was sweating quarts and, bare-topped by now, I had on only my jeans, baseball cap – back to front – and my shades as I was sitting with my arse against the wall of the bridge. Cars lined up to my left as I looked back up the road I had just come from. Some cars turned right onto the N-340, and some turned left. It looked as broad as it was long to go one way or the other. Underneath the bridge was a small stream running through a bed made for a wide river. It looked inviting, and I could do with a cool wash. A momentary trance was broken by a lady in a white BMW who appeared to give me eye contact. She was about twenty feet away. I looked around and thought, 'She aint' lookin' at me... is she?' But she was. She drove her motor over the road and back around and pointed with her finger towards a car park just set back from the junction, and behind some trees that covered the nearby hillside. She parked her car there and beckoned me with a quick wave. What could she want with me? Directions? What else could she want from me? She looked about mid-thirties, with big peroxide hair up in a bunch, and with huge dark eyes; and as I got nearer I realised she may have been nearer forty and very busty. I leaned on the roof of the car and she lit a cigarette. I asked her if I could have one.

"*Si*, no problem," she replied, passing me a 'Ducat'.

As she gave me a cig and as we talked, she made no bones about leaning towards me and exposing more-than-ample breasts, minus a bra, in the heat of the day. Why was she starting a conversation with a fella on a bike who was wearing nothing but scruffy jeans, shades and a baseball cap? I was well tanned from working outdoors in the Portuguese sun for months and might have looked younger than I actually was from a distance, once I had removed my layers of top clothing midday.

Then I spotted something: not all of this woman was a woman! I couldn't tell at first as her voice sounded so feminine. But there was the slightest amount of facial hair poking through her thick make-up! She asked me what I was doing. I told her. She then offered to let me have a shower in her place and told me she owned a nearby salon. I gently asked her if 'those' were implants...

"*Si*. You like?" At that point she cupped her very ample implants and asked me if they made me feel like some "jiggy, jiggy"!

Quite shocked by now, I almost swallowed my ciggy and coughed out a giggle at the same time! I used the lame excuse that my wife wouldn't approve, which was bullshit – it was just the quickest excuse I could think of at the time. I was separated from my wife by my own choice. 'She' was actually prettier than my wife, who would also 'do' anyone, male or female, any time.

Trying not to laugh, I told her, in the context of 'thanks but no thanks', that I needed my strength for my journey. But 'she' became quite insistent that I could rest at her house and then go 'later', or tomorrow!

"Sorry, I've got to go now!" I looked towards the direction of Barbate.

"OK, *como quanto*?" she quickly added.

This got funnier: she was asking me 'how much?' The briefest of thoughts flashed through my mind bearing in mind I was skint and starving by now – but then, with a bang, I realised what I might be having to agree to!! Regardless of what cash she might be offering, it was time to make a sharp exit.

I rode off towards the coastal town of Barbate and more than a couple of times looked back over my shoulder for a white BMW!

After a bath in the sea, using my almost empty shampoo bottle, I washed my clothes again, wrung them out, and rode on whilst they dried out on me in the sunshine of the day. Out of Barbate, I went along a minor coastal road, the A 2231, which climbed back inland and rejoined with the N-340 in a wide valley on sweeping roads between some incredible steep rocky mountains, on which were fast motorbikes and local lads on big four-stroke quad bikes which flew by, exploiting the wide corners for all their worth. This scene was beautiful: long, fast bends gently rising and dropping down and around this very long valley going off into the mountainous distance down towards the next coastal town.

After a couple of hours, I eventually reached a town called Tarifa, down off the N-340. I could have travelled a lot further that day but the road ahead was mega steep for miles up into the rocky mountains and my body was craving calories pretty desperately by now. I had travelled one hundred and twelve kilometres (seventy miles) across a mixture of hills and valleys in the heat on a couple of biscuits and a couple of oranges. Got to find some eats. I could see a supermarket near the road into the town just after the junction off the main drag. Looking towards the hills that would take me over to Gibraltar, I instantly thought I would leave those until fed and rested. This turned out to be a good choice because the bins behind this place had a pile of fresh oranges still in their nets, and six litres of UHT milk with one of the pack split open. I checked the sell-by date: no problem, so I tried one – splendigedig! I was that thirsty by then I drank two of 'em straight off. I stuffed the oranges and cartons, together with some biscuits and five fromage frais, into my crammed bag and headed down town.

Tarifa had bars, discos and streets of joined-up white villas and terraces along ever-steepening streets with posters on walls advertising various European DJs playing at the various clubs in this cool town appealing to the dance and club music scene. I could imagine Tiesto playing here on his winter break before he became a megastar.

Right at the seafront next to a sea wall I found a couple of benches placed near a little cul-de-sac just out of the wind, which seemed to gust around this place. I was at the end of a street leading to the beach with a car parking area and small bars next to it. Looking south-east out to sea, I saw a rocky island which looked accessible only when the tide is out. Across the bay, looking east towards the Gib direction, were boats and a harbour in the distance. As the light was fading and I was getting tired, I decided to arrange my bed for the night and had my 'supper', watching a hydrofoil ship quietly coming across the harbour from the direction of (maybe) Morocco. The lights now on across the harbour away to the east gave the whole area an expensive, cool Euro look. The night fell and it wasn't too cold either, unlike the last few nights. A distant lighthouse briefly lit up the images far away and one side of the island. I flipped on the tiny radio and listened to Kabin FM and slept a deep sleep until the chill woke me at dead on 7.45 a.m.

Chapter Eight
Tarifa to Gibraltar

Tarifa to Gibraltar – 46 Kilometres.
14ᵗʰ April 2007 to 15ᵗʰ April 2007

It was a good job I had that feed the night before. My legs needed it for the hills out of Tarifa. They must rise at least a thousand feet from sea level on a three-lane highway that crosses the hills to Algeciras and Gibraltar. It was a crisp and fresh sunny morning, clear and bright – one of those which make you feel good to be alive. I thought Gib couldn't be more than twenty kilometres away but, boy! I climbed the main road up inclines I hadn't seen back in Wales unless they were well off the beaten track. The road climbed over the rocks, roughly parallel to the sea. What a view for hundreds of kilometres! As the morning wore on the traffic became a little busier, mainly with motorcyclists, bikeys, cars and the occasional large-engined lorry straining flat out up these hills. Up and up the road climbed, with the odd short crest that gives a short relief before climbing still further up and around the next crest. The road flattened very slightly over little dips bridged by concrete road-carrying structures, and then it would continue up to another brow just when I thought I was at the top, and then there would be another... and another. There were steep drop-offs to my right looking out over the sea, and steep jagged rocky peaks lit up by the bright early-morning sun. To my left and facing west, literally hundreds of wind turbines came into view like marching monsters, all shapes and sizes, some thirty or forty foot high – older in appearance and built with steel frames, to newer, gigantic ones uttering their steady 'Whoosh! Whoosh!' I would crest another apex or round a bend, and there would be more turbines, which were initially hidden from view. The sight and sound brought the mountains to life.

A couple of hours of straining and pushing the bike, then the road maxed out past a cliff-side café. I would have loved to have stopped for a drink and a look across the bay to Gibraltar and across to Morocco, with money to pay for the drink too!

The road descended steeply for a kilometre or so, then rose up a final, well-steep, kilometre. On this last climb, a Spaniard on his up-to-date high-tech mountain bike in full kit passed me and handed me an energy bar. He shouted from over his shoulder, "*Muint forca por trabalho*!" (Strength for work!)

"*Obrigado, er... Gracias, Senor*!" I shouted to him, offering my thanks, first in Portuguese and then in Spanish. With that, he raised his arm and kept pumping away at his pedals up the hill. A chocolate-and-magnesium energy bar... sound!

Eventually I crested this last murderous hill and found a rewarding downhill for at least three or four kilometres down to Algeciras. I couldn't get much speed up though, bearing in mind how steep it was, and I realised I had... another slow puncture! Across the bay, I could see that famous Rock of Gibraltar, with a cloud glued to its northern peak. That was my goal today – maybe a better chance of a job and some money to get things straight. The puncture was a slow one and I wasn't stopping now – Gib didn't look far and I was sure to find a petrol station on the way, where I could blow the tyre up. I sweated along the well-used road alongside the mixture of thickly packed suburbs and built-up industry right next to the bay and sea transport. This road was dusty and dirty tarmac, which became dual carriageway most of the way around the bay. Traffic flew by me, blowing grit and dust into my eyes and sticking dirt to the sweat on my forehead. The carriageway steepened up to San Roque – a place littered with flyovers and clone retail megastores.

Eventually I turned towards Gibraltar. I couldn't find any signs for it until I was almost at the place – only a sign for La Lina de la Conception. I stopped at a garage, blew the tyre rock hard again, and made the point of shaking the hand of a Gibraltarian fella in his sixties who was getting fuel for his old white Merc with a UK-style Gibraltarian black-on-yellow number plate. I told him he was the first person I had spoken to since Portugal. (Well, apart from the tranny!)

The fella looked surprised. Looking back, I think he must have thought I was a tramp who thought he had just crossed the Sahara desert or something, but to me such a lot seemed to have happened since I left Portugal. It seemed ages ago, but was really only a few days ago.

As I arrived at the border crossing in Gibraltar, which is the actual runway that runs east to west, as you cross it, the police checked my passport. I doubted if they would know if I was an on-the-run criminal, having dozens of passport holders to check in minutes, but it was a strange feeling having it checked by a British bobby with a Gib suntan. Going onto Gibraltar for the first time was strange: it was like being in England, with English signs everywhere, a Shell garage, then a Morrisons, and Gib-registered vehicles everywhere. It is one overcrowded, busy place. Along the dock road I turned right and up through the city walls into the city centre. It is a maze of quaint old streets, shops and houses built on every bit of space reaching up to the steepest part of the rock cliff itself, with the town area spiralling up and around the crowded streets, lined with hundreds of scooters and mopeds. Great for tourists – if you have dosh. The main square is quite traditional except for Burger King, where I had my fill of second-hand burgers and fries and half a litre of Pepsi with ice in it, straight from the tables where people had left these items, and I lusted after this stuff like a patrolling seagull with a raging hunger and thirst. I even remember having an almost-perfect ice cream left on a plate to finish.

Sitting down to rest my tired legs and smoke a half-done Rothmans, I got hassled by a Polish guy who looked no better than I did. I had lived with a couple of Polish blokes. We all worked at the same place, where I repaired artic trailers and they were welders, at an Irish trailer manufacturers. I waited for his begging spiel then told him to "Fuck off! I have no money." This made the guy stay for a while, as though I was hiding something because how would I be able to eat here without money?

"*Kurva, eu tinho nao dinerho!*" I said in a mixture of Polish and Portuguese. Just then a tall, rough-looking fella came over and told the Pole to 'do one!' I asked him, "Are you a Brit, Pal? I'm Welsh. Tell your mate to fuck off. I ain't in the mood. You got any fags?" I then cheekily added, not wishing to miss an opportunity.

"Aah, a Brit!" He sounded surprised.

He then handed me a half-empty packet of twenty Dunhills and offered me half a bottle full of brandy, which I declined. Tony was the guy's name. He was about six foot two, with a gruff voice and general gruff look.

The beggars ended up giving to the person they were begging from!

It turned out that Tony had a police 'problem' and a drink problem. He had been all up the Spanish *sols* looking for work, and had resorted to petty theft to get by. He had also done a tour of the Spanish coastal jails and been roughed up in most of 'em, which made me laugh because he said it as though it was part of life – a necessary evil to get by! Anyway, he had talked to 'Father Charlie', a local Catholic who was giving him the plane fare, and he may be flying home soon.

"You can see Father Charlie too if you want to go home. He will book you a ticket just like that!" He flicked his fingers. Just then I thought, 'That's how easy it would be to cop out!'

I decided to spend a few hours job hunting. Tony had spent months job searching around Gib and all up the Spanish *sols*. But I thought his manner and obvious drink problem would have held him back... What the fuck did I know?! I visited every business with manual labour and mechanical skills involved, as well as the local job centre, where the wages were advertised in pounds as well as Euros. Three hundred and three quid seemed to be what most employers paid. But, just like that city Huelva, I needed a permit, as well as an address. According to the local passport office: no address, no permit; no permit, no job etc. Same old story. I tried to persuade a couple of dockside businesses to bend the rules a little bit, but they informed me Gibraltar has these rules to stop the Brits coming for 'working holidays' and disappearing afterwards, plus there are plenty of Gibraltarians who need jobs anyhow. Fair point.

On the way round the island through one of the many one-lane tunnels a hundred years or more old, I found a little concrete electric shed next to a quiet cove facing the bay and the mountains I had crossed that day. Construction was going on down below the road next to the shed, just near the pebble beach, and workers were abandoning the place for the day. I scaled the flat roof via the cliff side the house was built against, as the evening came. I kind of 'cosied' up on this roof. It was sheltered and warm. I could see the various ships anchored up around the bay, all with their lights on by now. It was calm and quiet, only disturbed by the occasional boy racer bombing through the tunnel. Some things don't change that much. Under the sodium lighting I studied the dog-eared map again, and then ate some Jaffa cakes still left over from Tarifa and thought, I'm sure it's Monday tomorrow.

After no, no and plenty more no's in response to my job enquiries, I thought I would kip the night there and maybe head up the *sols* tomorrow. I bet I could nail a job down, unlike Tony my alcoholic mate. If tomorrow was a working day maybe I would have more of a chance. By now, I was half thinking of how long it would take me to ride to France.

Dumping my junk, I went back into the centre of Gib, and being on the lookout for freebies I noticed a sign on the door of a small Methodist chapel. It said 'Open for service 7.00 p.m. Refreshments afterwards. All welcome'. So today had to be Sunday. This was my supper. It was almost 7.00 p.m. by now so I went in. There was a sort of little courtyard next to some stairs. I went up a couple of flights of stairs, leaving the bike at the bottom. The congregation were crammed into a sort of cafe bar. I crept in and a few smiling faces welcomed me without saying anything but offered me a chair to sit on. There were about thirty people there and the Gibraltarian pastor was talking about Doubting Thomas, who needed physical proof of the marks on Christ's hands and feet before he would believe the fact that he had been nailed up, then resurrected. The pastor was very profound, with a well-calming voice. I felt completely calm and stress free in the company of these people. The pastor went on to say how his faith had been challenged by people from all backgrounds and the events of the world of today but, with faith in this wise bloke who lived two thousand years ago, the darkest times are survivable. These words were well comforting, seeing as I was about two thousand miles from home. I'm glad I had a few crafty prayers here and there.

Being around this atmosphere I forgot, for a moment, my troubles and where I was, feeling calm, unwound, and loose with the same sort of feeling I'd previously got from a good smoke... or a skinful of alcohol.

I had to earn my cuppa and cakes by shifting a pile of chairs back into their main room, where their services were normally held. They had just re-decked and varnished the floor. I met some of the people: a couple of Germans, some Gibraltarians, Irish, English and, I think, a Belgian. They were sound and friendly. They asked me why I was in Gib? I told 'em I was "just visiting"!

Why I was on that journey and why things are the way they are, I thought of as I returned to the concrete roof of the electric shed. It was well after dark; with the little cove now lit up by the orangey-yellow lights between the exits from one tunnel in the cliff face twenty metres away, and the next tunnel. There was a small single-track road in between, and cliffs behind, and a pebbled shore in front, about twenty metres down. I looked out to Algeciras Bay, which was dotted with cargo ships with their lights on. All-round calm and warmth made me appreciate I was alive and healthy, warm and fed. I began to appreciate the stuff I had previously taken for granted. I then flicked on the little radio and drifted off to a peaceful sleep, with the sounds of the waves lapping onto the pebbles. I offered up a prayer – just in case!

Chapter Nine

Costas, Curves, Sunsets and Absolution

16th April 2007 Gibraltar to Marbella – 80 Kilometres,
17th April 2007 Marbella to Canuello – 119 Kilometres,
18th April 2007 La Herradura to Barriode de San Juan – 125
Kilometres,
19th April 2007 Aguadulce to Aguilas – 134 Kilometres

Up 7.45 a.m. and on the road out of Gib to La Lina. I had quietly mentally decided to ride along and up the *sols* to France. I would worry about crossing France when I got there. Besides, France didn't look that far away on the map I had!

There were plenty of beaches to sleep on and the sea to wash in. Whatever happened, I believed I was being looked after. I'd got this far with the things I'd got free from life. That bloke Chris Ryan walked hundreds of kilometres with bugger all, and at night in the freezing cold. Here the weather was warm enough. I just needed to keep this bike pedalling and find food along the way. From the crap map, I reckoned I could get to the border in about ten days or so. Surely the worst was behind me now. The biggest problem I had to face was finding enough food to match the amount of calories I began to burn up. The straight hot roads for hours and hours gave me a ravenous appetite, so I would eat anything and everything I could find, which mainly came from supermarket bins, at every chance I would get because I never knew where the next food might be. It seemed strange then but food seemed to be easy enough to find when I was desperate enough.

Despite a bit of headwind on the coast road out of La Lina on the A-383, the road was devoid of major hills; and having a goal of ten days to France, I plodded on at a natural pace I had begun to find. Also the endorphins would kick in and defeat the constant backache and the fact that the position I rode in, together with the sometimes rough tarmac and bumps, began to numb both outer two fingers on each hand. These fingers would have pins and needles way after I had got off the bike for the night. The road I followed generally ran parallel to the main *autovia*, the E-15 (the Autovia del Mediterraneo), sometimes for miles. It ran on one side and sometimes on the other side. This ran roughly along the coast. When it didn't I usually got lost or made lots of detours, up, down and around, until I felt the direction was the right one. I grew to love the names of places I would ride through. Some places looked idyllic; and some, 'package hols', with too many high-rise apartments and hundreds of little recently built villas. Any chance I could I would run along right next to the sea, sometimes finding supermarkets on the way, and sometimes not. I went through San Enrique over the Rio Guadiaro, then down along the coast past places with names like San Diego and Estepona, eventually finding the N-340, my favourite familiar coast road. By then I was almost in Marbella and the beginnings of the Spain I disliked the most: the tourist traps.

Having covered roughly eighty-two kilometres (fifty-one miles) since I left Gib, I was well hungry. I remember riding under that sign which bridges the dual carriageway into Marbella. It looks, for all the world, straight out of Bedrock: designed by the bloke who invented *The Flintstones*. I had seen it somewhere before and couldn't remember where, probably on some telly – yeah: *The Garage* on Sky, with the Scots fella, whose garage, 'English Mechanics', was based in Marbella.

This place was a lot like Rhyl or Blackpool but with more expensive cars, suntans and tattoos! I eventually noticed an Aldi on the right of the main drag, just up a slip road with a roundabout crossing the well-worn carriageway. All around were hundreds of clone apartments for holidaymakers and expats from various countries. I turned off and entered the road leading around to the loading bays, where the large bins were kept. As I went around, I noticed a teenage kid of about sixteen, with long hair. He had a skateboard and a hat next to him, and was on the 'cadge' for cash. If he was that hungry he should have looked around the back like I did. Just on top of the large wheelie bins, still in their plastic boxes and nicely defrosted were – wow! – three huge tiramisus and four gateaux, as though someone had put them there either as a stash or left 'em for a deserving recipient which, at that particular moment, happened to be me! I didn't waste any time, not even to check the sell-by dates. Ripping the first tiramisu open, I almost face dived straight into it. I ate it like a glutton and almost finished it before starting on a gateau. Not quite finishing that one either, I went back to the tiramisu, its light cheesecake texture cold and sweet on my tongue and face, filling my belly with a massive burst of sugar and energy. I began to get full after a bash at a chocolate log thing about a foot long. I couldn't carry this stuff – it would just melt into a big mess and go off – but I couldn't finish it either. I had to stop to give my gut a chance to cope with the shock of so much rich sweetness and cream; it was already complaining. I felt like that dog with a bone in his mouth who'd seen a reflection of himself in a pond – he wanted the other dog's bone but would have to lose his own. I wanted the rest of the cakes but my belly was saying, "No more, please!" I tried some more chocolate log and nearly threw up. I just couldn't do with the pain of leaving food, because the long spells between finding the stuff were frustrating. Before I eventually burst, I decided to ride on. After an hour or so, I stopped heaving too!

The day grew late and longer. Shadows were present, and I passed through the resort, with its shops, hotels and businesses, until I reached the outskirts going towards Malaga. My legs got a bit tired and my back was aching. I could see the beach about fifty feet below down a dirt track, looking accessible and quiet. This was where I would kip tonight. Down the dusty track I went and bedded down near to a shallow sand-dune next to a beach bar which looked like a neglected Hawaiian bar with its tatty palm frond roof and about ten tables and chairs. I think it was called Cafe Mambo. It was deserted. So was the beach, apart from me and a young couple in their early twenties canoodling in the sand without a care in the world. I looked out to the sea, jealous of those two. I thought, 'It's gonna be a long time before I ever get to do that again!'

Next day I rose from my sand-dune bed to a bit of chill at 7.45 a.m., with a goal of at least a hundred kilometres. I had eaten well the day before, so as long as I could find water I reckoned it should be easily achievable. The roads were flatter and straighter now and they also followed the coast, which meant I shouldn't get lost or shot at etc. This hundred kilometres was my daily goal from now on. A bit more would be a bonus, and a bit less to account for punctures and the like would still be progress. I reckoned I should be able to get to the French border by about the end of the month.

Before I climbed up onto the main road, I wandered over to the beach bar, which was not yet open. It had a sheltered area with benches and tables. I looked around for liquids and as I was doing this a fella entered, eyeing me suspiciously, so I shrugged my shoulders at him and got the bike mobile, up to the main road out of Marbella and onto the A7 *autovia* towards Malaga. It followed the coast, passing various golf clubs and 'country clubs' and endless villas and expensive-looking homes, all well kept and with smart cars and gardens. The coppers didn't bother with me on these coastal *autovias* except for when there was a tunnel involved or if the main road left civilisation for a bit.

The places looked the same on this stretch past Costabella, Elviria, Artola, Tore de Calahonda, El Faro, Fuengirola, and Punta Negra. Somewhere there I noticed a sign for San Francisco. After these the N-340 went inland a little, through Torremolinos, which was a busy, packed place with nothing but that typical package holiday look and feel, with tree-lined boulevards, apartments and shops. The costas weren't too bad though: mainly tourist traps and heat, which I rode on through. Everyone was on their hols or idly walking around shops, cafes, bars or driving their SUVs, black Jeeps, X5s, Jags or Mercs. I guess people find these things 'essential'. It just felt so far from how I had been living and existing for months. It is stuff I previously thought I had needed, 'cos, after all, who are we trying to impress? People we don't like and with things we don't need. Keeping up with the fucking Joneses. "Look what I've got." Status: a refuge for a fucking fool! But without all that stuff I realised small pleasures mean as much as expensive belongings. I would think about this on the long drag out from Malaga, along the coast road, which was seemingly endless with its curves winding in and out of coves glued to the coast for mile after long hot mile, some with hot gradients and some with rewarding downhills. Like the one which crossed a deep valley entering La Rabita. One of the many high concrete bridges spanning totally dry river beds; but all with the Mediterranean feel drilled into my brain through the sights and sounds, hour after perspiring hour, with the mountains rising sharply to my left, sun-baked and sparsely covered with hot scrub and cacti looking like spiky 'triffids'. Always with a satisfying view towards the calm blue sea, sometimes over little hamlets of terracotta villa roofs surrounded by neat patchwork ploughed fields towards the sea. You could pay thousands and not ever see the sights I was privileged to see on this journey, though at the time I thought it was just pain and struggle to do the miles. Nibbling away at each metre, yard, kilometre, it felt that, inch by inch, I was getting somewhere, although many times I just wanted to stop and sit in the sun and say "bugger it" 'cos my arse was hurting so much and my back was always aching, no matter what position I could wriggle into. Then I would think, 'Well, I've got to keep going; what if the next town is hours away and it gets dark and I'm without food and, more importantly, water?' At this point, I began to drift off and think of anything to keep my mind off my leg and back pain, and would stop only if I absolutely had to.

The vast areas between the tourist traps were hot and seemingly with no end at times. I would only stop if there was a convenient dossing place to treat as a 'reward'. At times, there was no reward – just a few more miles, then a few more, then a few more. This became a great way of covering the distance once I learned to time my stops to coincide with a bench or a bit of flat concrete out of the wind to spend the night on. Unfortunately, tonight wasn't one of them.

As the sun began to slowly dip behind the mountains, I was still negotiating curves and coves around the edge of the coast, seeing no sign of life except for little groups of villas dotted here and there, mainly down below the road to my right. It got darker, and my arse and legs would complain loudly in direct proportion to the dying light and increasing silence. More bends, long and tiring, with no concrete or flat rocks – nothing. I stopped at a spot where the old road once used to be before the N-340 had been straightened out. It was around a very tight curve, and was now cast aside for nature to gradually take it back. This might do for tonight. It was on a piece of headland jutting out, with a steep drop looking right down about a hundred feet into the Med. It was the only place where I noticed I could see the sun setting over the faraway headland. I must have been facing almost west on this tight, abandoned bend. Dropping the bike, I sat right on the edge of the drop, and got out an orange and a dog-end as a reward. My legs didn't want to go any further. Looking at this faraway huge, bright, orange blob just mesmerised me, with the orangey-pink sky and darkening, flat, calm sea blending into the headland. At that point, I noticed that the orange blob was actually sinking into the horizon as I looked at it. Lower and lower the orange orb could be visibly seen to vanish! I was forty-three years old, and in none of those fifteen-thousand-seven-hundred days, did I ever take time to watch a sunset! And until I saw one I never realised it goes down in a few magic minutes. Wow! I wanted to tell someone but there wasn't anyone around. If there was they probably wouldn't share my amazement. It didn't matter anyway – I'd just seen my first sunset on the edge of a cliff on a deserted road in southern Spain.

Being well transfixed, I didn't notice the ants invading my legs and arms. Shit! I can't stay on the ground tonight; got to find somewhere off the ground. I didn't want to get back on that bike, and neither did my legs. At the first attempt I stumbled and overbalanced, and then fell over. I was more tired than I thought. I was near a place called La Herredura and at this point I had ridden a hundred and thirty-plus kilometres that day, and couldn't figure out why my legs weren't obeying my brain. As I strained to get going on the slight incline up the N-340 the chain jumped, making me aware of blisters starting on my feet. I really didn't want this now; I just wanted to rest. The light was almost gone by now, which made it a big anticlimax to a day of distance and that sunset. After climbing around a few more bends, I was sort of back in the groove, a bit slower and just hoping for somewhere to stop for the night. As I slowly biked around another slight uphill wide curve, I noticed a lay-by. It was too dark to see if there were any rocks and the lay-by had only a giant wheelie bin and a bit of rubbish strewn near it, with two big dark shapes nearby which I first thought were animals. It made me up my pace a bit and look back to see if the shapes moved. Hang on! Are those chairs? I eventually stopped and turned around to investigate. They were chairs – two leather armchairs, one a bit taped up. This was my bed! I pulled them both away from the bin and positioned them facing each other, stuck the bike next to them, got my bag off and dug out my radio. But there was no reception here. I found another orange and a few biscuits and washed 'em all down with a mouthful of water I had saved for my supper and to rinse my mouth of the ever-decreasing amounts of toothpaste I could use to give my teeth a scrub. Comfy as hell was this, as I looked out over the dark sea, and noticing every sound from the nearby dark mountain. Peaceful but a bit spooky... Ever seen *The Hills Have Eyes*? Whatever, I drifted off, happy to find a bit of horizontal kip, and slept well deep until being woken by a chill, mixed with rain spitting on me. It was well after midnight and I was well into my sleep. If I stayed I would get wet; if I went I would get wet. So once again, I rose from my almost-comfy leather armchairs, loaded the bike up, and rode on. Tired and miserable now, I could hardly see because the cloud and rain were obscuring the moonlight and stars. I just rode on slowly around more curves for maybe five or six kilometres as the rain got heavier. Those abandoned leather armchairs discarded from a nearby café overlooked a beach called Playa del Canuelo. After a long straight and around an uphill left-hand bend I found a garage with a jet wash further up the road. The garage had a four-metre-square canopy for petrol pumps, built next to a slightly smaller canopy between it and the white walls surrounding the garage. It was lit up. I leaned the bike against the wall and sat with my back to it, crouching, with only the soles of my feet in contact with the ground as water dripped off my jeans and anywhere it hadn't soaked into. I was a bit tired and 'naggy' now. I guess it must have been about four or five in the morning and I was shivering a bit, but almost falling asleep. I guess I must have nodded off a couple of times momentarily, and snapped awake when I fell from my position sideways, putting my hand down on the wet concrete to stop myself from a further soaking. I tried to get comfy and get a return on my sleep deficit, but there was no chance unless it stopped raining and I had somewhere decent to send zeds up to the sky whilst flat out instead of crunched up like a shivering foetus needing warmth.

It must have been getting somewhere near dawn, as a few artic fridge lorries were braking hard for the steep wet corner I had not long ridden around. They sounded loaded, with the distinctive sound of engine exhaust brake on and footbrakes being punished simultaneously, with the loud hiss of the road's surface rain being squashed out from underneath forty tonnes of tractor unit and trailer on their morning run to deliver southern Spain's produce. They used the early-morning deserted roads to make progress for a few hours. I noticed Volvo 'Wendy House' FL10s go past, then six-wheeler FL6s. Sad, I thought to myself, that I know those lorries from beneath so well, having been a truck mechanic, using that work as a fall-back position in between starting various businesses. I hated the job – sweating and struggling in the summer with oversize metal components, and cold spanners covered with smelly diesel in the winter. These memories actually gave me comfort for a second – at least I could afford to eat then and go home to comfort. Hell, I would love to be able to do that now! Even the wages for a truck mechanic, which have dropped and dropped over years, with the three- and five-year warranties on new lorries, which drove fitters' wages down, would feel like big bucks now. Several garages I worked in paid the cleaners more than I got per hour. Thinking remote random thoughts like this temporarily took my mind off the damp, wet and cold tiredness as I stared into space in a trance for a while.

Back to reality, I noticed a slight lightening of the sky, together with the rain subsiding to a spit. Here we go – another day.

I was now on my way towards Almuneca, still on the winding N-340 around more 180-degree curves and tunnels through the mountain rock as it occasionally spilled into the sea across my path. The early-morning dead calm was cool enough to get a good pace on but the many uphills still made me sweat before a cooling downhill meant I could look out to sea and straighten my back for a few easy moments.

Up ahead I would catch a glimpse of the next town, which would be sort of a comforting sight, almost exciting – only because my belly might get a treat and water – especially after the huge amount of pedalling between places and the endless tarmac and rough terrain, for this coastal area was far from being a flat road journey. Anything to drink or eat would help the miles pass.

By now, I would enjoy the days, the constant varied and changing scenery and sometimes the conditions, but the distance would once again send me into a trance. I would stray and almost think of how I got here on this journey in the first place, but that would produce a downer so to maintain progress I just could not afford the luxury of thinking negatively. Much the same as in life and the sports anyone has been at any sort of level in, you've just gotta think of good things. That is the only way you get through bad stuff. Think badly and no matter how well off you are or whoever you are or however clever you are, bad stuff will drag you down. It's fatal. Drop a blob of black paint into a tin of white paint and it discolours the white, and it takes a lot more white to make it as white as it was before. My tin of white was contaminated. Being on this journey, very far from problems, was like looking at my hometown from the top of Minera Mountain: the little streets, people and things were still there but I could see the whole picture… eventually.

Today I had travelled from La Herradura along the twisting coast road – the N-340 – then out of the curves and hills for a while. Past Adra and Balanegra and towards the vast plain where the A-7 cuts straight across the Comarca de el Poniente, which is almost flat and completely covered in fruit and vegetable fields sheltered by plastic sheets, themselves miles across. A massive silver-and-white squared-off sea of man-made produce. It was boring and straight, with no view, in contrast to the coastal roads, but a lot more direct. It crossed from Balanegra, past El Ejido, all the way to Aguadulce, where the mountains cut it off from taking the entire coastline with these fields. This area was thirty-six kilometres across, making in total, a hundred and twenty-five kilometres from where I had chickened out of the rain under that jet wash canopy at La Herradura. I only stopped for one decent break across this place, getting sick of the *autovia*, and as a rest from people complaining with their horns 'cos I shouldn't have been riding on the *autovia* anyway. But by now I was in a 'fuck 'em' mood. I stopped where the A-7 is crossed by the A-358. It went underneath and I sat on the middle of a hot roundabout to drink some water and eat an orange or two, picked up from the roadside. I sat facing an agricultural machinery garage on the east side of the A-358 and watched the lads repair and grease small tractors for half an hour – rest for my tired legs. I then decided to see if I could follow the *autovia* along minor roads, but the road ran perpendicular and not in parallel to the major road. Finding some extra fruit to stick in my bag, I turned back toward the A-7 at a place called Barriode San Juan where, after going through another sparsely populated place with a few shops and lots of cheaply built houses, I ended back next to the *autovia*, with no option but to stay on it to make headway. I could see mountains blocking the way in the far distance but there had to be a way around. According to my crap map, Almeria was the other side of this mountain. Being marked on the map, it must have been pretty big. That was my next destination.

Because of the previous day's distance and today's I was jiggered tramping along this long road, and the day grew late. I began dropping down the off ramps and looking around for suitable beds nearby. I must have done this a few times but couldn't find anything really out of the way or comfy and by now the light was ebbing away. I was shot so I picked a concrete plinth around a couple of manhole covers near to a roundabout in front of someone's fenced-in home. This smart home had big Doberman-type dogs roaming the high fenced-off garden. They barked at me for a while before either getting bored or used to me. I was just too tired to give a shit. Prematurely I lay back on my rags to rest my body. I could lie flat out, which was a bonus. It was quite warm and unintentionally I dropped off to sleep rapidly. I remember that sleep as one of the best. It felt to me that sleeps like that were the best because they were well earned. This one was because it was a hundred and twenty-five kilometres from La Herradura.

If that was one of the best sleeps I had had so far, it was in contrast to how I woke. I came to with a shock. It was still dark and I felt a prod and heard a fella's voice saying, *"Estes homme morte?"*

No, I wasn't fucking dead and jumped up, scaring two Spanish coppers and maybe relieving them at the same time.

"Iesta bien, Senor?" (Everything OK, Sir?)

"Si, eu unico necesidade sono, foder sei! Que horas?" (Yes, I need sleep… fuck… what's the time?)

Pointing to my absent watch, the copper told me it was just after 6.00 a.m. They didn't question me, and left me to my own devices. I couldn't go back to sleep. I felt a slight chill by now, so on the road it was. Shit! My back tyre was flat. I had topped up my litre pop bottle and blown my tyres rock hard in a truck stop service-type station, but that was quite a few miles back. I hate going back on a journey. I walked up and down looking for any dwellings which might be near. They might have a pump of sorts just to give me a start. I could rely on finding a garage with an air line after that. There was nothing but agricultural plastic green houses for miles on this side, so I went under the *autovia* and up a short rise. I found some houses just up on the left, with a couple of cars parked next to them, and across from the houses there were two ramshackle garages, with one smart BMW and another old car parked next to it. These people were bound to have a foot-pump somewhere. I knocked on the door of the first house a couple of times. There was no answer so I tried the second with a loud

"Desculpar, exusar, Senor, Senora!"

No reply, no one around, but the garage door was open... Bugger it, what have I got to lose? Peering inside, I saw a metal stack of dexion-type shelving with paint tins and various tools and bits and bobs stacked randomly, together with a blue cheapo foot-pump. Yes! I 'borrowed' it – permanently – my need being far greater than theirs. Quietly I walked out of the dirt yard and back down to the *autovia*, where I spent a tired and irritable hour trying to repair two or three punctures, unsuccessfully, with wind blowing dust into my eyes in the early-morning cold. This day would be hard. Any time there is wind the day is slow and hard. Rain is bad but wind is worse, especially if you are battling against it. It is a right pain in the arse.

Eventually I was ready to roll, taking a good hour or so today to find my natural pace. After a time I was sure the *autovia* went towards the mountains so I tried to find my way towards the corner of Aguadulce where it met the sea, to find a road around the mountains. Conveniently, the main road went directly in a straight line, cutting through Aguadulce and right to the very corner I needed to be. The suburbs I passed through were large and the road turned into miles of boulevard with suburban small businesses giving way to the larger retail outlets and a shopping centre in this large town with plenty of money about and places where I could scout for fruit and good-nick thrown-out food. I had found plenty of bits to fill my wrecked rucksack, and plenty of barely-used nicotine. By the looks of that mountain, I bet there was another pile of curves and deserted roads before Almeria.

As I got nearer to the built-up commercial centre of Aguadulce the buildings around me grew taller. Some of them seemed made of glass, and filled with more fashion and useless stuff that would be of no use from my point of view. It was like another world but different to the tourist cities on the earlier costas – more four-wheel drives than in the Serengeti, and people engaged in buying more stuff to satisfy the urge to empty their wallets and purses in exchange for goods they believe they needed. I could only see this now. In my past life, we did it because that's what people do. As I rode on this long straight through this place, I noticed I was on the N-340 again. The wind was getting stronger, almost as if the buildings were funnelling the air in some sort of outdoor wind tunnel. I was sweating with the effort of fighting against it. I decided to stop near the end of town to have a reward of nicotine. I stopped next to a major bank which had some steps I could sit on. Pulling up at the kerbside, I found a whole new cig. Great! As I was sitting down on the steps some people walked up past me to use a cash machine. A smart Spanish lady dressed in a skirt suit and with her sunglasses on, even though it was overcast now, was caught by the gust of wind and almost lost her footing and her scarf. The gust blew her long dark hair out of place and for a second she lost her 'cool' look and looked uncomfortably at the tramp sitting on the steps and with a fag in his left hand, eyeing her. At that point, this fag was blown out of my hand, which made me scramble for it before someone trod on it. I *ain't* losing the first full fag since Gibraltar, I thought to myself, as a guy stepped over to avoid me. Fag finished, I negotiated the wind and had to physically push the bike against it until I got clear of the highest building at the end of the town. I must have been on the leeside of the mountain now because the wind had all but died. I could hear the nearby *autovia* disappearing into the mountainside somewhere up to my left as I found the coast road out from Aguadulce. The day was grey and well overcast. This road was within twenty metres of the sea, which was choppy with the wind blowing from the east, and slowed my progress except when I was sheltered by a bit of headland or a nearby tunnel, which there were more than a few of.

The dull morning made this tunnel entrance remind me of the north Wales coast road before it was violated by the A-55 road, which cut out the unique bends and old tunnels around the rock faces near Penmaenmawr, just after Conwy. On this similar-looking Spanish coastal road, you could see the waves crashing on the rocks below. Even the colour of the vegetation clinging to the steep Spanish hillside looked similar to that familiar Welsh coastline. About an hour into this part of the journey, the weather felt the same as well. It just rained gently, then heavily, and then became wet and windy. I was back home for a bit. The wet journey to Almeria was only just over eleven kilometres and a slow drag. Entering Almeria, it rained harder, but in a faraway weird feeling it was kind of comforting remembering trips with Mam Four and Seren, Mam Three with Ceri, and trips with Dunc, my mate, who looked like the mad scientist out of *Back to the Future*. Jobs then were just a method of funding the weekly trips to fly off cliffs, scavenge shipwrecks off the coast, or ride dirt bikes through Wales's finest deep muddy bogs for over a decade. My Nain back in those days would put a fiver of petrol in her old '63 Moggie Minor, or later her wreck of a '68 DAF 33 estate car, together with army surplus blankets, a plastic box with sugar and tea bags, and a gas stove, and take us on an 'adventure' around north Wales for a weekend. She had no fear of breaking down or disaster, and no AA or RAC cover, mobile phone or satnav. That stuff didn't exist. She just sat us in the back with my Taid in the front and went miles, giving me memories and a map of north Wales's nooks and crannies, mountains and lakes, and a love of Welsh culture that has stayed with me forever. We were all brought up skint, but still any spare cash would be invested in memories which would last forever, even if it was our last tenner. My Nain would always say, "You don't know when God will take you," so that was probably why she had faith that whatever happened, we would be looked after. People ain't got that today: only faith in technology and cash – well, in our Western world anyway. Most people in the Third World still have some kind of faith because they don't have the privilege of dosh and ready food or the nanny state mentality. We are lucky or 'blessed' or however you see it in your own opinion. Our lives are a lot easier than those of most of the world's population. Even at this point I thought I could easily be well worse off.

I was free – for now. I could find food, wasn't about to have my family raped, shot or abused, or have to travel miles for water; and this journey was because of my stupidity and my reaction to events.

I was beginning to get my head around the shit I was so far away from. It was like being cured of some disease – a right cleansing process or 'rehab' even. The long hours spent on this wreck of a bike were doing the same job as using Domestos down a bog that's not been cleaned for a long time. It ate away at the build-up bit by bit, which was then flushed away and replaced with fresh and vivid sights, smells and sounds which would be there to keep no matter what happens in the future. These sights, sounds and smells were being seared into my brain.

The rain stopped, which lifted my mood together with the temperature, but not till I was almost clear of Almeria. I had no need to stop in Almeria, only stopping to pick up a set of panniers off a bike that had fallen off something. Another fella had stopped in a van and he was trying to break the bike lock, which was holding this bike against a two-metre-long plank of wood, but he gave up when he wrecked the back wheel and the rain became heavier at that moment. Those panniers draped over the rack of the bike I was on made it look like a real tourer now. I could carry a lot more food to keep me going. Another few hundred kilometres. Later on in hindsight, I wished I had slung them there and then. They added a lot more weight as I filled them with junk and they constantly caught the wind, slowing me down.

It was still early in the day and the wind seemed to die but the rain didn't for a while. Rechecking my map, I could see there was seemingly an obstacle preventing me from getting around the bottom corner of Spain to the faraway cities of Alicante, Valencia and Tarragona, which were too far away to even imagine right then. My map just showed a red line cutting across a corner, but no apparent route around the coast. Stopping to look up at the looming hills in the near distance, I thought for almost a second before my desire to get over what lay ahead overcame hesitation. Everything topped up, and the bike with hard tyres, I reckoned I could bridge that gap and get across to the other side of the coast by nightfall. It must have been about early midday. I 'felt' I could do it, and after all, I bet there were a few towns here and there. Trying to ignore any distractions in the port town of Almeria, such as bins and dossing areas, I just remember going for it. This was going to be a distance day but with grim wetness to ride through. I remember getting that strange excited feeling again – the same as when I decided to leave that campsite in Olhao on that small bike – not knowing where I would end up or what lay ahead, just wet roads climbing into more mountains.

Today was 19th April 2007. I climbed and pushed for a few hours and the rain eventually stopped. I was making my way along the N-344 up into the sparse scrubland with bare sandy plains on either side. I had to join the A-7 *autovia*, having no choice. This road felt like forever but was just a taste of what was to come. To my right were gently rising plains of nothingness – no houses, people, animals or any tarmac roads – just open free areas where the sun must be a killer at the height of summer. The road rose slightly for miles but I managed to concentrate, plodding on rhythmically with a determination to reach somewhere up ahead in the distance. It got very hot, and I dried out. Distant features such as a little culvert or a wire fence across a plain or a solitary dirt track would merge into view and be left behind. This was after thousands of revolutions of the pedals adding to my sore bum from hours of sitting on a bare-bone plastic seat with no padding. I would wrap my leather 'do it all' bomber jacket around it and that would be comfy for a couple more hours. There was a very slight climb, but a climb up towards the plateau or plain with absolutely nothing around was draining, not just physically, but mentally, with nothing around to look at or focus on. It was another time for dealing with things I had put off, being distracted by the variety of sights. Here there was nothing, just distance.

I needed water; I realised I needed a drink. I hadn't had a sip since it had stopped raining, before I topped up in Almeria. A quick stop at the roadside to undo the bungee chord holding my litre-and-a-half pop bottle full of *agua*, and I took off my baseball cap and drank, tipping my head back, enormously enjoying this slightly warmish water. At that moment, it was the best thing in the world: clean refreshing water fuelling me up; and swigging it down more and more, it was as though I'd been given a bigger man's capacity to drink. Then, a moment of clarity: I needed to drink more but stopped to check how much was left. The bottle was just below half full. A few seconds ago, it was full. Did some leak out? No. I looked up ahead into the distance. The road just disappeared into the hot horizon, and behind me was the same. I decided I'd better take my time with this: it was hot and I must have been pushing harder than I thought. Well, there was bound to be something up ahead. But there wasn't, not for a long time. Doubt crept in, which suddenly made the endless plodding sore and hard and unsure. I let my thoughts drift into negative ramblings like "Why am I here?" I reasoned with myself that to cope with the distances up ahead and the coming days, maybe weeks, I would have to deal with the nagging issues I had been ignoring by coping with everyday stuff. This stuff kept me far too busy to deal with such bollocks.

But I would have to deal with these issues sooner or later.

"Listen," I said, speaking to myself out loud. "If you do make it back to the UK, it's not going to be a happy ending with a bath and a welcome or a rest or back to work or to see loved ones. It is going to be another ordeal. Hang on, no. I will definitely be clean everyday, have three square meals and maybe the chance to learn new things. That is the part to look forward to. And you will have been on the adventure of your life, with no money and virtually no comforts. If you can deal with this journey, you can deal with anything, so use these long hours to deal with stuff now. Does that sound right? Yeah, course it does."

Saying this out loud usually worked for me, like having someone to discuss things with. No one around would think I was a nutter because there was fuck all around for miles, and who cared anyway? This time it didn't work. Like when someone cannot talk you out of a pit of gloom. Up until now, I was too proud to think of this mental monster, too cavalier. If there was any time to get it out it would be now; some things you have got to deal with or they may drop on you in worse moments. I had to deal with these things now.

There was still the slightly smarting matter of why did I get so 'shafted' by my girl, and the unjust feeling of all of the confusing and painful issues in such a short space of time, bending my resolve like a brittle plastic ruler. Why? Well, they just did, and I just cracked, had enough. What's done is done. I could have reacted better, but I didn't. Too much had happened in such a short time, like a dam burst sweeping your best efforts away. I needed to get these things out of my system.

I couldn't blame anyone, could I? Not even my girl's brother-in-law, who I caught 'doing' her on New Year's Eve 2006, minutes after thinking, 2007 has got to be better than last year, hasn't it?

He had the opportunity. His trusting and naive, unsuspecting wife worked days while he worked nights. He also had the motive. His sister-in-law was slim, attractive, and dressed much younger compared to his wife. His sister-in-law was also promiscuous, and free in the daytime. His wife was a lovely woman who had gained a few pounds and dressed to reflect how secure she obviously felt in her marriage.

He was a right toad with a wet fish handshake and no eye contact in conversation, but it didn't matter now. I felt sorry for my ex-girl for a while afterwards. She had suffered terrible sexual abuse by a trusted relative when she was in her teens, and only chose to tell me this a couple of days previous to New Year's Eve, as though trying to tell me she confused love and sex, or was she just a nymphomaniac? Nah, it wasn't her fault.

The poor girl's head was messed up years ago. The copious amount of drugs she ran her life with should have told me that. But outwardly you wouldn't know. She was a hard working clean freak and a good mam. She craved the sexual attention of anyone. But behind closed doors she could make you feel no one else but yourselves existed.

That relationship was a mistake but, well on the rebound, I chose to accept her hospitable invite a short month after leaving my wife. Marrying her, in August 2005, was my worst mistake of all. I had made a total misjudgement of character. I thought she had climbed out of her promiscuous past lifestyle. I thought we respected each other for both having done well since meeting over a decade previous as skint party people. As far as my misinformed thinking went, once you married, that was it – you put away the fleeting desires of the past and no one else mattered. No. To her it was like having a new car, but once the ashtrays were full she wanted a new one.

She had gained an 'ology' – a government-sponsored degree – since I had last met her. She impressed me with her basic legal knowledge, and outwardly shiny personality, until I really got to know how this sexually aggressive, loud, alcoholic bottle-blonde behaved in unguarded moments. She would put on boxing gloves and punch the back walls of her house when she had had too much to drink. She would fly into a narcissistic rage if I *dared* to defy her will.

It took me a while to realise that life with an egoistic, amoral wife is totally confusing. Seductive on the outside, she, almost subconsciously, forever moved the boundaries on what I had to do to please her. She had a job which put other people in her care, "But that is just a job. I can do what I wish in my personal life!"

A sense of morals in her personal life didn't appear to exist. However, I had fully thrown myself into trusting her. Especially after discovering she had frequent black outs and fits. She was almost in denial of these fits. So were council employers, the Social Services. She was a skilled and down-to-earth practitioner, so it seemed. She was still my wife. I tried my best after I had made that commitment, but in her personal life, she began acting like a character out of *Shameless*.

I should have spotted the warning signs when:

- The person thought ecstasy was wrong but loved speed and coke. (Aren't all drugs bad?)
- Close friends the person met through me, either got a little 'too' close to her or distant towards me.
- She was boning a work colleague behind my back for months whilst I baby-sat the person's son after long hard days of running a business.
- Other people you know, usually blokes, had a sly grin when they found out who your partner was.
- Just like the line in the Glasvegas song: 'And how my missus is fucking every guy she looks at'.
- Finding the person took no interest in the hard-won business I ran, but plenty of interest in the gold and cash it provided for her.
- The person was violent towards you, usually when you were passed out. This also happened one time when her young son was present.
- This person was a narcissist, a female version of an incubus.

I left this dog-eared milf. I chose to live in a van in a scrap yard rather than be near her – and having to put up with what she might do next whilst I would be sleeping. She was a very frightening woman; a truly vindictive 'bunny boiler'.

Months later I met the woman who I found 'shared' her brother-in-law with her sister.

This woman was immoral but told me she didn't give a fuck what people thought. She was entirely too attractive to possess such an attitude without incurring lifelong problems.

But at least you could see what was coming… unless the recipient was mainly too stoned or drunk or tired, or a combo of all three.

And I ignored the better judgement of my previous long-suffering partners, who put up with the years of graft, study and hard times and then saw me blow it on the insipid person I married: the bottle blonde.

The 'post-wife refuge', I loved and thought she was the one, though I doubt she felt the same way. What a dick: to become fooled twice in a row!

Of course it never occurred to me that my flagging sex drive might have caused all of this, together with not being able to cope with these events:

- My dead and dying close relatives.
- The loss of access to my young daughters.
- Almost no holidays in well over a decade.
- The brief disappointment of 'Shortie' Senior finding me after twenty-two years, and who only wanted to use my abilities and Operator's Licence for his own financial advancement.
- The pressure of being self-employed in a busy, skilled business.
- The discovery of another teenage daughter I didn't know existed.

All of this happened all at once in a short period at the end of 2006 – a time when my faculties were beyond reason. I had the choice not to have drunk and smoked so much on the night of the 31st. I was offered depressants and had the choice as to how much I would drink and smoke – no one forced me. The toad gave me copious amounts, and so did my girl during a family get together, and during a spree around the local pubs. This was not out of kindness as I thought: it was because they both knew full-well I would drink and smoke until I would barely be able to stand or know what I was doing or seeing. Only I *did* see. Those both engaged in an act in the first hours of a new year. This resulted in the toad rapidly disappearing home to tell his trusting wife, "Shortie's a nutter" to cover his own rear end. My girl would not let me near a phone and certainly would not be pressed into a confrontation about her toad and his infidelity. No matter how hard I tried to drag her after her brother-in-law, she would not face her sister or him on this night. It wasn't the first time she had done this with him. The Rumours I had heard and denied were true.

Completely drunk and frustrated, a sentence passed through my mind: Go alone and cost *him*; hit him in the pocket.

His nice silver Vectra he had just bought ended up with very few intact windows or mirrors, which I don't regret, though I do regret doing almost the same to his wife's car. Why? She was a victim of the situation. My reasoning had gone – as had the front windows of their home and, apparently, the garden shed windows as well. There was just no need.

Now under sentence of the local magistrate, and having just lost the last person who I thought I meant something to, plus everything else that makes a worthwhile life,

I had passed the point of no return. I had gone beyond costing the toad his five minutes of pleasure.

I then decided to even things up for all the hard work and money invested in the insipid wife who had cost me my business, years of my life, money, friends and access to my young daughters. She had moved on to sub-twenty-year-old lads, without batting an eyelid, as she had done for years, as though it was like picking up a jar of coffee from the shop on the way from work.

My life was ruined. I didn't care.

Under cover of darkness I wobbled across the large village on a bike and proceeded to wreck her nice shiny new car I had helped her so many times to pay for because of her habit of spending most of her overpaid wages on vanity. The old Vee Dub bus I had spent months underneath welding and repairing in order to complete her collection of possessions was gone – she had sold that. I then wrecked all the windows of her house, which I had paid her thousands of pounds for the privilege of living in for a few years whilst she carried out affairs with various colleagues, both male and female. I then wrecked another car, which I thought was her fella's but it wasn't, thus creating another innocent victim of the situation.

The words of one of her ex-husbands I had previously overheard flashed through my head: "She will fuck him up. She fucked up my life. There's something wrong way back in the past."

My life was ruined. I didn't care.

Under cover of darkness, I decided to steal a lorry and drive to the nearest airport early next day; and considered stealing a nearby full-weight artic. Too slow though, and besides, I may not have time to disable the speed limiter. Then I thought about taking a thirty-ton eight-wheeler because I thought it might provide an effective 'battering ram' if I ran into trouble. I needed time to think.

I found a hidey-hole, drank some water and sobered up, with the full weight of consequences now on my head. It was flight mode. I did steal a lorry: one I knew would be in a remote location, was insured and which I knew the mechanics of well. Plus, it was usually unloaded. In minutes, a steel bar and some hot-wiring, and I was on my way.

My life was in ruins. I didn't care.

I was too much on my own ego trip to take the final straw on the chin so I went, hard faced and determined. We all react differently, and my resolve was gone. I decided I'd do what it takes to get away from this country, there and then!

Within days I was in Portugal, eating from bins, sleeping in doorways, skint, alone, hungry and desperate.

It's very easy to form an opinion when you don't feel the emotions of the situation.

Within weeks I had found everything I needed, and within months I could speak another language, but I had a conscience and knew I would have to pay for what I had done. But the easier and better things got, the more I drank to forget. But I couldn't forget.

All these thoughts had hit me all at once whilst tired through no proper sleep on this long, hot highway. My spirit dropped. The heat, the hills and dehydration got to me. I was a failure in a foreign country on a stolen wrecked bike, with rags for possessions, no cash, no home to go back to, diminishing family and friends, with the shame of my crimes, and with no happy ending in sight, sweating and struggling up this dead road. Nothing is worth what I did.

I broke down right on the side of this deserted unforgiving road, with equal remorse for the malice I had felt when losing it totally in those dark few hours. Not only could others see what I had done, but the people I respected could see: my Nain and my Taid. I threw the bike to the ground and fell to my knees. With my elbows and forearms in the dust, I dropped my head onto them and cried like a baby, begging them both to forgive me, then begging God to help me, in an absolutely earnest moment.

"Please, God, help me! Forgive me. Let me get back and put my life back together. I've got nothing and don't deserve anything!"

I could taste the saltiness of tears in my mouth as my kids' happy faces flashed in front of me and then my Nain's forgiving face, and my Taid's honest smile and voice; and sobbed deeper than I had done since they had died.

"Forgive me, if there is a god up there, please!"

At that moment I felt a determination to get up, and a new resolve – a moment where what felt like a massive coil spring in my brain, which had been tightened and tightened for months inside my head, had just unwound. I felt total peace like I had never felt before – not a vision, not a blinding light – just total peace, as though my slate was wiped clean. Nothing else mattered now. I stood up and took a gigantic breath. I was still thirsty, hungry, sore and tired but my mind was now clear and I had a sense that I would definitely get through.

If I asked for help, I would get it. It was a case of having the balls to swallow my pride.

I got back on the bike and rode on, having a different feeling altogether. I would be OK; there was no doubt now.

I would just get on with it, put it all in a box and throw it off a cliff into the sea, keep that thought as a picture in my mind, then walk away and start again. This is what the struggle across very long hot distances, cold nights and no communication with anyone but my own mind did: it cleared out the trash.

This regurgitating of mental garbage and giving it up to another higher power was the best thing I ever did. There was more distance and difficulties to cope with and a clear mind was the only way to deal with whatever lay ahead. Like a landfill newly covered with topsoil, the rubbish was now buried and occasionally, when it rained, like a landfill, the rubbish would poke through. But only briefly.

I now felt a huge weight off my mind. I could now concentrate on the struggle ahead and that brief 'interlude' had taken the best part of an hour to think about. I had done about another twenty or so kilometres without noticing my dry throat and tiring limbs. I was better off emotionally now than when I was actually with these women, and only had myself to be concerned with.

Yeah, this journey, even at its very worst points, was incomparably better than life with those people. Plus, I was outside, in conditions which I had never had the time to enjoy for a long time. Yep, this sweating and struggling and survival felt a million times better than being emotionally and financially ripped off. This was simple, uncomplicated and just physically hard now.

With new resolve, I would get on with the job in hand.

The *autovia* swept around in a huge eastern arc and I noticed signs for Nijar. A couple of kilometres later it was time for a check of the basic map. I had plodded along a fair distance after drifting away with my mind, and was now feeling no nearer to the coast. Glancing at the red line threading its way across the south-eastern tip of Spain was no help at all, as usual, so I just persisted and hoped that eventually I would come across a turning or junction towards the east or to Sorbas and then Vera, which were at least marked, further up on the map. Vera, I eventually found, was my turning point for the coast again, once I had taken a few detours. I had gotten off that l-o-n-g AP 7 *autovia*, with its long straights and wide curves, and the anonymity of endless indistinguishable cars and fridge trucks passing by quietly, with good road manners. Unlike in the UK, where they pass you with the thickness of a Rizla paper, and with no thought of death by the dangerous charge they are dicing with. Not to mention the trauma to the family they would be causing. Life can change in a second. I felt they gave me some quarter here.

At last, back on a road towards the coast, I was now on the A-332 heading for Cartagena, with the familiar and more comfortable, less urgent atmosphere of a two-laner with white lines up the middle instead of a metal Armco barrier dividing the oncoming traffic. There were more gradual rises and falls, with olive plantations, and sparse parched grass covering most of the irregular field areas; and the beautiful smell became more apparent. It would stay as my permanent link with Spain – orange blossom. The sweet sickly aroma drifts across your path for miles, even when you can't see any orange groves at all. Sometimes I would go to sleep with it in my nostrils, wake up with it and sometimes get sick of the smell, especially when not in the mood for it. But it's a smell never forgotten. Now it beckons me back and stops me in my tracks. It makes me drift off and think of the lonesome spaces, but without the pain of unrested legs, back and arse; and the hunger which lasted for maybe six or seven hours at a time and sometimes a whole day. It gives me the best bits of this journey but without the mentally painful, physically draining, monotonous hours of travel. And times searching for bins that may or may not have had a couple of half-decent pieces of fruit or any sort of just about edible food, in towns I had never seen before, in places I had never heard of before. A smell really fetches pictures and feelings back in your mind, whether you want it to or not.

I began sighting the sea again. It was a relief. I knew it was there but actually seeing it again confirmed I was going in the right direction, changing from due east to north-east. The sun began dipping more to my left instead of almost right behind me. My shadow would be just ahead and to my right in the dying hours of the day. I would glance at the slightly elongated one-dimensional figure pedalling away next to me, with scruffy wisps of hair blowing and its arms fixed to the straight bars and with a matching pedal rhythm to my own. I could also see a shadow of junk, bungee-chorded to the lashed-on rack moving side to side a couple of inches as the bits of electrical wire tying it to the bike wore thinner before it would occasionally snap, prompting a quick roadside repair. If it was hot the shadow reflected a dark shape almost covering the back wheel and seat as the bomber jacket would be draped across the rear of the bike, and the rider had his sleeves rolled up. I would keep looking at this fella at my side. He always rode with me on sunny days but I couldn't stay ahead of him as the sun went down. I liked riding with him and I think he liked riding with me.

At this time of the day, my batteries would start to die. My pace slowed and I would begin looking for somewhere to rest for the night, which would be coming soon. If I was really tired, any place would do, but if the places I passed were a little more built up I would keep plodding on until I found somewhere out of the way or which had a good wide bench to put my feet up on, and off the ground, away from ants. The road suddenly took a detour away from the coast. It was skirting a place called Aguilas. I came to a roundabout, almost riding on, but then realised it was too late now and this place was a coastal town. There might be some bins, benches and dog-ends for temporary relief from the bike and its rock-hard seat. I took the road signposted into the centre, then rode down a couple of dead straight overcrowded streets that narrowed and steepened so much I lost sight of the sea totally.

The apartments near the centre were for Spanish nationals, well lived in, with trails of washing draped everywhere and small wrecked cars at the road-side. Getting disoriented, I stopped and asked a couple the way to the beach. They pointed up a set of steps, well steep to contemplate with my shot legs so I rode around the next block of apartments and up a less steep road, coming out into the marina area. But it was a busy place and I needed peace tonight, maybe somewhere nearer the quieter part of town at its north end. I rode around the curving marina road, but not before I smoked a fag I had found and had an orange from the few collected after jumping over a wall in Vera into a roadside orange grove. I could see a sort of headland with some smart apartments built near to it. I bet that it was a bit quieter there. On investigating this, I found a quiet cove overlooking another bay. It was as flat as a millpond and sheltered. It seemed to be hemmed in with red rocks rising out of the sea. Facing me was a slightly elevated flagstone area with a circular cul-de-sac with four benches. To my right or the east, the terracotta rocky headland rose up not more than about thirty metres. To my left were the apartments far away – nothing to ruin the scene straight ahead of me. Evening lights flickered on across the bay. I sat and turned my radio on, really enjoying this scene at the end of another day of travelling. I was completely weary and tired but felt I'd achieved something and had got a bit nearer to where I was going. To add to these good feelings I had found a couple of apples I had forgotten about, and another orange. What a bonus! I even found a couple of dog-ends. As the light died, it was warm. I was satisfied with my efforts and then one of my favourite recent tunes came on Kabin FM – Tiesto with 'Adagio for Strings' – followed by Ultrabeat with 'Pretty Green Eyes', both last heard in happier times. These sounds took me back to those times but were slightly painful too in that I could hear these familiar tracks so far away from the places I wouldn't be hearing them again for a while. No matter: I had just made another lifelong memory which is not going to fade. At this time, I had travelled from the far side of Aguadulce to Aguilas – a hundred and forty-seven kilometres – and crossed that hot dead place, the Sierra de Gata. And after a bad start, with punctures, rain and headwind, I was chuffed to arrive in this warm windless place, settling down lying across this bench, almost comfortable, into peace, with the sound of faraway music and almost nothing to disturb a settled kip. Said my prayers though.

Chapter Ten
Charity, Hunger and Scary Reflections

20ᵗʰ April 2007 Aguilas to Los Alcazares – 132 Kilometres

I woke at the usual 7.45 a.m., loaded my stuff and headed out on a fresh sunny morning towards Cartagena, the next city along the coast, according to the map. I wanted to stay off the *autovia* and hug the coast, expecting an easier day today. My legs were feeling the effects of yesterday so I went north-east on the D-15, but not before the local cops pulled me, did a passport check etc, and then let the suspicious scruffbag go on his way.

As much as I tried to avoid the *autovia*, I would many times 'guess' or 'feel' that lots of effort would be spared by using certain more direct-looking routes, especially if they headed into tunnels in the mountains, and plenty did. Also plenty of times the traffic cops would 'advise' me to get off these roads so for the most part I would kind of forget that cyclists weren't allowed on them until I was forced off, again. If I did this enough times, with any luck they might arrest me, thus providing me with a night in the warmth and a chance of a shower. Didn't happen though – just a daily process of bobbies doing their job and checking a suspicious/unusual character or getting me off the *autovias* and out of the tunnels. It was a fun game, like could I get away with a few kilometres here and there by riding on the *autovia* through a mountain instead of all the way around it? I've forgotten the number of times I did this.

I went through this process and sometimes was so concerned with when the 'feds' would be stopping me that I would be alert and going for it, pedalling hard to reach another intersection back to the N-332 or whatever two-way road was nearest. This stretch of mileage crossed several small hills and mountains between Aguilas and Cartagena. The first was over a two-hundred-metre hill into a small agricultural valley area, with the only road out being a newly built *autovia* tunnel via some tollbooths. I stopped to survey the area. The hills ahead of me rose steeply and dropped sharply into the sea to the east, with no visible road around. This was going to be another cop game incident. The little lane I was on ran down, winding around the little farms. The place was called Garrobillo. Up to my left, I could see where the high bank supporting the *autovia* could be accessed next to a little tunnel built through the embankment. The tollbooths were about a quarter of a kilometre back from the tunnel entrance and this little tunnel through the Autovia embankment was halfway between the tollbooths and the tunnel through the hill. Right: this will save me a lot of struggle. I found a humble farm track, which eventually took me to the edge of the fifteen-metre embankment. I lifted the bike over the barbed-wire fence and climbed the steep dirt-and-gravel slope with difficulty because there was no vegetation to get a purchase on. Almost at the top, I had to negotiate another barbed-wire fence before I got onto this new section of road, scratching myself and tearing a hole in the arse of my wrecked black jeans in the process. Mounting the bike and quickly straightening the stuff on the wobbly rack, I went for it and sweated to reach the tunnel entrance before the coppers would stop me and make me go on another, longer route – stuff that! Within minutes, I was entering the tunnel, which was brand-new and about a half-kilometre long; a two-laner, with one tunnel going south and the one I was in going north. Yes, pedalling faster than my usual pace, I was panting a bit. Not quite halfway, I giggled to myself like a naughty schoolboy who's just broken a window with his catapult. Behind me, there was a rumble getting louder – a motor was bearing down on me. I glimpsed around, thinking it was a truck. You can never tell in a tunnel of this length – it magnifies the sound of the wheels and the engine. It was a car which zoomed past, blowing its horn for good measure. Didn't half sound noisy though. I was about a hundred metres from the exit of the tunnel and felt myself gathering speed so it must have been slightly downhill. I was nearly there, then, BING BONG! – A message from the friendly tollbooth staff I couldn't quite understand but got the gist of: Get out of the tunnel! What did they expect me to do? Go back? Not likely: I was nearly out now. There was another rumble coming behind me again. This one grew louder and louder as I got near to the brightness of the sun. I glanced around again, pedalling more urgently, and saw the truck, a lot further behind me than it sounded. I then glanced back in front of me, but not quite quickly enough to avoid my front wheel trying to mount the kerbing or a raised portion at the edge of the tunnel, which made me overbalance and hit the deck fast and hard, hurting my knee, losing a couple of bits off the rack, and twisting the handlebars. No time to piss about. I was up and riding to the end of the tunnel before the ear-splitting lorry noise made the situation more vivid, and seemed to add to the fun and the small drama.

Just outside of the tunnel, I straightened out the bike and carried on down a large downhill, gathering speed, which cooled me down in the process. I felt elated, chuffed, until I came across the next off ramp, where two motorcycle cops were sat, one with his hand up. Here we go again, with passport, who, what, why etc. I tried the "I cannot speak Spanish, I only speak English" but the first copper, with a tache and sunglasses, dismounted his BMW and approached me with an amused smile on his face, saying, "That's OK, *Senor*, I can speak English", so that excuse didn't work. Then the "My map is crap" didn't work either. Slightly smirking to his colleague by now, he could see I was bullshitting, mainly because I was smirking too. He asked me in a calm voice,

"*Senor*, how did you get onto the *autovia*?"

Now I was on a loser, so with a giggle I told him more bullshit about the staff in the tollbooth not noticing me ride through, to which he replied, "They seen you climbing the embankment with your cycle. Oh, *Senor*, did you hurt yourself when you fell off inside de tunnel?"

At this I giggled a bit more, which set them both guffawing. The cop then asked me, "You wish to go to prison?" to which I thought for a split second and said, "*Si, por favor, Senor*", which made them both laugh. Oh, how we all laughed! Today: cops one, me one.

Back on the N-332 it fell gently between the mountains, which were casting slightly cool early-morning shadows across the highway as it snaked right and then left around steep terracotta mountain cliffs and hills all around me on the road near to Canada de Gallego, which became flat as it neared Mazarron – a small coastal farming town. There were more mountains up ahead, which were a bit disappointing to see by now. Well, if I was to make it to Cartagena I'd have to cross 'em. Along the route of the N-332 another *autovia* was being completed, presumably to complete the length of the Autopista del Mediterraneo coastal motorway, or the AP-7, that I got thrown off regularly. The nearer I got to Mazarron, the bigger the set of mountains became, and the thirstier and hungrier I became. It was early afternoon by now. It may have been too early for out-of-date or damaged stock to be binned but I was due for a search. But as I rode down into the little town towards the beach road it was disappointing in equal measure to my empty belly, which was complaining, as well as my tongue, which was like a dry-baked flip-flop. I did a brief detour down a few roads and along the beachfront, checking every wheelie bin as I went. I found them all empty. I didn't want to wait here till the next day – it was just too early. Cartagena couldn't be too far away. It was those hot, parched-looking hills up ahead putting doubt in my mind. I gingerly rode further out of the town and with things on my mind, looking straight up at the mountains, trying to suss out the distance up ahead, not noticing the set-back petrol station on my right, which had an 'agua' and an air line. I then reasoned that if I didn't have food to get over those hills I definitely needed a full bottle of water as there was no wind and the sun was hammering my head. I swung around without really checking the traffic. The bike would take ages to stop because my one back brake was completely feeble, with non-existent brake blocks by now, and was even worse in the wet. I headed back twenty metres, moved to the centre of the road and impatiently waved a black-and-orange sprinter van to get out of my way as I almost hit his rear end in my haste to get across the forecourt to the water pipe.

As I leaned the bike between the water pipe and the air line and took a long and much-needed drink from the water pipe, the guy in the van parked nearby, got out and slowly walked over to me while his female companion went into the small garage shop. By now, I was filling my battered one-and-a-half-litre plastic bottle with water labelled 'Not suitable for drinking'! The fella came over to complain about my road manners, going on a rant as I began inflating my tyres back up to seventy PSI (far too much in that heat). He went on for a bit before I explained to him in my pigeon Portuguese and Spanish mix where I had come from and was going to, and that I was tired, hungry and skint and I'm sorry but I've got to get to Cartagena over the hills by evening. He said with surprise, "*Para UK como estas cycleta – nao dinero?*" (To the UK with this bike – no money?)

He must have taken pity on me because his girl came out of the shop and over to him just as I asked if he would give me a ciggy. He then told her to go back inside and buy a drink and something to eat. With that, he gave me half a packet of ten fags, then told me I was crazy – *loco* – and laughed. He then gave me a small meat wrap, a sort of energy drink, and a couple more fags.

"*Aqui. Estas frio.*" (Here. This is cold.)

After he handed me the cold drink I gave my thanks to him in the usual Spanish and Portuguese. With that he shook his head, smiled, and got in the van and drove off, not before bidding me, "*Bon voyage, Amigo!*"

Then I continued on towards that long, slow, winding uphill journey in the post-midday sun, up an unpopulated mountain pass with lots of basking lizards roadside, and a few foot-long dark green snakes a bit smaller than the ones I had seen in Portugal. In a couple of kilometres, the pass climbed from sea level to three hundred and forty-one metres, with dry tarmac and no wind. I was melting, half pushing half riding, where the gears would allow. As the pass became steeper, the bends became more tortuous. It seemed to encourage the Spanish drivers to see if they could peel the tyres off the rims of their wheels, squealing round the almost-full lock bends at the top of the pass. The record being taken by a guy in a black Audi with a fag in his grimacing mouth, shades on, with both hands giving the steering the full 'whoa!' treatment as though he either knew the road very well or had overdone it. This was almost at the summit on another 180-degree curve with a steep wall holding the mountain from falling down onto the road.

On these dozen or more curves I got fooled into thinking the summit was around the next bend at least five or six times. By the time I finally crested it a cool breeze greeted me, which I was s-o-o grateful for. I could see hundreds of kilometres of Spanish sun-baked fields, olive groves, orange groves, and villages, towns and far-off cities; but had to concentrate because the road was steeper going down than coming up, but just as curvy. My rear brake complained noisily but it just about coped with the first few bends. More than once I found the brake lever right against the stop and my bike running out of tarmac to grip on as I kicked up dust and stones from the rough road edges with my inside leg out, motocross style, purely for balance, which I still almost lost two or three times before the steepness and bends subsided. I had my coat open and my top and T-shirt rolled up, exposing my sweaty chest and belly. They were welcoming this temporary cool breeze as it dried my forehead.

As the mountain levelled out, I followed a straight road through long and wide olive groves. It was near a place called Los Ruices. The road was easy and kept dropping away gradually for miles, past small hamlets, towards Cartagena. As I passed by a little roadside taverna I noticed a UK-registration green Suzuki Jeep. It was worth stopping and meeting these people. I liked to think there might be some empathy for another UK national in Spain. I struck up a conversation with a southern English bloke and the Spanish landlady, who was silver haired and exquisite. Without saying anything, she offered me some ice-cold water. The fella's wife remained silent. Bloke just said, "You're Welsh, aren't you, Mate?" in a dark unimpressed tone.

He then proceeded to tell me how much he was making and that I was making a big mistake trying to cross those Pyrenees Mountains.

"Rather you than me, Mate!" said he as he turned back to the bar.

Ignoring this tosspot, I thanked the Spanish lady for her kindness and went on my way. This part of the journey to Cartagena would have been quite pleasant with the gentle breeze and a good pace in top gear on roads dropping a few metres every kilometre or so most of the way – that's if my arse wasn't hurting like a wounded plum. That's how I arrived in the centre of the city. I had followed the N-332 from Mazarron right over the last mountain, and arrived well thirsty and well hungry. Cartagena is a large port city with large streets, flyovers, and boulevards, with a station near to it. I searched in the bins of several supermarkets. Mostly I had missed the bin-emptying completely, or the bins were locked inside wire cages, presumably to stop the 'freegans' of the city looting them. I was gutted and my legs were giving out so I went up a tree-lined boulevard with roads running up either side and benches to rest on, and found a couple of dog-ends. Sitting down was such a relief I didn't ever want to move again – literally. I sucked on a three-quarter-length used Marlboro and it sent me into a trance with its addictive hit. I stared at an old-style eighteenth century office building the other side of the trees, wondering how many people had worked in it over the years and how many times people had gone in and out of its doors to and from work, with wages to spend and lives to live over the years, dull but contented. Random thought.

I just didn't want to move but had to find some food. I was about to start eating tree bark – it looked tasty and edible – much like a pregnant woman would find coal ash craveable and have other strange cravings. My hunger overcame my tiredness so, on the bike, I crept around the streets using plan two – takeaways, cafes and delis: there was bound to be a burger or bread thrown out. If I was to keep a pace up, I had to have something.

My feet were now stinging, obviously blisters, to add to an aching back, arse and legs. They were moving up the league table of pain. I tried to ignore these aches and pains until they stopped me or I cried. I wasn't far off both.

I summoned up the energy to swing my leg over the bike again, and visited another fruitless bin outside a 'Dia'. Around another side street, I raked through four or five bins until I found another one outside a baguette shop. In the wheelie bin was a pile of cardboard with two large long breads cut in half. I jumped up and stretched inside to reach the bread, which was dirty and hard. This would do if I broke off the dirty bits. It was like digging for diamonds. As I reached in to clasp the bread, chuffed with my find, someone tapped me on the back. I drew the bread out of the bin and looked round. There was a smart Spanish lad about mid-twenties standing behind me.

"*Senor.*" He then offered me a crisp five-euro note. I remembering clasping my hands and thanking God. "*Muchas Gracias, Senor,*" I said in a loud and enthusiastic manner.

A few feet behind him was a blonde big-breasted lady of maybe fifty, very smart, standing next to the open door of her silver Mercedes car. She was dressed in a silver jacket top and a tight silver skirt and offered me a smile. Her conscience was clear for the day with that gesture, and I was very grateful.

Right now, it was on to the next place. I found signs to the N-332 and resisted the temptation to blow the five Euros in the city, wanting to settle for the night at somewhere quieter than in this place. Plus, my energy was renewed because I had a supper to look forward to now. I had to get nearer to the coast. The map only showed a tip of land jutting out not far east of this city, next to the sea. That is where I would save this money for and have a real fresh supper. My mouth watered at the thought of fresh long breads, tomato juice and fresh apples with a pile of biscuits. That's all I could think of. It was the best thought in the world. Better than sex, better than a Sunday dinner, better than a sausage butty with brown sauce on a Sunday morn. Bread, tomato juice and fresh apples!

I headed out of the city and up a bridge carrying the A-30, and over to the *autovia*, heading east until I came to a run-off packed with commuters going home. Not being able to find a suitable road running in parallel with it, I had to carry on along it until I found an eastern loop off it. This took me for a kilometre on the N-343 up to a junction where I followed a road right next to a single railway track back on the N-332. I found a little town called La Union, where I saw signs for Los Alcazares. According to the map, La Union was next to the sea. In reality, it was miles away. I only found this out by asking a local, who told me Los Alcazares was next to the sea.

As he explained a short cut to me, I noticed a Dia. That's where I went in to get my scram: the fruit and food I could see lit up through the windows. With a grin on my face, I went in. Boy, did it feel strange to actually go into a shop with money. Licensed to buy. As I made my way to the fruit aisle a mam with a little lad went by. The mam gave me a double take and the little 'un kept his stare firmly fixed on me as his mam went past, tugging on his hand as the boy craned to look at me… for some reason! A few more people looked at me more than once. I was too interested in adding up the price of the stuff I was buying, making sure it added up to five Euros. It came to €4.96. As I made my way out of the store I realised why the people were giving me double takes. I noticed my full body reflection in a mirror and didn't recognise myself for a second. I saw a grubby blackened red baseball cap with matted wisps of almost shoulder-length grey-and-black hair that had not been cut since I left the UK on 9th January. My face was deeply tanned, with two scary stripes like tiger stripes starting at the bottom of my eyes and running round to my neck and ears, from days of rain, dust and sweating, matching my scruffy clothes. Around my waist I had tied my leather bomber jacket, and was wearing a dirty grey woollen jumper with roughly hacked off sleeves ending just below my shoulders. Under this were the black arms of a Benfica tracksuit top. My black jeans were misshapen and their colour hid most of the dirt they had accumulated but contrasted with my tan leather work-boots. To top it all I had a right load of thick 'non-designer' stubble on my chin. I looked like a right desperado!

I hadn't had a wash since Los Palacios, or was it Barbate? It didn't really matter now – every other consideration apart from distance wasn't important. Now I had fuel. Next, a place to scoff, and kip.

I followed roads that ran alongside fruit and veg fields for six or seven kilometres, where my legs began to fail and my pace dropped at the same time as my backache amplified the numbness in my outer fingers. The body was telling me to rest for today but I carried on because I could sense I was near the sea on a minor road, which began running almost parallel to the *autovia*. After noticing Mr Shadow riding alongside me as I changed direction along a few kilometres, I spotted the sea again, just short of a small town on the coast up ahead. I kept glancing at the shadow and wondered how he kept going at the same sort of regular pace. His legs and familiar sight were always there at the end of the day, just when I needed a bit of company. Sometimes I talked out loud to him, asking his opinion and why he was riding with me. He wasn't me; he was this impartial companion who decided to stick with me only when the sun suited him. I even complained to him,

"You're just a fair-weather friend... Yeah, you."

He never replied.

Other times I would share the victory of getting over a big hill with him, or when I reached a place where I had intended to be eight or nine hours ago. Or sing at him bits of music that made me feel good.

"YOU'RE A DIRTY SON OF A GUN, OOH YEAH...!" That always made me feel good, and N-Trance's 'Only love can set you free...' and Rui da Silva's 'Touch me in the morning...'. 'Old skool' and dance classics which I never learned all the words to but which sounded great in a good club with decent sound, and far too much alcohol, and a sexy woman to dance with, and some drugs.

Bad things to remember that made me feel good.

Hang on, it's stuff like that which got me here in the first place. So I gave Shadow a grimace and remember growling at him, as though it was his fault!

Shadow didn't give a toss; he just kept plodding, like forever. He never even complained about my singing.

Today was 20 April 2007 – a hot, hard and hilly day. I felt I had come far. My legs definitely felt it with a lot of hills today, which slowed me up. I had only done just over a hundred kilometres – give or take one or two to account for searching, and wrong turnings.

I was on the N-332 heading towards Los Alcazares, alongside the AP-7. It eventually left the huge agricultural fields and ran alongside a coastal nature reserve that looked inviting as the sun was fading. Just before the road ran into the built-up coastal town I turned off and went as close to the sea as I could be. I then turned off the road and onto the path leading away from a parking area and up the rough path that ran next to the sea. I stopped to find a spot a bit sheltered from the sea breeze. It wasn't cold and I had a false sense of security from the residual heat of cycling. There was a small embankment running next to the path, with sand and dried mud and sparse seaside plants growing on it. This is where I might settle tonight. The sea was literally about ten feet behind me. Dumping the bike, I got out my scram. I didn't care what happened after this. It was a moment I had denied myself for over an hour to add to the long hours since that van fella gave me the small snack meat wrap in Mazarron earlier that day. It was what I had taught myself for years: the more you wait for something the better it would feel when you got it. And this was like heaven: leaning my back against the small embankment watching the sun dropping away west whilst I necked fresh tomato juice and fresh bread, which was like medicine purging my empty belly of the hunger and emptiness and replacing it with vitamin C and the carbs I needed so badly. Two long bread sticks and a litre of juice later, I wolfed down two succulent, juicy, fresh, huge green-and-red apples and savoured the juice running down my chin; then a couple of fresh yoghurts; and, to finish with, a pile of biscuits with my water. Full, happy and 'accomplished', I watched the remainder of the sunset far away over the flat gigantic horizon. The sky, with its darkening shades of light blue then darker blue with pieces of solitary stretched-out cloud, formed a scene which looked like a distant memory of sunsets at the seaside as a kid.

The sky back then, I would think of as a giant reflection of the tidal pools and sand left behind by the retreating sea in Morfa Bychan (Black Rock). With its mile-long, flat beach empty by seven or eight in the evening on a long summer day, deserted just like this deserted sky I was entranced by for about an hour. I never noticed it was fucking cold by now and the wind had got right up. I guess I just felt fat and happy enough to forget.

It was time to find somewhere to shelter for the night. Up, and grabbing the bike, I fell over a lump of driftwood in the darkness. I made my way back to the road and headed up into Los Alcazares. This town looked well lit up at night and had plenty of life, with bright neon lights advertising restaurants and seedy-looking clubs and bars. It was at least a kilometre long, with black four-wheel-drives, palm trees lining the streets, and pretentious twats walking around at night with shades on to the sound of the Balearic beat. Yep! It was my kind of place if I had the dosh. I felt caught between two worlds. My bad side craved this superficial music-filled sensory-seeking veil of bullshit which was just show with no soul.

And the other world. The real feeling of being caught in a rainstorm whilst biking down a muddy Welsh mountain as it went dark, or running off a cliff edge with the paraglider, not knowing whether I would land safely or be killed.

Or taking a big risk with a new business at the expense of family and friends.

Or leaving a woman who loved me for one night of passion with some stranger who looked good at the time.

Or going to bits when meeting some kid with no dad or no mam.

Or a dying kid. Who wouldn't melt if they met a child with cancer? What would flashy clothes, shades and car mean then – fuck all! God forbid, what if it was your own child? I would ride the world to pay for a cure for 'em. I no longer gave a shit about flashy cars, money or status – they all rust and rot and we get old. But good, fulfilling memories stay with you as long as your mind is able to recall them. And so does your conscience.

We've all done one or more of the things I've mentioned but there are people who don't give a shit –until something happens to them.

Don't knock any faith or pass a homeless person by. You just don't know where life can take you. Or how it can all change in a moment.

Done good or done bad, at least this was one memory I could use forever if I made it and if I survived it.

Losing the shelter of the buildings that lined the straight boulevard through Los Alcazares, I felt the chill of the inshore breeze along a dual carriageway, then spotted a supermarket on its own – newly built with nothing but flat land behind it. Being black of night and me being cold now, I went across the car park round the back, and into the darkness of the lee side of the building. Finding it totally windless there, I arranged a pallet and furnished it with cardboard to settle on for the night. The building faced the dark flat nothingness behind the sunset boulevard of this town. I settled down but not before I rifled through the wheelie bin on a concrete access road around the corner. I might have had a good feed earlier but tomorrow I would need fuel. As I searched for anything of use to my belly, the staff unlocked the back doors and were leaving for the night. I didn't care what they thought as they gave me a look of 'We've seen it many times', as they walked away, leaving me to my search. I found a net of oranges. They would be useful tomorrow. I also found some Rocchetta cheese – about half a pound of the stuff, gone a bit hard but well tasty. As I settled down on my pallet, I thought that all I needed now was Pavarotti and some bone-dry Chablis. I drifted off to sleep to the music of a concrete pump across the fields to my right erecting another block of apartments, with eastern Europeans and Spanish no doubt labouring away to finish the concrete pour. I had even been the workshop manager of Dublin Concrete, pumping; and later a concrete mixer truck owner. I knew full well, the urgency and contingency of completing a big pour in one long day. Regardless of problems, you could not leave a pour and finish it the next day as this would leave a cold joint, susceptible to failure. Even here, I was reminded of previous jobs and businesses – over thirty in all. I could imagine those lads slaving away, struggling, with their wellies deep in thick wet concrete. Slipping and tripping on the reinforcing bars laid within the wet cement, whilst they fought with a seven-inch-wide and thirty-foot-long pulsating black rubber snake gushing out its grey stony mush. Whilst the self-righteous concrete pump operator stood with his remote control, quietly moaning to himself about his tea being in the dog again and he still had to wash the pipes out and put them away and then drive the rig home. Ha ha! I laughed to myself. This tramp could do all those jobs and had done – delivered concrete, been on the crew and even repaired the pumps. Another faraway, past memory. This was a day of charity, hunger and scary reflections, physically and metaphorically. The pumping stopped and I fell into black.

Chapter Eleven
High Gears and Headway

21st April 2007 Los Alcazares to Altea – 157 Kilometres

That night the wind changed from an onshore to an offshore breeze, cold and stiff, blowing directly off the cold plain and hitting the rear of this supermarket, waking me from my slumber with biting feet. It was still dark and I knew I would have to find another place to kip for a couple of hours or so, or risk exposure. I loaded up and rode to another location further up the road, my hands and feet biting with cold, and feeling a massive need for some more sleep. I found a Chinese restaurant just before a huge concrete flyover out of town. It had two big, set-back, glass doors guarded by two huge golden lions of about five foot high, each with one foot on a small golden pig. This was just about out of the main blast of wind – enough for me to doze for a while but without falling fully asleep. The chill became too much and the light began to appear. It was no use staying here. I may as well move on and promote some blood flow around my body.

Off I went, tackling the rise over the flyover, which was a prelude to a flatter journey today, almost entirely coastal. An hour later the sun had made the early-morning wind die off a little. I reached a pace where the bike needed higher gearing. I was making good progress, and the hills were rises with shallow dips between them, if they existed at all. I stopped and changed the derailleur onto the smallest cog on the back wheel. For most of this day, it was all I needed, plus a quick adjustment of the bungee chord that was almost worn through by the chain. I remember picking another up off the road and using it to keep the tension on the gear mechanism so that it would stay in top gear. As the tension became less, or as it wore through the elastic, the chain would jump into a lower gear. If it did this later in the day I just couldn't be bothered getting off the bike; I would just plod on in a lower gear. That would then annoy me because over an hour it was lost distance. I eventually settled on the cog next to the highest-geared one and used the front big cogs to give me a complete 'range' of two gears – one for hills and one for the flat. I couldn't stand up to pedal for more than a couple of beats without the chain jumping the sprockets by now, no matter how tight I could get the chain tension. That was painful because as well as giving my arse a sudden shock loading, my feet would remind me of the blisters I had developed over the past few days. I kind of tried to ignore those and hoped that they might go away. I would wriggle my feet in all sorts of positions but, sure as eggs are eggs, they hurt. So I used 'em as a kind of gauge, like with my back. When the pain increased to the point where no matter what I did I couldn't handle it, it was time to stop and take five. This would give me another hour or so of 'semi-pain' – not quite as painful but still only just about bearable – all in the name of distance. Also, because of this stretch of flatness, I didn't want to waste a morsel of energy stopping and starting. My brain was wrapped up in going somewhere. I didn't stop unless I absolutely had to. It was also really hard to get going again.

I knew that if I kept going all day I could go further than previously. Up ahead the road was as straight as a plumb line for the most part, with no mountains or hills for maybe a hundred kilometres or so. By now, I had reached a place called Torrevieja. Passing huge inland lakes, maybe salt lakes, I saw factories far away on the western shore. The road rose and fell slightly and I passed small roadside businesses and newly built apartments for foreigners – Brits, Germans or whoever – populated by the over-fifties walking their dogs and wearing clothes that looked like everyone had ordered them in shades of beige out of the *Daily Express* supplement. I rarely spotted a Spanish person here. These places I passed were characterless and humdrum. Every structure looked the same, with the most prominent shops being estate agents and hair salons for the blue rinse brigade. Totally uninteresting. By the time the sun was almost overhead, it was time for a stop and a break I found a large supermarket, which I checked out for food, only to find an empty auto lawnmower box and some grass cuttings. This summed up the whole area to me. Maybe it was a retirement area for older 'Stepford wives'? Yep, these people know how to live!

Finding a bench next to some more mundane apartments with their backs to the N-332, I rested my legs and bum for about half an hour. It wasn't worth staying any longer – I had no food or water or fag stumps. It was back to the familiar pain, which I would placate by telling myself that I was nibbling away at the miles bit by bit – better than sitting down and doing nothing. I noticed a sign for Alicante. I think it was about fifty or so kilometres away, and knew if everything went OK I would be there by late afternoon.

These parts of the journey were visually the most boring but physically the most useful with no hills to contend with, just distance and pain. The pain was to be temporarily appeased by the almost-full pack of twenty Camels I found discarded at the roadside – what a bonus! Stopping and finding one of the three different half-used or almost-finished discarded lighters stashed around my person, I lit up one fag and raised my head to the sky, taking in that addictive but so pacifying hit which took away the tension and aches for a small eternity. Once again, I fell over backwards, gripping the bars of the bike tighter, thinking it was falling when it was actually me losing balance and pulling the bike over, with me landing flat on my back in the roadside vegetation with a thump. It must have looked funny to passing motorists. I somehow managed to bust the yellow shades, which I had relied on so much against the fierce daytime sunshine.

This was the start of the bigger distances bearing in mind I was riding a shed, but at the time it didn't matter – it was a means of getting somewhere considerably quicker than walking. I would try to draw a parallel to think about on the long flat distance. This was another attempt at 'boxing' the past and analysing why things went good or bad.

I learned from a couple of failed attempts at businesses that you don't wait for the perfect conditions or latest technology, enough money, the right people to come along, the right 'breaks', time of year, family or friends' approval, equipment or any other excuse which will hold you back from the time you have NOW. You just get off your butt, and your *buts*, and fucking do it! You go with what is available at the time. This bike was what was 'available' to me at the time. That's why I had already done over a thousand kilometres on it at this point. It didn't matter how it was done; it was done. That's all I was bothered about. All the other rubbish didn't matter at the time. Future or past was being dealt with bit by bit and I never even realised it at the time. All that mattered was the road ahead, keeping going, and staying alive. It was a great dumping ground for the rubbish of the recent past but it also made me value things like my legs and my health and my brain, my kids, and the things I wish I had done and said whilst valuable people were still alive.

None of us are perfect – we've all got big defects. Those of us who think they haven't will have a big shock one day when finally confronted with themselves.

I would have loved to have been content like my Taid was, for example, but it sends me off my rocker. His contentment was having a crafty roll-up in the outside toilet. Now I feel really guilty for the many times as a ten-year-old when I grassed him up to my Nain, who was trying to force him into giving up smoking. He had done his bit, brought up and paid for a family of five during wartime, working as a crane driver above the main ladle in Brymbo steelworks. He rode to work up steep hills on his old black heavy pushbike, with his canvas workbag with his 'snappin' tin inside, which usually contained lard-and-salt butties and a battered thermos flask full of neat tea with no sugar or milk, for forty-five years. He retired a couple of years before he wanted to due to chronic emphysema, certainly not helped by twelve hours a day sucking in the fumes, dust and smoke entering his cabin perched above the molten metal. Mind you, the twenty-a-day Capstan Full Strength and Golden Virginia habit didn't help, or his daily habit of cooking everything half an inch deep in lard – especially cheese, and then, once finished, mopping the remaining contents of his plate dry with bread, desperate not to waste a morsel of tripe, brawn and other animal by-products he lived on. He was a throwback to rationing during the Second World War, where he and his protein-hungry mates weren't scared to eat anything which gave them sustenance for another grim, black day. He came from seven generations of Brymbo (which means Hill of the Bow) and Ffos-y-gof (Blacksmith's Ditch) families who worked the mines and steelworks that bound the communities together with strong accents, belonging, and identities. This little-heard-of steelworks, which shut, with the loss of over a thousand jobs, in 1985, was originally the home of John Wilkinson's steelmaking company for two hundred years. The machinery was exported to China. Even with profits of seven million the year, it was shut by the ruthless bean counters of the UES Steels.

When he died there must have been five hundred or so people at the funeral of this tall, white-haired, blue-eyed fella who secretly would polish my moto-cross boots the night before I raced, so my disapproving Nain didn't see. And would knock up another cock-eyed shelf, three inches by three feet, out of rough plywood, to hold the growing collection of trophies I fetched back each week unless I was in the casualty department of a Sunday night. This fella was the only person who was proud of anything I did though he never told me. He would just polish my boots with dubbin on Saturday night, then secretly drop 'em next to my bike, then squeeze another trophy onto the magnolia-painted woodchip wallpaper-covered corner shelves. Now and again I would secretly catch him standing back and looking pleased with himself whilst looking at the, usually, slightly crooked shelves. This was the only approval I would get but it meant a lot then. I howled like a little baby on the bottom steps of the stairs at my mates Dunc and Gill's house after seeing him lying lifeless, with his sharp eyes half open, one leg on the bed and one leg off the bed. I fled 'cos I couldn't show my Nain this sort of emotion – she was mentally and spiritually as tough as old boots. She lasted another twenty years or so. He wouldn't have lasted five minutes without her. The old generation – we just don't compare with. We are wusses compared to them but I guess relative to them we have far more unneeded stresses forced on us by twenty-first century living. Their generation must have had 'mental monsters' to deal with but more physically, with food shortages, early deaths of children, fear of sickness, and poverty. They just seemed more content without the electronic and techno crap we think we need today!

Whatever you are like, we all have to deal with our own 'mental monsters' relative to ourselves one day. It's how you deal with them that counts. And when things do go pear-shaped from time to time, it's how you deal with it. No possessions, holiday, car, clothes, boob job, bank account or sense of humour will protect you from your own fuck-ups one day. But if you've got the balls to admit you were wrong with a capital W, it's like a tightly coiled-up spring inside you being unwound until it does not matter what people say about you or what's happened. It's not where you are, it's where you are going that counts, whether it's now, next year or in five years' time. If you deal with things an inch or a centimetre at a time you will get there. Tit about with too much drink, good times or drugs, and you will lose all you've gained. It's like trying to run up a greased slope – it's a lot harder than walking or running up stairs. The crap things that you may be thinking about this actual minute now: will they matter in six months' time, or five years from now? – NO: they will fade like toothache does, though at the time you may not think so. I reacted badly, and emotionally, so it cost me. But it also taught me that all that glitters isn't gold. I wouldn't swap the current experiences for anything; I just wish I had found a different way to get where I had got.

More flat long miles took me through the cool city of Alicante, so much on a high because it was still early and I had covered more today than I had done for days. I cycled right down the main street to the marina area and continued out along a tree-lined boulevard out towards Villajoysa and Benidorm, where I might find food and continue right past the place. I had no plans to kip there – it's just a concrete jungle with sunshine, even worse than I imagined it to be, like a clone of every commercialised city but with more concrete skyscrapers and apartment blocks. My legs, bum and back were pretty shot by the time I got there and I almost bedded down behind a car dealership next to a giant supermarket and a retail park overlooking a maze of concrete flyovers, hotels and apartment blocks which obscured the sea. But the boy racers, groups of drunks, and litter everywhere forced me to bed somewhere further up the coast. I had roughed it in better places and this place ruined the feel. I had developed 'tramp snobbery': if I was going to doss on a bench, it was going to be on a more 'exclusive' doss...

Getting going again was hard, but every time I decided to get resume the journey was hard. My muscles and joints had cooled down and felt stiff. Benidorm was over a hundred kilometres from Los Alcazares and I had gone for it today so my limbs weren't going to be co-operative. I didn't care – I wasn't staying here tonight. On I went, complaining to the shadow man, who joined me on the last few miles.

"Where the fuck have you been all day, Pal? You're only here when it suits you. I bet you went on the train to Benidorm. No wonder you're always just in front of me. You ain't tired like me, huh."

He had nothing to say, as usual. Not getting further than ten more kilometres, I found a convenient bench near the sea at a place called Altea. I went no further that day because up ahead were steep rocky mountains which weren't huge but formed a mental picture enough for me to say, "I'll try that after a rest, *manana*!" A hundred and fifty-seven kilometres from Los Alcazares wasn't bad progress. Just a day of killing the long distance.

Feet, bum and back were very sore at this point, and I also had well-numb fingers. The two outermost were completely numb. I contemplated these before nodding off pretty suddenly. The evening was warm enough to get a good full night's kip and I needed it by the look of tomorrow's first obstacle. Before I bedded down I had a long slow Camel 'bonus' after a few oranges and some biscuits and crackers raided from a nearby small supermarket bin; and rummaged for the little bit of superglue and resurrected the yellow shades by reaffixing the lens into the frame and gluing the one side arm so it was now permanently open. This didn't matter: they were on most of the time, daily.

Chapter Twelve

Unable to Sit on a Dying Bike

22nd April 2007 Altea to Valencia – 156 Kilometres,

23rd April 2007 Valencia to Vinaros – 136 Kilometres,

24th April 2007 Vinaros to Cambrills – 88 Kilometres,

25th April 2007 Cambrills to Castelldefels – 95 Kilometres

Up at 7.45, I had a breakfast fag before contemplating the rocky cliffs up ahead. After loading up I cycled along the seafront of Altea and stopped at the end of the seafront road, placing my leg on the pavement whilst sitting astride the bike, and surveyed the scene ahead. It looked more ominous the closer I got, and steep. I couldn't see the roads climbing it because of trees and vegetation. Ah! I'll find a way; there must be a way, I thought to myself. The old English fella who rode up to me agreed there was a way. He had a shiny unused mountain bike and I half wished he would offer to swap me if I told him how far I had to go. I could have done with his brakes and gears.

Off I went in the early morning. It was fresh with bright sun, a bit cool but no wind. Let's tackle these hills. Wow, they were hills! They climbed from sea level around a series of sweeps and loops, to over a hundred and thirty metres in less than a couple of kilometres, over one of the most striking sections of road, through tunnels and over gorges hewn out of the steep jagged rocks. At the bottom of the climb, I altered the gears down to the lowest position and this got me up most of the way until I hit the first tunnel. It went at a steep angle into the rock, with the main *autovia* another twenty or so metres above me, on another ledge, and the train track somewhere below me following the same path. There were beautiful views and costly homes with terracotta roofs strewn around this green and rocky area. This was Calpe.

The sweat of the climb was dried up by the tremendous force of wind coming through the tunnels, which funnelled the early-morning air and made my ears hurt. I put my bomber jacket back on for a bit. The second tunnel was hundreds of feet above the rock crevasses, and on either side, other bridges carrying train track and *autovia* crossed this magnificent void of sheer rock cliffs. What a sight! – bendy and inspiring. After this climb across the rocks the road steadily climbed Spanish hills with farms converted into villas for the wealthy – beautiful and secluded, with views, peace and the need for two BMWs, a four-wheel drive and Swiss bank account.

I was crossing these hills towards the Gata de Gorgos, climbing to two hundred and seventy-five metres (nine hundred feet). As the road finally levelled, I reached a tiny town called Benissa, where I stopped at a crossroads for a fag and a rest. Hungry by now, I looked around for any shops and noticed an Aldi down a side street. On checking this out it was – bingo! – full of edible food. I found a net-full of almost perfect oranges, some cheese, biscuits, UHT milk and a huge, still-cold yoghurt, which all went down well bar the oranges, which I saved for later on. After a fag and 'five' I moved on and noticed a hefty farm girl with a fat tanned face investigating the bin as I left. The road out of Benissa went straight towards some more rocky mountains but I was glad: with fuel inside me, they wouldn't be a problem. I encountered some curves and straight agricultural areas before I hit the rocky pass. With the sunshine back out and beaming down on the surroundings, a night's rest and a belly full of food, I had another of those rare 'things can't get better than this' feelings. No bills, stress, mortgage, bank loans, routine or the same glum faces and grim weather. Free as I could possibly be… for now.

As I climbed into the mountain pass, I found it didn't actually climb up much because after a short time it descended quite steeply into a twisting, dark, rocky and well-windy depression, passing entrances to quarries. I stopped at one entrance to put on my bomber jacket again. The cold wind being funnelled uphill at me was like ice after the last few hours. It was a strange feeling having to pedal down a steep hill against the oncoming wind. This was another place which reminded me of the rocky valleys near Blaenau Ffestiniog, close to home for me. Blaenau was the home of the world's largest slate mine, and this place too had a grey and lonely forbidding charm matched with cold. To me it was beautiful: chilly, rocky and almost unchanged by time. All I needed was a downpour and I could have been in north Wales!

Nah, not today. Snap out of it, Shortie! The steep rocky sides and wind eventually gave way to the familiar flat road dropping away to almost sea level over about twenty kilometres through Ondara, and then endless straights running completely straight like Roman roads alongside the *autovia* – the AP-7. I stopped once in maybe two hours at a truck stop to fill my water bottle and blow my tyres up in anticipation of reaching Valencia – a major city – today. Regular road signs helped me to count down the miles and check my daily progress, and I was seeing names like Tarragona and Barcelona, still hundreds of kilometres away but reachable in terms of days. Now I felt a master of distance. I was reaching these goals daily, thus completing a separate adventure, and not being so impressed by my surroundings that I would gawp and waste time. I began enjoying the pain and effort and the small rewards at the end of a long day. There was no feeling like it. I learned to survive the distances, the regular problems of finding food, the punctures, which were too many to mention, all while remaining completely skint apart from a couple of Euros here and there. I passed Oliva, then Gandia, Xeresa, and Xeraco with the sea to my right, and fields and *autovia*, flat, on and on and on until I made a mistake of not going the last kilometres into Valencia by following the N-332 inland near a place called Cullera. Because on days like this with loads of steady progress it was too much effort to cross a busy road and go off track for a couple of kilometres, I decided to stay on the N-332. It went inland, away from the coast, and the signs indicated that Valencia was on this road so I followed it. Besides, the crap map indicated that I was on the right road. This took me past Sueca and on until I had no choice but to join the *autovia* for the last kilometres towards the city. Bugger it! I was too close to go all the way back and find the coast road proper. The Spanish would have to blow their horns at me or the cops pull me. I could smell Valencia now, and as I had a full stomach, I would use the last of my energy today on this *autovia*. I pedalled in the hard shoulder faster than I had for a while. It was fast and flat and my legs were moving up and down in top gear as fast as I was able to make 'em. I definitely thought I had been on this *autovia* (the V-31) for over an hour before I decided to get off it. When I did, it was into an industrial area where the giant Ford factories were situated. Nearing Valencia, I seemed to ride on little access roads mainly used by car transporters carrying new Ford Focuses and the like, until I found a way over the *autovia* over a rough bit of dead olive-growing field towards the city's nearby rough arse end. I went up, down and around quiet lanes with the surrounding fields tended by workers few-and-far between. Eventually I spotted a little non-tarmac track leading into the back of some buildings coming out next to a back-end industrial road behind a truck garage, that led dead straight into the city. I stood next to a 35-cubic-yard metal skip, which had a discarded old sofa with no cushions next to it. I leaned the bike against it, got out a half-used Marlboro and slumped into the comfy seat whilst pulling out the dog-eared, sweaty, crap map, filling it in with the time and date of where I had got today. I reckoned it was about a hundred and fifty kilometres from Benidorm, on 22nd April at about 5.00 p.m. – all wrong but not far off either. I was a new kind of tired today – absolutely and completely bolloxed, with my arse really saying now that this was too much. My back just throbbed to the beat of the blood flowing from my heart, and my feet were burning with the pain of the blisters I was too chicken to look at in case I found something I didn't want to see. I just wanted some good news and feelings for now. On went the radio and I listened to Kabin FM. I was that worn out I would have stayed there if it wasn't for the flies and gnats buzzing around me as I blew smoke their way.

I had reached a major city so I would find food here. Though being tired enough to crash where I was, the lure of food nearer the centre or, better still, the thought of waking up a few more kilometres across the city, would once again get me up off my sore, weary arse and chance a couple more kilometres.

Off down the straight road out of the industrial area and battered road, I slowly plodded towards the city centre. Just before an intersection I noticed a little Aldi set back from the road, with a quiet small loading area with wheelie bins full mostly of cardboard, but a lucky find was a bunch of well-ripe bananas and four 'Rola Cola' bottles – one of 'em leaking – and all bound together with nylon banding. Great! My tongue was as dry as Ghandi's flip-flop. It must have been eighty degrees Fahrenheit or more. I couldn't get the bands cut quick enough. Even though the cola was warm, it would be sugary and thirst quench-ing. In my haste, I sliced through one of the litre plastic bottles and BOOM!

It exploded all over me with a good force, emptying almost its entire contents in milliseconds. I stood there for a second with my knife in hand and shook myself, then laughed. Not only was I hot and sweaty, but completely sticky as well now. I opened the next bottle and almost finished it on the spot, and I bagged the last for later. I also found a decent packet of UHT to go. Further on into the city I went down a dead straight, increasingly busy street, narrow and packed with Spanish working folk shopping in every type of place, but as I neared the centre the cars, people and shops became more exclusive and the buildings posh! The road became a boulevard with neatly kept vegetation, and palm trees lining the central area. Still with major pangs of hunger by now, I stopped next to a Burger King, which had its wheelie bins outside next to the pavement. Definitely worth a look.

As I rifled through the discarded rubbish I netted at least a dozen ketchup sachets and a couple of bags of untouched cold fries. These all went straight down my throat without a minute's hesitation, my hunger and need for energy overcoming all discretion. Standing next to the bins, I washed the food down with a couple of big gulps of Rola Cola and belched loudly. I then lit another half-used Marlboro and leaned on the bin, my eyes slowly panning around the immediate surroundings. Across the road were smart shops, huge buildings, and a busy boulevard with cars all going somewhere. Round to my right and across was a huge brass-and-glass tinted-window building. In the middle were cool-looking large, tall palm trees. Round to my left, the oncoming traffic coming into the city was less busy by now as it was early evening. Then almost behind me – in front of the Burger King – there were about twenty little aluminium tables and chairs filled with lots of Spanish families and younger well-dressed people with their glares, non-smiling, fixed directly at the tramp who had just had his evening meal before their eyes. Who was now enjoying an after-dinner cigarette whilst surveying his surroundings from underneath a grotty red base-ball cap and mirror yellow shades; one elbow on the bin and one on hip. None of 'em moved their glances away for a bit, or ate. This gave me a laugh.

"*Buenas noches*," I said with a big smile, then finished my stump and moved on.

I didn't go far – just almost to the end of the boulevard where the city buildings ended and the *autovia* out started. There was a paved area with four benches in front of some apartments right next to the road. It was going dark and my body was still needing a little more nourishment. I then had a supper of bananas and almost half a bottle of Rola Cola, brushed my teeth and hit the bench flat, completely tired again. I dropped off into a warm sleep with the sound of the city in my ears.

Next morning at 7.45, as I checked my radio for the time, I was dying for a pee – too much Rola Cola. I loaded up the bike to the sound of car horns and engines and noticed the cars on the boulevard directly behind the bench queuing up and not moving on their morning journey into this cool city. You couldn't have fitted a Rizla paper between them. Two lanes one way, and two lanes the other.

These commuters were then treated to the sight of me conspicuously peeing behind the nearest tree.

On the road again I cycled not a hundred metres or so and tried to cross the gridlocked junction at the northern edge of the city, where I spoke to a flustered traffic cop who was directing four lanes of traffic, two abreast, all seemingly trying to penetrate the city at once.

"*Senor, carratera por Castilio*?" (Road for Castillon?) To which he pointed to the northbound *autovia*. Quite logical really but he had just given me official permission to ride on it. I went on ahead at top speed in top gear, pedalling as quickly as my legs would allow me while taking advantage of the daily freshness in them. On this dead flat straight four-laner towards Castillon about seventy kilometres away, I felt like I had kept this pace up for a few hours, though it was probably only about just over an hour, to the junction where I got off the V-21 *autovia* and back onto the N-340 heading back towards the coast on an intersection. The road seemed to drop off really straight, up ahead, slightly downhill, then slightly uphill, off into the flat hot distance with plenty of sandy-coloured level Spain either side of the road. Dotted with modern industry sporadically illustrating the space available in this country to plonk a large business and bring a dead area to life, or to 'ruin' the vast peaceful distance with workplaces we all need, depending on your viewpoint.

This sort of road stretching up ahead would mentally drain me a little because of the immediate distance I would have to cover, but I got used to thinking about anything but this sight up in front so before I knew it I would think, 'That didn't take long – next!' Things we don't want to do are always intimidating when you think too much about them, but if you just get on with it, it's never as bad as you think. As I was riding up this slight rise on the wide and long stretch, I stopped to change the gears down a few cogs to make it easier on my legs and the slack chain, and found I was developing yet another slow puncture. Better move on. This is where I found a sleeveless Brazil T-shirt, with oil marks on it, cast aside at the roadside. This I picked up as it would be useful on hot days like this for protection from the sun and also make it unnecessary for me to wear my woollen jumper with rolled up sleeves which chafed my neck and itched with sweat. Brazil were my favourite world-beaters at this time. Some time the previous year I was bought a Brazil shirt with 'Ronaldinho' on the back, and the Brazilians also spoke Portuguese so I guess this find was somehow my link with the past and the future. This shirt stayed with me for some years. I did wash it though!

Another several kilometres along dead flat, straight, hot, dusty roads, I came across a fuel station at an intersection of busy roads in the middle of nowhere. This place had a tyre bay, an air line and a water pipe. Right – time for a spot of maintenance before the rest of the day's journey, and to get this heap spot on. I borrowed a spanner off one of the tyre fitters, removed both wheels and tyres, used their tyre bath to find the slow puncture, and blagged a decent patch to fix it, off Miguel, one of the fitters. I swapped the front tyre with the back one, which had taken all the weight and was showing signs of cracking up and wear. I also tightened every spoke on both wheels and sorted the tension on the derailleur, giving the chain a drop of oil too. I then took five minutes whilst smoking a cigarette I got off a fella who had pulled in to fuel his car up... *Gracias*!

On I went with the bike (almost) 100 per cent. With my full water bottle, making progress along desert roads, easily negotiating a couple of hills here and there, and being overtaken by mad Spanish speed freaks in their motors, one of which was pulled up whilst racing another character, by a police car up ahead in front of me along a quiet straight road. As I passed the shade-wearing sheepish-looking youngster being booked by the copper I thought, 'That's a familiar memory!' I remembered that just before I left the UK, one of the only good things happening that year was having a clean licence for the first time since I was sixteen. That didn't last long.

Flyin' today, I took in a load of distance, with direction and a complete lack of sightseeing, just focusing on as many miles as I could do before the heat, pain and tiredness would once again end the daily journey. For hours, I passed through flat countryside, with land either side covered as far as the eye could see with grape and olive plantations, roadside agricultural buildings and haulage yards, through places such as Nules and then the slightly larger Villarreal, following the N-340a through Castillon de la Plana. I remember briefly stopping to raid a supermarket bin somewhere en route, and finding a pile of bananas and oranges, but without wasting a minute, as I wanted to keep going and take advantage of the flat roads, and make the most of the day.

Somewhere this day I stopped for water on a straight which rose gently up into far-off hills surrounded by neat agricultural land and a mixture of scrub-covered land which resembled the scenery out of *Close Encounters of the Third Kind*, with a dead straight tarmac road disappearing up into the horizon. I found a little electric substation with a clean flat concrete area with shade. I sat and drank water and ate one of the last oranges and searched for biscuit crumbs, enjoying the only whole one. Looking back the direction I came, it was as straight down into the distance as it was the other way. I spent a few moments watching a disoriented ant that fell out of my bag. I'd carried it from some-where, probably the last bench I had slept on. It wandered to and fro, unable to find a trail or traces or any direction, so it just stayed in one place for a bit, stroking its antennae. I had a lot in common with it.

"We're in the same boat, Pal!"

What the fuck was I doing talking to an ant in the middle of nowhere? Time to get going. I loaded up and hit the road again, leaving Mr Ant behind. Instinct would keep him goin', same as me, except I had a map and knew how to pray. A quick scan of the map showed me I wasn't more than maybe two days' riding away from Barcelona, the city which had looked so far away about a week previous. It was a day's drive in a car but on this 'adventure', it was a quest, a massive boost to the feeling of completing something big, a great feeling. The French border was now a reality. If anyone had suggested a ride on a bike around half of Spain in the past, I wouldn't have even given it a second thought. But this was the most important journey I had ever done at this moment, and I was almost loving every pain-filled mile because I was going somewhere. The journey was more important than the destination.

I went on through Opressa del Mar then, as my legs and back needed to take in some rest, I took a stop briefly at the side of the road in a place called Santa

Magdalena de Polpis. It was getting on in the afternoon by now and this tiny, quaint Spanish town looked as if it was still back in the eighteenth century. With tiny streets and a traditional chapel with a bell at the top of its steeple; and the homes, painted white, with old fellas leaning against the inside of their roadside wooden front doors, with their old chequered shirts and caps, and cigs dangling from one side of their moustachioed lips – a different world from the coastal resorts. This was traditional Spain – quiet and beautiful. In a little shade from the small mountain behind the town, which formed a natural barrier between it and the Costa Dorada, I took a moment to smoke a stump and have a drink of water, then got back on the road again. No food or water there. It didn't look too far to a place called Benicario next to the sea. The late-afternoon arse ache and tired legs getting the better of me by now, I thought this place might be the one to rest in tonight so I made the last few kilometres a good effort to wring the most out of my tiring legs in order to get to my 'bed'. I had made good progress today but wasn't sure how much yet. But with Tarragona only a day's ride away, I didn't plan to slacken off tomorrow's distance.

The long periods without food of any substantial amount had taken their toll. The long last few straights before Benicario were mostly downhill but my legs tired quicker than a dead Eveready battery. My mind wanted to go a little further but my legs were slow and heavy. Even my bum wasn't complaining that badly. Not until I could see the whole picture of daily distance travelled could I see the pattern of a couple of days of progress followed by a low-mileage day. At this moment I struggled to make small progress; my legs were getting that weak. I had another moment in Benicario where I rested, then decided the N-340 looked too inviting as it ran right next to the sea for another couple of idyllic kilometres. Mr Shadow joined me for a short while as the sun began to die. I realised why he was there late in the day: he was never without his other mates – pain and hunger – and they all conspired to slow me down, eventually getting the better of me. I couldn't drag 'em all along the road so I stopped at a place with a large paved area which had benches near an open standpipe where people filled up five-gallon plastic drums with water. This was great: as well as filling my bottle with clean fresh water I had a good long drink in between several pauses. I was able to rehydrate myself several times before I chose a bench next to a small public fenced-off park with a view of mountains, which looked about two or three kilometres away across the road, which was busy with large continental artic trucks with their lights on. I ate my 'supper' of about four oranges, enjoying the sweetness and fibre and juices entering my body, which was completely tired tonight after almost another hundred and fifty kilometres. This place was called Vinaroz. I definitely felt God was my 'buddy' by now, as I looked at the silhouette of the huge mountain, black against the now-darkening clear blue sky. I had not had any punctures in a while, the bike was trouble-free, the chain hadn't jumped or come off, my arse didn't feel like a wounded plum entirely, and my legs felt almost indestructible – very tired but reliably refreshed after a night's rest. Lying flat, with my head on my makeshift pillow rucksack which looked tatty and battered, I flicked on the little radio and listened to Spanish flamenco music, which suited the scene as I scanned the distant horizon.

The nearby N-340 was far enough away so the traffic lulled me off into random thoughts. I could hear the faraway noise of familiar individual, big-capacity truck engines. Scania 143s with the offbeat rumbles of their fourteen-litre V8s; MANs with their unhurried six-pot whisper of million-mile reliability; and Mercedes Actroses with their distinct faraway engine notes, all driving goods to faraway destinations, for ten hours plus per day, five or six days a week, or twenty-four seven if they were double manned, as many European rigs are. I had repaired and driven so many diverse makes and types of trucks over the years I could tell what they were with my eyes closed. I thought a couple of times of hitching a ride but thought that would just be cheating myself by now. I was gonna do this journey and was convinced I had a greater force on my side by now. It was like some kind of mission I knew I couldn't fail. But times up to now had had me on the roadside begging for help, and more times like that were to come. Maybe I just felt I would get there somehow.

This was another one of those chats inside my head, telling myself I had been through worse in the past. Just like everyone predicted, I was on course for self-destruction – well, I guess you can't sink much lower than I had done. The difference was I believed I was a lot tougher than most people gave me credit for. And by now I also believed in what I was saying. Totally! No negative talk from anyone to discourage or remind me of past mistakes, only physical experiences to overcome, with a determination from inside my head, nibbling the distance in metric and imperial at the same time. This trip was beautiful, exciting, frightening, exhausting and rewarding all at the same time; better than all the previous achievements I had ever had. But I had to be completely tired at the end of a complete day's struggle to appreciate it, and then drift off after wallowing in the good feelings and thanking God for the abilities I've got whilst my eyes slowly shut looking up at a bright and warm starry night.

The end of a successful long day was always like that: my brain totally submerged in endorphins and good feelings, like a giant sensory room taking you far from reality and troubles, summing up the good stuff and enjoying the mental reward where you would forget what was up ahead and what was behind. In front: bring it on! Behind: a past that can't be changed. The bad stuff: forget it, dump it and move on.

You don't drive forward whilst looking in the rear-view mirror or you will soon crash. You are either going forward and getting better, or looking backwards and moving nowhere – simple as that. But you just can't do it all on your own and sometimes you can't find anybody to help you either. I prayed and uncanny things happened. I had never been a spiritual person before this journey: too pragmatic and far too reliant on things and money. Atheists, you lot can fuck off. All the modern technology, money and things can't protect you from personal loss and tragedy. You may think so right now and be totally blind to this, but shit happens. There's something none of us can fully understand – way bigger than ourselves, and our powers are finite. Asking for help worked for me bit by bit. Faith in something intangible, whatever faith you believe in, works not in the way we expect because many of us play 'safe', never getting into situations where we may experience total despair. Most of us have our own little comfort zone where we can believe in our own narrow self-righteousness. It's only losing your comforts that makes you desperate enough to swallow your pride and ask for some kind of help. I never want to be so far up my own arse again that I can never ask for help. We all know of someone who is not waving – but drowning; I personally knew a few. They are dead now. Too proud and too tough to ask for help.

Too much over-zealousness in the various faiths around the world causes trouble and wraps people up in guilt, only for 'Holier than Thou' to point the finger and put people off just when we need it most. It's between you and what you believe may or may not be there somewhere, not any intermediary or 'go between' or anything else. It's between you and what you believe in. Fuck what anyone else says – they are not in your personal situation. If you believe it works for you, then it works! Simple as.

Up at 7.45 again and on the road. I rode through miles of deserted areas en route to Tarragona, and then through miles of well-heeled areas with large homes and palm-tree-lined roads. The desolate beauty of the south-eastern coast of Spain became more like the costas from the holiday brochures. Food was easier to find: there would always be a *supermarchedo*: a Plus, an Aldi or a Lidl, just when I was hungry. Hunger became less of a problem but I felt the previous couple of days' mileage in my legs today so I dropped my pace to give them a rest. It was approximately a hundred and thirty-six kilometres from Valencia to Vinaroz and a hundred and fifty-six kilometres from Altea to Valencia. Barcelona was approximately two hundred kilometres away but I knew my legs just weren't going to get me there today. Anywhere up this coast today I would be happy with; I would be nearer Barcelona than I would have been if I did nothing. I covered less kilometres today than for about a week. Apart for some brief trips uphill, no more than a hundred and fifty metres high, my legs just didn't want to fire up and my bum was really beginning to hurt. The nearer I got to Barcelona the more my legs felt like jelly, and the slightest of slopes would make the bike jump the cogs sometimes. The chain was at the end of its life by now and a quick inspection of the cogs on the back showed that most were getting well hooked, so the chain was loose on them. This bike was not going to get over the lowest of the Pyrenees without being pushed. I was frustrated but almost resigned to this situation: how could I get angry with myself and blame things? I would find a way. When I stopped and thought about it, I even excitedly anticipated the problems, and it took the boredom of the distance away sometimes. The problems were a pain in the arse – literally and metaphorically, but sorting them out was a buzz!

Most of the day I rode, stopped, rode and stopped for long rests for the sake of my rear end and my back, and I would stare at the bike and try to find solutions in my mind to make these gears work a little better. By now the brakes just didn't exist at all. If I came down a big hill at speed, I would hope there would be no obstructions to crash into, or if I needed to lose speed, my boots would be the brakes. But at least the wheels were still round! And the fuel stations still had water (sometimes with bits in it) so I would have a chuckle at the situation and move on. This reflected in the mileage today. I only managed about ninety kilometres before settling down between Cambrills and Salou, thinking things would be better in the morning. They weren't though: the bike was still knackered and my arse was still giving in early. I was only one day's ride away from Barcelona and no way was I giving that goal up. The only real challenges that day were the hills after the Delta de la E'bre, which gradually rose no more than a hundred and sixty metres where the N-340 left the coast for a brief spell. Then, just as briefly, I was back on the coast road at sea level, to the relief of the chain and my legs. And that was it, apart from little rises, until Cambrills after Miami Platja, where I bedded. Doing about ninety-five kilometres that day, I could have borne the pain to go a little further; but if I had a good rest, Cambrills to Barcelona shouldn't be a problem. I don't know what I was expecting to find there. It had just been such a goal for so long it was almost a big halfway point in my head, and I was almost there, having looked at the place on the map for the first time since the 16th in Gibraltar.

A couple of hours later I found myself at Sitges, just south of Barcelona, looking at a barrier of cliffs and hills in front of me where my coastal N-340 disappeared inland into more tunnels or over the top. On the map, the city just seemed to be around the corner, but the map showed no way along the edge of the cliffs and at this point I couldn't see a way around; there didn't seem to be one. Maybe the road was there but was too small to be shown on the map. I needed nourishment so I switched on the bin food antennae. It was late in the afternoon in this quaint Spanish resort town so I rode slowly, with my eyes waiting for the orange flash of a Plus or the dark-blue and yellow colours of an Aldi. I remember climbing under a gate into a loading bay and having my fill of chocolate mousses, biscuits and apples there. With bag and gut full, it was time for the city. At least I had plenty of food to get me across the next leg...

Losing my way slightly, I climbed out of the town, with a railway on my left, and then spotted the cliff-edge road the other side, over the railway and about a couple of kilometres to the right. People were everywhere in their best tourist get-ups, getting off coaches for the nearby hotels behind me. I felt a rapid bowel movement: the fruit and yoghurts just suddenly took effect. Oh no... not another repeat of that episode after Seville! No. Luckily there was some thick scrub near the railway embankment, and an unused pack of luxury tissues next to a discarded, almost full pack of cigarettes, which were sitting on the side of the pavement, lying there as though someone had spotted my plight. As well as being desperate, I was desperate for nicotine relief – it was my only relief from the pain at some points. What I wanted were both sitting on the paving that made up the edge of this road crossing the railway bridge, just when I needed 'em both. Maybe this was a 'you had to be there' type of explanation but after hours without food and maybe almost two days without a decent smoke, this moment was a big relief in more ways than one!

Now everything was right, so I had a new, unused cigarette at leisure, and a full belly, and looked across at the road exiting Sitges towards the edge of the hills next to the sea. It couldn't be far around those cliffs. I was bound to make it before dark, so, onwards. As I rounded the headland the road climbed and perched itself along the edges of the cliffs. This road was probably one tidy road to ride a motorbike on if it wasn't for every man and his dog doing a pleasure drive. This was the C-31 coast road. It hugged the cliffs for maybe ten kilometres or so. It was early evening, and the sun sinking was away somewhere over the hills to the west. It might have been about eighty degrees Fahrenheit by now – cooling down compared to today's journey. The Med to my right was flat and calm, with the odd sun seeker boat on its own in the deep blue. This cliff-edge road was one sight I can't forget. A low metal Armco barrier was the only thing between me and about a hundred metres of sheer drop into the sea. Cars and trucks couldn't give me more than a foot or so as they passed me uphill and downhill on this busy road. It snaked around the edges of the cliffs, which shot directly up another hundred or so metres to my left – no kerb and no room to go anywhere.

This seemed to go on forever, into coves cutting into the cliffs with tiny beaches below. In one place there was a giant 'Cemex' cement factory, which accounted for the amount of full-weight tipper artics, which had to squeeze past me along the edge. I wondered how many had gone over the edge over the years. An hour or so later the road began dropping down towards civilisation, but not before I was nearly squashed a few times. The hills down became steeper and the artics would pass me, two or three at a time. They must either have been on their last loads, or loaded with a set-up for next day, and were all heading into a huge haulage yard. Another familiar memory came to mind: flying round the north Wales and north-west motorways with an artic tipper, and chasing your arse all day, bored and tired.

I could see into the yard on my right as I dropped down next to the railway, which ran parallel to the sea. Further in, the main *autovia* emerged from a tunnel out from the cliffs. This was Castelldefels. Across, the main rail and road, hotels and residences ran right across the coast in a wide curve on a flat area set back from the sea. It looked like Llandudno with its hotels and B&Bs strewn right across a bay up to the next set of rocks two or three kilometres distant. I stood up on the foot pegs and allowed the wind to cool my throbbing arse as the road dropped to almost sea level away from the main Barcelona road. I decided I was going to kip here tonight: the stinging rear end just hurt too much to sit on, even sidesaddle. Somehow, I had to find a bridge across this railway, to the sheltered dark-looking part of town where the hills met the back of Castelldefels. I could see cars heading along the road, with their lights on now, and the streetlamps were flickering on. Riding along a road alongside the railway I came across a footbridge and eventually stopped, almost falling over when the full weight of my body landed on my right foot. Really goosed now, I just didn't want to face carrying the bike over this bridge. Up ahead, a street or two away, there might be a subway. I didn't know this for definite but I would rather have ridden another kilometre than climb over the bridge: my legs had died suddenly. Also, I just couldn't sit on that saddle anymore. I walked the bike through the subway, only because I could not get my leg over it to ride it. At the first opportunity, I was going to die on a bench or a flat piece of concrete. Crossing the main road, I kind of stumbled back onto the pedals, and half pedalled and half freewheeled along the front of homes and houses along a lengthy straight, without daring to sit down. It felt like sitting on needles.

With my eyes on the lookout for anything to lie on, preferably face down, I noticed an old mattress standing next to some wheelie bins set back from the road, with the cliffs directly behind them. There was a short road running up to them. On the right, there was an old folks' retirement home and on the left a closed-down shop with a small corner entrance, which someone had attempted to brick up but had given up on the idea. It was a little windy, with a chill in the air. I went over and peered into this entrance. It was about five feet square and out of the wind, with about twenty bricks forming a barrier. In went the old mattress for comfort. I leaned my bike against the small wall and threw my kit inside. Great! I pulled out one of those candles I had had in my bag since Cartaya, which I had used whilst sleeping in that office shed. I lit up and had my supper to the sounds on the little radio, which echoed around my little shelter. I had a couple of those new fags I had found on the roadside at the bridge in Sitges the other side of the headland. After that I ate an apple and an orange, some biscuits and two choccy mousses; and said a little prayer of thanks for food and this little shelter, and the mattress for my sore arse, out of the wind. I filled in my map: '8.30 p.m. 25/4/07. Arse hurt too much' and had a good long softer sleep out of the wind.

Chapter Thirteen
Pain, Punctures and Part Exchange

26ᵗʰ April 2007 Castelldefels to Barcelona, &
Santa Susanna to Girona – 136 Kilometres

7.45 a.m., always 7.45! Don't know why. Dumped my rubbish back next to the bins, loaded up, and back on the road. Not far to the big city now, but a lot further than I actually thought. The road followed more cliffs but with bigger carriageways than the previous day's roads. The surroundings took me back to the north Wales coast road, especially since it rained most of the way, the only difference being the colour of the terracotta stone, which made the cliff look different. There were more tunnels, cliffs and a rough sea with surf bashing against the rocks for about twenty kilometres. The nearer I got to Barcelona on the *autovia* the more roadworks there seemed to be going on, just like in any major city. The narrow *autovia* was fast and busy with a heavy rush hour, early-morning commuter traffic of cars, buses and trucks, all bombing towards its centre. A huge city, it took me well over half an hour to get anywhere near the centre, even on the direct *autovia*, where people complained with their horns, not that I cared: it saved me time. After cycling past the centre jams up alongside the deadlocked traffic I made my way down one of the main streets, which was wide and well busy with all manner of people looking as though they were all going somewhere, serious looking, and most having an early-morning fag or some wrapped snack.

This city is one cool place with magnificent-looking buildings, all in a distinct style. I stopped to take it in and noticed a rusting bike, one of several left chained to various cast-iron vintage lampposts up and down. The bikes all seemed to have one wheel or a seat missing, so the owners had just left 'em. I spent a wasted fifteen minutes or so trying to get the chain off one, in front of a big queue of people waiting for a bus, but split links are a thing of the past now so, not having a chain splitter, I gave up. I had no adjustable or any function-ing spanners to take off the derailleur either. Bugger it! There would be other opportunities. I headed towards the sea along the boulevard-type surroundings down this huge street, enjoying the sights, sounds and smells of this fantastic city of culture. Valencia was a cool-looking place, and so were Tarragona and Alicante, but Barcelona is something else. I hope one day I can return in better circumstances. It seemed to take me ages to ride across the place. I stopped near the sea and sat on a welcoming bench, which let the wildly complaining blisters on my feet, rest and my arse gather its composure. My numb four outer fingers (two on each hand) were still numb and my back was aching badly, and it was only about midday – factors which really dented my enthusiasm for the next day's journey. I ate an orange and an almost-black banana I had found in the recesses of the bottomless bag and sat, not tired from riding but very much in pain, thinking, 'Is my body actually going to last across France?' I looked at the map once again, as if looking at it would make France come nearer or give me some sort of psychological boost to make the pain subside, but it didn't. My left foot hurt the most, throbbing with my heartbeat, just like my back would at the end of a day. I had to get on the bike again to ride and find some sort of solution. Lazily moving across the long seafront that makes up Barcelona, I ventured across a kind of gigantic exhibition centre with a giant paved area underneath. It had television trucks outside, and dudes with skateboards running to and fro underneath. Part of the centre was on concrete stilts and quite fascinating to look at, and vast – indeed so fascinating to look at that I didn't notice the two or three metal posts standing about shin height as I gathered speed when leaving the paved area for the pavement alongside the road… Thump! One of these posts stopped me dead, almost cracking my shin, and bending a pedal in the process as well as throwing me right over the front of my handlebars in front of bodies unloading from a coach at the roadside. I landed in a heap of bike, various bits and pieces, and oranges rolling all over. An elderly fella came over to see if I was OK. Just as soon, a guy in his twenties pulled him away, muttering something about *el vagobundo*! My shin was bashed and I skinned my left knuckle but I was more bothered about the bike. The handlebars easily straightened but I now had a bent pedal, which was bent down at an angle. No question about it: this bike was now about fit for the scrappy.

I slowly plodded on again along the coast, using my last fag before checking out a bin near a shop on the opposite side of the road. I discovered, to top it all, I had another puncture, always on the rear, and wasn't able to remove the rear wheel because I had broken my box spanner hundreds of kilometres back and had lost a 150-millimetre adjustable whilst I slept on a bench even further back on the journey. I would remove the wheel and mend the puncture *in situ*. I was outside a Red Cross (*Cruz Rouge*). A fella came outside for a fag and I blagged one off him as I had smoked my last, and got into a conversation with him. He let me use his toilet to have a wash, answer the call of nature and fill up my water bottle. I went and fretted about the state of the bike and France being an unknown quantity, and recalled the words of that Brit I had met in that roadside bar near Cartagena:

"Rather you than me, Mate!"

Arsehole, I thought to myself. I went on across the road and down into the marina and out again along the boulevard, which goes out of the city. This carried on for a few hours, or so it seemed, with ample benches for rest and supermarkets for food and easy, flat, fast road which would enable me to stay in top gear. I covered plenty of distance, got very sore feet, and my bum gave me premature grief. I eventually stopped at an Aldi near Mataro, next to a college. They had just emptied stuff into a bin, which I tried to redeem. and settled on a seafront bench thinking that I could pass off as a tourist. That is if I didn't look like a transatlantic tramp with a bike that looked like it had just crossed the Gobi desert, and with oranges and old rags bungeed all over the back of it, and the frame with two shades of tanned mud still there from the night-time incident outside of Sevilla.

I ate a perfect and cold one-litre tub of choc chip yoghurt, then eleven fromage frais of all flavours. Totally full, I got the map out and tried to work out exactly how far I had come the previous day. No matter what, a great many of the 'A to B' distances would be inaccurate until I had a decent map. These wouldn't record the searches for bin food or when I frequently got lost in and out of places, but they would give me some idea of distances travelled.

This would have to be left for another time. Where I was now would be the last of the easy roads before the Pyrenees and France. I took another survey of my bum – hurting; my feet – hurting loud; my back – bearable; my fingers – still numb but no hindrance to progress; the bike – shagged out, which was becoming a worry. I had never looked at the Pyrenees before but expected 'em to be well steep and difficult. Between my body and the bike, it was bothering me exactly how I would get over them. Hmmm.

On I went along the coast road – the N-11 – through Arenys de Mar and Callela until I overshot the turning to Girona by a kilometre or so, having pulled the map out to check. It looked like I would be going uphill for some time and this bike would jump the chain on the slightest of slopes now, really giving my blisters grief. I stopped at a place called Santa Susanna and sat on a bench with my back to railway tracks and the sea, looking at the bike leaning against the kerbside. The chain was stretched longer than a well-chewed Wrigley's. It hung down off the bike. I breathed a large sigh and looked up and across the road towards a large block of flats. There was a half-decent adult-size mountain bike leaning against the wall across there. I bet it had gears, brakes and a comfy seat. I would love a bike like that. I said a little prayer asking for a solution: this was my last resort. Then I let my head fall back and dozed for an hour or so. I then woke up, looking straight at the mountain bike still against the wall. Seeing as the day was at an end, I was going nowhere. Neither was that bike, which had no lock on it. Without thinking about it I took my bike across the road, plonked it lower down against the wall, swapped my gear, plus the loosely tied-on rack, over, and off I went without looking back. My need being greater than theirs, it was a 'part exchange' I had to do: why was it that I chose to sit across from the only unlocked bike I had seen in Spain, then kipped and went off with it without anyone batting an eyelid? Why did that puncture outfit turn up when it did after I had returned to the same bin after about two hours? Why did I seem to find things just when I really needed them? Always after a little prayer, and I am only stating the facts here. Many things would happen on this journey I wouldn't forget – some big, some small – but the whole feeling of comfort and wellbeing at the end of a day, no matter what had happened, came from somewhere. I have no explanation for it, but it worked. I already had a plan to replace what I had to take, which will be underway now as this is read. Yep, just like karma in *My Name is Earl*.

I blew up the tyres hard and adjusted the gears, and realised this was my vehicle for France and the Pyrenees. It had a full set of gears, two brakes, a good chain and a comfy seat. I would be in Girona tonight.

I definitely wouldn't have made all the inclines along the N-11 towards Girona away from the coast on the old bike: all I seemed to do was go up and up steadily. I was so glad of a soft seat and a set of gears that I almost forgot my various pains and problems.

The roads and surroundings could have easily been on the borderlands of England and Wales – the Shropshire farmlands. They were green-hedged and slightly hilly and steep in places, with mostly farms all around. Any hill could be taken in second or third gear. With good brakes, I was covering ground much easier than for the last couple of days. Every couple of bends there would be an entrance to a farm trail. Many had white plastic chairs at the end of them. I rested on one of these and enjoyed a half-used fag for a couple of minutes. It was early evening, warm and sunny but cooler than when I left the coast. The next white seat had a gorgeous *senorita* sitting on it. She had shades on, long black hair, tight top and short denim skirt.

"*Ola, Senorita,*" I shouted as I rode by. She smiled, replied, and made my day.

A little further on there was another one sitting in another white plastic chair, and after a few more kilometres another, then another. All seemed to be texting on their mobiles, maybe waiting for their fellas or boyfriends. The later it got the more I saw. Farming can't be that much on its back, can it?!

The N-11 became straighter and more direct, with gentle inclines stretching for miles, largely agricultural all around. The distant Spanish mountains far away in the west began beckoning the sun, which was heading further towards them every time I looked at them. The atmosphere was like going home after a summer day's work somewhere in the UK – not hot, and a slight breeze. The now abundant French black-on-yellow number plates on passing trucks and cars would soon become an even more familiar sight.

The light began disappearing altogether. Along this straight towards Girona aeroplanes flew overhead towards the airport and to my left, a new *autovia* was under construction, still in the dirt stage, with surveyor's posts along its length and huge graders and six-wheel dump trucks parked here and there.

Traffic was quite busy and brisk along this straight, which rose and fell only a couple of metres for miles, it seemed. I was determined to reach Girona. I rode through the dusk. Trucks and cars would take their glowing red taillights far off into the horizon ahead of me. I was tiring and sweating slightly but still making good progress. I had to get somewhere that had a bench or flat concrete because there were only fields here. The nearer and nearer I got, the darker and darker it became. It was the first time I had ridden in the complete dark since that freaky night in the rain after that encounter with the Sevillan shootist! There was almost no light from the stars or the moon. Trees and hedges with thick vegetation made it blacker than before. Only vehicles would momentarily light the way before fading away up front. I stopped to put on my orange-and-black Benfica *casico*, or tracky top, as it was getting cooler. A motorist stopped up in front of me to ask if I was OK in the blackness on a bike at night – which was nice. I then rode on, thinking, 'Where is this Girona?' I couldn't see any lights or signs, just empty blackness. This evening journey for the last couple of kilometres seemed to go on forever. I eventually spotted some orange sodium lights to my left in what seemed like a tree-covered valley a couple of kilometres away – not the huge city I had expected. This was Girona and it lay in a deep river valley with steep cliffs lining its sides, and trees all around. I drew nearer and had to climb a road and then loop around on an off ramp, which spiralled down to allow me access down into the city. Across a roundabout or two, I was ready to hit the first bench I came to. I was so tired I was almost nodding off and would shut my eyes for a second or two on predictable straight bits. The first set of traffic lights near a junction with the river and trees on my right and a raised playing field on my left had a bench overlooking this junction. Good enough for me! I headed up, leaned the bike against the back of the bench, and with a bungee cord around the frame I tied the bike to the bench in case someone part-exchanged it in the night. I then placed my red blanket on the bench, and filled in on my map: '26/4/07 9.30 p.m.' and sat with the radio on. I cut a thick, hard sausage about ten centimetres long and about three centimetres thick with the little knife I had found amongst other roadside treasure, then ate the sausage with some biscuits and oranges. I slept more soundly than I had done for at least a week, to the sound of sodium-lit boy racers revving up their quad bikes and motors as they drag-raced away from the nearby light twenty metres or so away below me. Dead beat, I just died.

Chapter Fourteen

Across the Border

I Get Wet and Learn Some French

27th to 28th April 2007 Girona to Perpignan – 107 Kilometres, Perpignan to Carcassonne – 125 Kilometres

I woke up at 7.45(?) without the alarm, loaded up the bike and headed into the centre of Girona – a cool, smart place built along the river, with a lot of homes and buildings which seemed fixed to the cliffs. As well as smart modern places, there were little cobbled streets with shops and cafes. This city was fought over so many times historically between the Moors and the Christians that the little streets ran red with the blood of conflict. Many more cities did, but catching a glimpse of these little streets, that haven't changed much for centuries, you can imagine it happening here.

Lance Armstrong, the cancer sufferer who lived here prior to winning his fifth consecutive Tour de France, and winning his sixth after recovering from testicular cancer, stated that the fellow sufferers, old and young, he met from all around the world are more important and significant to him than his tour victories were. He realised how difficult it is to beat cancer, for young 'uns and old alike. He got to the point of thinking, 'Every second counts.' This journey across, and his words, would inspire me towards the plight of cancer sufferers, and figure in my head for the near future.

A quick call at a city centre garage for some *agua* and off I went, just as it started raining. I rode along the hillier and green surroundings on the N-1 towards La Frontera via Figueras and the Midi-Pyrenees, for France. The inclines became steeper and the showers more frequent, but I was pleased with my progress. According to the loose schedule I had set myself, I was about four days ahead of my goal of being across the border by the end of the month, so now I hoped to be across France in ten days or so. I was making much more comfortable headway on this bike, covering almost as much mileage over the hills towards the border as I had done on the flat on the 'shed' of junk which only had two working gears and a tenth of one back brake.

Girona to Figueras became wetter – a sign of impending France to come. The nights were colder too. The roads were more like British roads, the vegetation being more familiar and the motors of all types newer. Every second motorcar or truck appeared to have come straight out of a showroom. I made Figueras about midday and on heading closer to the border I came across many truck stops and parking areas chocker with truckers asleep in their rigs, or resting. Shops, bars and rest areas became more frequent, and roadside prostitutes lurked under concrete bridges. Within a couple of kilometres of the border, the road would again steepen and each side was full of tourists shopping at the roadside, where anything could be bought cheaper, according to the enthusias-tic vendors. The sun beat down now and I reached the border crossing point, where all vehicles and people passed through without having passport checks. The old check booths were still there but were not in use, though police lurked around the whole place. It was a busy, interesting sight with families shopping and travelling, and business types and truckers all going one way or the other. This was La Jonquera, at a hundred and forty-seven metres. Further up, after a couple of kilometres, I noticed tunnel construction going on away and down to my left, not least because of the distant dull 'boom' of explosives being used to construct the tunnel through the Midi-Pyrenees.

As I climbed the little two-laner, which climbed to a little place called Le Perthus, the road got well steep, eventually topping out at two hundred and eighty-seven metres through a tiny street packed with shoppers and tourists buying everything from sunglasses and jewellery to clothes of all descriptions. There was even a shop selling mini motorbikes, as if the products sold in the shop had been scaled down to fit the narrowness of the hillside street. Next door to these shops, there were restaurants and cafes. All this crammed along the little road, which sat on the apex of the hill. It was like this was your last chance to bag a bargain before entering either country. I crossed the border at 2.30 p.m. on 27th April 2007. Right, now let's deal with France. I was determined to ride over this little steep hill. I pushed on in first gear and eventually crested the top, then dropped down a tight curvy tree-lined pass for miles on a switchback of tarmac surrounded by the green of southern France. These curves cooled the sweat all over me, as I was doing at least forty to fifty kilometres per hour – great! The road went down and around forever, and all around was leafy green.

Up ahead a giant anvil-shaped cloud was looming: a humongous rain bearer, miles across, ready to dump its load. The road became wet with puddles as I left the tree-lined road and crossed a bridge into a place called Le Boulou and found a sheltered area next to a pizza emporium. There was a little wall to sit on under a roof supported by concrete pillars. The worst of the storm lashed straight down as I sat and watched the traffic go back and forth for a while. A couple of gendarmes went by slowly, giving me a look. I gave them a Gallic shrug whilst glancing up to the weather. The shrug was reciprocated by the gendarme. I was not just a grim-looking cycle vagrant but a wet one too.

The rain calmed down and almost stopped so on I went, following signs to Perpignan. My map of Spain was now useless. The clouds moved away west and the sun shone on the French surroundings, with neat agriculture, well-kept buildings, and everything in good nick and well watered, as though the Pyrenees dried out Spain and watered France.

The twenty or so kilometres I rode slowly from Le Boulou were in the afternoon sunshine. Everything felt generally OK: my left foot was a little sore from the blisters but my bum was in a lot better form, having benefitted from a soft seat. So, it was onwards to Perpignan, where I would find a bench, have a good kip, and then go for it as far as I could across France. On this afternoon journey, I began hearing the regular squeak of one of my pedal cranks. The further I went, the louder the squeak, until I could feel the crank loosening on its spindle. Also, there was the continuous squeaking of the now-dry chain after riding in the rain. The squeaks were at their loudest as I arrived in the centre of Perpignan. What a place! I thought, as I picked up a hardly-used fag in the main square near the fountains. The late-afternoon sun cast long shadows and I had to find some kind of garage or bike shop to help me out. Eventually I found a motorcycle shop which serviced mopeds, next to a tyre shop along the main avenue going out over the main bridge, where the whole city seemed to be on its way home, judging by the traffic. I went in, and asking for some oil for the chain and a small ratchet, I realised my Portuguese and Spanish were virtually useless now. It took me about five minutes of gestures to obtain a small squirt of oil, for which I was grateful, but I gave up on the ratchet. I tried a nearby garage and the French owner tightened my nearside spindle nut with a huge breaker bar. That wouldn't come off in a hurry – I hoped. I was to eventually wish I had thought of doing the other side at the same time. Great! I now had a squeak-free bike once more. The road out of the city looked long and busy. I knew it might be better to bed down here tonight but I desperately needed to know a direct route across the middle of France so I wandered around, looking for a business that might have a map I could look at. As I did, I found a park with benches and banked the place in my mind for now for in the event of me not finding anywhere better. I must have ridden up and down a few roads for a couple of kilometres until I found a car washing and valeting place. It was warm and still hot at this time. I approached a large fella who looked like the owner and, with my old map, explained where I had ridden from and what I wanted. He then got out a large map and almost completely drew me a map across the centre of France – south to north – before relenting and giving me the whole map as a gift. Me being hot and sweaty, I reckon he must have been downwind from me and either couldn't stand it any longer, or took pity, realising how far I had to travel, and decided I needed the map more than he did, just like I had decided I needed the bike I had 'part exchanged' a day earlier…

I decided to call it a day. I had a map and the bike was sorted, as was a place to kip tonight. I hit the bench in the little park on the north-west of the bridge out of the city. It was about 7.00 p.m. and I began to settle, not long before being moved on by the park keeper as he was locking up.

"No sleep here," he informed me, in his haste to lock up.

"OK," I replied, after which I thought, How did he know I couldn't speak French? I never thought about it until later. I then found a bus shelter outside the park, which got a little busy. I didn't leave until after I had a chat with a couple of friendly French ladies, who I showed where I was going and where I had come from. I blagged a couple of cigs off 'em for after 'supper', then I noticed that across the road there was a shut down hotel of sorts, where I found a deserted flat and sheltered porch area around the side of it. It even had a flat entrance mat that would do for tonight. It was off a quiet street behind a hedge. The flat marble base was my bed. I could just see the last of the sun going down. My supper of oranges and apples and biccies, with a couple of mousses from the bins of a local supermarket, was washed down with half a litre of very welcome clear cold French water. The garage taps had clean water here: a great personal relief. The evening light was calming. I gave thanks for the things I'd got: my sight, my health, the food inside me, for getting this far, and for the six packets of chocolate-covered finger things I had found at a big service station somewhere between Girona and Figueras. I also asked for an opportunity to have a good clean soon… and the strength to keep going...

A great end to a good day! Feeling totally satisfied, warm and fed gave me that feel-good all-over buzz so much lacking in many people today, with all their self-inflicted debts and pressure to appear 'normal' to others. Normal is however you see it, but never again would I want multiple vehicles not paid for and so many payments to meet that you get credit blur, not actually knowing exactly where your hard-won cash is draining away to, and never being more than a few weeks away from total bankruptcy. I just want to have food in my belly and to be clean and warm: that would be the first thing. Everything else is a blessing.

Days like this made me realise how lucky I was to survive without major injuries other than bone breakages. To be able to feel this good with the many chances I had taken up to now was definitely a blessing of some sort.

As I lay on this marble floor entrance, I thought about motorcycles – I don't know why. There were a lot of bikes around this city – great weather for them here, I guess. I thought about the crazy physical chances I had taken over the last two decades, which had become a habit much like any vice is.

Until recently, I was regularly bombing down a boulder-strewn, muddy Welsh mountain on an XR 600 Enduro bike or a mountain bike, especially in the rain and dark in the winter. The place and the conditions were remote, forbidding and beautiful. The routes I would choose would be increasingly difficult, testing and satisfying. There was no hope of rescue, or being found, if the worst happened, but I would never consider that sort of thing.

The gear I wore was shit. It would not be the stuff you may see a responsible mountain biker or dirt biker wearing for protection – I considered that 'get-up' embarrassing. I wore no helmet on a mountain bike: just maybe a Thinsulate hat in the rain or cold and a black ragged polar neck, wollen sweater with welding burn holes and a pair of wrecked surf shorts. My footwear would be knackered trainers with no socks. On the Enduro bike I would wear jeans, helmet, worn-out boots and a scruffy hi-viz coat 'cos it had pockets for a few tools in case of a puncture, and maybe baccy.

It was heaven with a fast heartbeat.

On the road I would go *far* too quickly, on fast bikes in 'wrong' situations such as filming the speedo showing well over three figures, one-handed with one of those early mobile phones, just to prove a particular bike would do a particular speed – usually round a long sweeping bend whilst passing traffic. That was just stupid. Bouncing down a misty, wet, muddy mountainside was where I was happiest.

My favourite for the best part of one decade would be leaping off a particular cliff, near Moel Morfydd up in the Berwyn hills, on a big motocrosser. It was the ultimate test for at least thirty of the bikes I owned. This precipice had a drop-off of at least a hundred feet or so. Eventually the authorities placed a stout fence across the cliff face. The gradual landing which sloped off at about forty-five degrees was gritty, steep and boulder covered. I would land after a long drop off the precipice with a thumping of bottomed-out suspension, and tyres squashed flat against their rims with the sound of stones, grit and mud contacting metal and plastic as they were thrown in all directions. If it was windy or raining then you would be blown sideways and land in deep rain ruts, which you couldn't see from the top as you left the edge blind. Your landing was almost in God's hands by then.

I regularly flew my nineteen-year-old condemned, sellotaped and stitched up paraglider off this cliff, usually with my mate Dunc, who considered himself slightly less irresponsible than me, though no one else did. In one place we worked at, some of the lads had taken to calling us The Dangerous Brothers, after a series of accidents involving hospital custody. In later years, I would fly and ride on my own in more remote places, as Duncan sold his paraglider to concentrate on building a huge steel yacht. I reckon he must have thought he was Noah.

This was how I unwound every weekend for well over fifteen years. These crazy things I did had become the norm and were a blow-off valve for frustrations, and maybe not the actions of a sane and happy soul. Physical contact sports and five-a-side were boring but kept me fit as a 'savings bank' of fitness for my 'real' fun. All this would help give me discipline and a vent for problems. Stopping this regular sort of activity and having no other outlet for energy other than drinking and drug usage, was looking for trouble.

But all that self gratifying stuff is bollocks, really, compared to a little 'un calling you 'Dad', or having a lie-in on a Saturday with someone you love. I am always impressed by people who work hard to keep it together and have an unselfish balance of life.

Thrill seeking is a fucking burden and bores people. *Nos da.* (Good night.) Zzzzz.

After a good kip, I was up at 7.45 a.m. and on the road. I think it was a Saturday. Bike sorted, I would get a move on today before my feet would start caving in and my butt would come out in sympathy, usually early afternoon.

The long flat straight roads to Narbonne, and through the little places along the way, ran alongside vast fields of either olives or grapes, small trees and other vegetation. Absolutely horizontal, gigantic fields and long roads with a tailwind enabled me to cover plenty of distance with easy effort, as though I had almost no chain, just a crank. I hit Narbonne and then changed direction slightly, towards Carcasonne, with the wind now slightly to my left side, but I was still able to fly along. Not far out of Narbonne I came to a large motor- and truck-stop with tables and a café. I took the opportunity to make my tyres rock solid, top my water bottle up, and sit and have a fag or two from the sand bucket full of stumps. I selected the longest I could find and sat near a bunch of cool-looking, shade-wearing dudes who were having a joint and gassing with each other. I ate an orange and offered them a painted 'piccy' of a VW bus I had fetched with me for the purpose of bartering. I bagged some ciggies off them and was offered a joint, half smoked. One of 'em had a VW and he was impressed with the piccy.

After a time I went on. A little more 'enlightened', I pressed on and really got into the ride, concentrating on every little action I could to make the bike cover distance. High as a kite, I rode, enjoying the carefree distance for about two hours or so. After a time I began imagining a slight 'squeak squeak', not very loud. Was it that pedal crank again or was it my mind reacting to that joint?

Shit! No tools except a bust flat screwdriver, a couple of blunt knives and two small tyre levers. I seemed to be miles from anywhere, and being a weekend afternoon every garage seemed to be shut. It was as though southern France had shut for the weekend.

Near Capendu I went off the main bypass road, stopped and rested with my back against the wall of an Aldi supermarket whilst a Scania driver unloaded his artic nearby. I dug into a still-warm chicken wrapped in plastic, which I'd just retrieved from the bin along with a couple of yoghurts. Half an hour's rest, then I headed on, with the sun getting longer and lower in the sky ahead and to the left of me in the west. France was sunny and warm here, and the wind was with me. I hoped it would be like this across France although subconsciously I knew I would hit a few drops soon. And judging by that ginormous rain cloud I'd seen just after the border, I was gonna be wet sooner or later. Still making good time before my feet started complaining, and my right-hand pedal now definitely creaking, I arrived in the quiet middle-class conservative-looking town of Carcasonne. It was a straight road through, and I stopped on the northern outskirts to sit on a wooden bench on neatly trimmed grass, next to the road. I got out the new map of France to contemplate my next move. It was almost six according to the radio display, not taking into account the time difference in the last two thousand kilometres, and my feet were screwed for the day. I took off my boots and surveyed my now sockless feet. I had binned the socks a long way back because they had fallen to pieces. My feet weren't far off being binned either: the blisters were numbering at least a dozen, and I also had deep blood blisters which were too far under the skin for me to be able to burst them. Just then a bloke of about thirty-five sat next to me, and we made small talk. He spoke rough English but better Portuguese and Spanish. I asked if he had fags and he gave me a few. He also offered me some strong cider from a litre-and-a-half bottle he had with him. He was fascinated by where I had come from, and offered his hand and introduced himself as David Mussecca.

Chapter Fifteen

The Alcoholic French Punk

29th April 2007 Carcassonne to Villanouvelle – 62 Kilometres,
30th April 2007 Villanouvelle to Cahors – 152 Kilometres

David Mussecca was a dead friendly guy, and told me Le Havre was near his 'home country'. He was a Breton and went on at length about Brittany. He told me his family were, by and large, alcoholics – a common problem up there apparently. This reinforced my mate Dunc's story of the local Breton postie who Dunc and his mate would prop up on his moped daily after he had sunk bottles of vino on his daily round en route to visiting Dunc and his friend, who were doing up a small house. Also a Welsh fella back in Portugal told me he had to put a sign up to stop locals bringing vino daily while he was working on another Breton house, 'cos they were getting nothing done as a result of the local hospitality each day. This appears to be the Breton way? This rang true for David too. He invited me to have a shower if I wanted plus a 'celebration', with a Gallic shrug, as though this was a necessity. Yeah, why not? So we walked about half a kilometre to the flat he lived in. This was right on the top of a nine-story block with green wooden shutters – a feature of most dwellings across France. After placing the bike in a dark storeroom at the bottom, we climbed the stairs to his sparsely furnished flat that had lots of alcohol around. He talked and showed me a picture of his daughter by his ex. His daughter's name was Melanie and she was nine: same as my Ceridwen (Ceri) was at that time. I told him she looked like my youngest daughter Seren. I gave him three twelve by ten inch paintings of VW buses, which he was chuffed with, and put one on the wall in his kitchen. He invited me to use his shower, for which I was so grateful. Together with a shave, I looked like a different bloke now. As I was scrubbing up in his 'open plan' bathroom David walked in and put my filthy black jeans in a bucket. It took three soaks before they stopped making the water black. As I was having a shave, wearing a pair of shorts he gave me, he handed me a few porn mags, saying, "If you need to masturbate, here you are, my guest" in his accent, without batting an eyelid, this being part of this Frenchman's extended hospitality!

After a scrub and some clean clothes, he pulled a cork on a bottle of white to celebrate the 'happiness' of having daughters, which we drank to and conversed, finding plenty of common ground. He made me a meal of fried potatoes and home-made meat, onion and garlic fritters. We had a bottle of red, then a bottle of rosé, and then cracked a couple of cans of Pilsner. By now we had got very pissed to the sound of AC/DC, Motorhead, Faith No More and punk music by The Sex Pistols, The Stranglers and Plastic Bertrand, all at volume. As he dealt with his complaining neighbour I leaned out of the south-facing window looking across a quiet, sunny, well-kept town, smoking a roll-up. I couldn't help but feel a traitor to myself, thinking how I should be lyin' on a bench somewhere smoking a 'dib' and looking at my map instead of being here, wasting time. Guilty? What's that about?

This dude gave me a sound Saturday night but I couldn't keep up with David's drinking, and the more he drank the more hyper he got and the louder the music got. This was me, a few years ago, in an almost identical situation.

"David, I'm gonna kip!" I said, over the racket of 'Epic' by Faith No More.

"Keep? What eez dis keep? You are tired?"

I silently nodded whilst cupping my face with my hands.

With that, he pointed to a mattress on the floor, with a blanket on it, in his bedroom. I crashed out on this and was asleep before you could say Jacques Chirac, as David played the last of The Collaborators: a controversial punk band despised by the older generation, for good reason.

I slept till almost eleven thirty next day, for probably the first time in about a year or more. I must have needed it. David, already up, made me a coffee and we smoked and talked in Portuguese and a little Spanish, and then about Wales's history and French history all in English. He told me about the candidates to be the new French president. It was a couple of days before the election and I had noticed posters in many places with Hitler moustaches black-penned onto a few of them. David's impression was that one of the candidates is regarded as a Fascist like Mussolini, as he put it. That's why people had chosen to defile his advertising posters. He thought this man would change many things, especially immigration laws, to the disadvantage of many. David then told me he respected the UK for standing up against the dictatorship of the Nazis in World War II – even though he played The Collaborators' punk music, but didn't acknowledge that if it wasn't for the Yanks it probably wouldn't have been that way.

I asked David why he was down here and he told me: only for his little girl. How often did he see her? He told me: once a month! We talked at length about the future and the past, exes and our daughters and the frustrations of being a distant dad anywhere. We both had a deep silent moment. I couldn't speak without getting a lump in my throat, and I don't think he could either. David eventually broke the silence and pulled yet another cork, and made me some food, and offered me hospitality for up to Monday. I half-heartedly agreed, but was thinking I should be on the road. As we ate and drank, I explained I would have to get back on the road – it would be too easy to take advantage of David's hospitality. At this point David became sad and actually started crying! He explained that he hated the solitude of being an outsider in this town. I empathised with him; he had only seen his reason for being here once in thirty days. Great reason, I explained to him. But wouldn't it be better to have the social support of family and friends around, and visit Melanie once a month, rather than living like this? It was a life I had tried, and which at one time became a desperate, sad life. We talked until about one o'clock. I then told David I had to go.

We went down and I loaded the bike. Outside the flats in the sun of a quiet Sunday in the south of France, David Mussecca embraced me in a Gallic 'man hug' and then said in English, "Thank you for your camaraderie, Shortie" which I felt so grateful for.

"And for yours, David. *Merci beaucoup*," I replied.

With that, he bade me *au revoir*. Then I was on the road once more.

With my body clean and my hair bushed up and getting long, I looked like I was riding to a rock gig as an over-age student of sorts. Slightly inebriated from the last bottle of wine I had drunk with David Mussecca, I rode out of

Carcasonne along a dual carriageway. Squeak! Squeak! I had forgotten to get that pedal spindle tightened. Then my seat pivoted back, as it had done once or twice since Narbonne, the retaining clamp coming loose. It was about 2.00 p.m. on a Sunday afternoon in southern France. Everything shut! I considered going back to David's. I stopped to check out a Marlboro 100s cigarette packet, which had one cigarette sticking out of it and was lying against the kerbside, and found the pack was almost full, having been discarded out of someone's car either after another resolution or because the smoker didn't like the taste.

I thought for a minute, with a smoke in hand, and stared directly across the carriageway at a big car dealership. Shut. I could see a couple of cars entering from a road running behind the dual carriageway and heard a woman's laugh, so perhaps there was a workshop or something behind. Upon investigation, opposite the car place was a huge café-restaurant packed with families, well dressed, eating their Sunday dinner. I don't know whether this was customary, or some special gathering – there were no signs on the restaurant at this converted 1940s building. A couple of people were outside having a ciggy so I asked if anyone spoke Portuguese or English. A chap went inside and fetched a pretty lady in her thirties who could speak Portuguese. I explained to her I needed a socket set. She explained this to a fella and he brought a brand-new one out. *Voila! Munto bien*. That sorted the bike. She asked if I was from England and, with pride, I explained I was from Pays de Galles! She asked if I was on holiday and I told her I wasn't exactly, but I was wanted in the UK. Freudian slip!

About twenty people had come out by now and were all chattering and asking what was going on. The pretty lady was busy translating and for once my cleanliness almost matched theirs. I probably would have got a different reception a day earlier; cheers, David! The ride that afternoon was probably one of the best I'd had since I left Portugal. The bike was going 100 per cent, I was clean with clean kecks, well fed, the sun wasn't too hot, and the roads were more or less straight and flat. A slight side wind meant less speed than yesterday but it was still a cool, distance-covering day. The odd uphill and windy roads through quiet villages never slowed my pace. The setting sun that evening was beautiful. Everything was right – or as right as it could be considering where I was headed. It was quiet on these roads: no trucks but mainly cars and plenty of bikers taking advantage of the sun. I was heading almost north through sleepy southern France's villages and towns. All the windows were shuttered either with flat painted wood or slats. You would think some of the places were deserted and shut down. I stopped rarely and only if I got well thirsty or very hungry. Today, despite the night's rest and late start I had, my butt began flagging early but I had covered a good distance considering I hadn't started until two-ish. It was early evening and the wind died. Along an endless straight, the only sound I would hear would be the whining of the hard knobbly tyres whirring on the rougher tarmac here, and only when going at a good pace in top gear.

Up ahead the road went on forever in a disappearing grey ruler, miles long, with only the odd shuttered farmhouse and vast well-kept fields with the odd tractor spreading nutrients away across the patchwork fields of different-coloured crops. I passed alongside the odd canal that ran parallel with this road. This place was like a holiday brochure, with perfect weather and civilised surroundings. The south was like this, though a bit less sweaty than Spain and greener; but the north, I was to find not much different to the UK.

I missed the bad weather conditions of home, though, thinking about it, they were only enjoyable when I was 'playing'. I loved the bad conditions on my terms: they remind you that you are alive. Bad or good, the wet conditions up Minera Mountain, with the few hours of being covered in mountain muck in the rain, was refreshing as long as I could have had a good hot bath afterwards. The desolate rawness of the high moorland, with its heather, ditches, drop-offs, tracks and streams; and its colours: purple, brown, and shades of green and copper; and in winter the snow: it was one of the only familiar unchanging things throughout my life. Contrasting it with the warmth of southern Europe at this time, it was a true oxymoron inside my head. But working in the rain as a mechanic/fabricator outside in all weathers was grim, unless I was in a large dealership in the winter with its heaters. Circumstances in the coming years are going to change after I deal with what I have to deal with…

The sun was becoming low in the sky to my left and Shadow Man was to my right, stretched and long, his unchanging form and pace keeping me company for a time. The weather being cooler and the road still endlessly straight, I decided to stop at a Perspex-covered bus stop that had a seat just about long and wide enough for me to perch my whole body on. I thought I might stay here tonight. I sat down, enjoying every moment of rest for my weary legs once again. I had pushed as far as I could for now and my bum was stinging once more. I think it was six or seven. I got out the French map and marked the date and the time but, as usual, after about twenty minutes or half an hour, my bum pain would subside and my legs would recover a little. I remembered the last sign saying seven kilometres to Villafranche de Lauragais and began thinking there might be an Aldi or a better bench to sleep on, plus, I would be a few kilometres up the road for the next day. Once again, even though I had stopped for the night lots of times, I would get up, load up and really struggle to sling my leg over the bike and slowly start my stiffening thighs moving again. For about half a kilometre or so my head would almost black out after crouching down or sitting. My heart told me to rest but now my brain wanted me to keep going for a bit. It was all right for my brain: he was just a passenger who gave orders from up top. Within another kilometre, I would get back into the swing again and then not want to stop. I reached the little roadside town just as it was almost dark, but rode across it to the northern side, not finding a suitable bench or spot quiet enough. Besides, it wasn't quite dark yet. I eventually settled in Villanouvelle. Its outskirts had bungalows and wide grass verges, with a perfect lone bench for a bed, set back in the trees. I dived onto it, got out my tranny radio, lit up a fag, said some prayers, and drifted off on the comfy bench with my international bomber jacket from River Island. As the sun set it got a bit cold. The sky was a pink salmon colour, with silver-and-grey lines of cloud spread out, going nowhere. Flash classic sports cars cruised by, with their grey-haired owners recapturing their youth but going a lot slower. All the little bungalows opposite showed no sign of life. No one spotted me and no one was bothered. All I could get on the radio was French classical music, which ain't my bag but it sort of went with the scene. My eyelids dropped across my eyeballs slowly and I had another sound night, having made a readjustment of the towel to wrap around my face to fend off the cold.

7.45 a.m. and I was up like a shot organically because my bowels told me to be. I found my feet were like blocks of ice – a sign of things to come. I cleaned my teeth using the diminished contents of my worn-out tube of toothpaste, which I would eke out until I found a new tube somewhere up north. I loaded up and hit the road again. I headed towards Toulouse on roads surrounded by mostly flat farmland. The N-113 was the last of the early-morning quiet roads, soon to be replaced by the busy roads heading more frequently downhill, wider and more congested and dusty, towards the giant motorway ring road that encircled this large city. Being in no mood for sightseeing and my map not being detailed enough to give me an easy route through the centre, I decided to ride as fast as I could on the ring road until the gendarmes threw me off at some point.

As I neared the ring road, I stopped near some road works by a small terraced row of houses where a chappie was doing some maintenance on his K100 motorbike. He let me use a 13-millimetre spanner to tighten my tilting seat, which had come loose again and had irritated me for some forty kilometres or so. I was now ready to go for it on the ring road, which was busy and fast. I rode along the hard shoulder as fast as I could until I reached the N-20 exit for Montauban. This took me a while but saved me a lot of time going through the city. I would get aggravation from the road users with their horns occasionally, but the 'feds' never stopped me. By the time I found the exit my legs were well tired and I was sweating, and feeling a bit deaf too from the busy, loud traffic. This ring road was mainly a raised concrete affair so I was glad to be back on real roads eventually.

I plodded on along the N-20 on more similar-looking roads, which seemed to rise steadily for most of the time. On this bike, I could now cover the distances without anywhere near as much effort as with the last one, and this was the first day of complete morning-to-night progress in France. My goal was to reach Cahors tonight and it looked good. The roads weren't too challenging, but climbed more the nearer I got to Cahors. After a few hours the road began dropping and dropping, which meant that tomorrow's journey out of Cahors would be up and up. I seemed to drop for miles, along a dual cariageway road down the wide river valley into the town. This road was surrounded by small cliffs of scrub and stone, which reminded me of the last of Spain. The road ran along a long valley with a train track to its right, and eventually passing under tall concrete viaducts, with graffiti decorating their columns. The graffiti looked out of place here.

When I eventually neared the centre, I spotted a tap outside a garage. I filled my water bottle with the sweetest tasting eau, which was a lot cleaner and fresher than some of the fill-ups I had drunk when desperate in Spain. I savoured this before I moved on – it tasted that refreshing. It was also free. France felt good just because of that water.

I was on the lookout for food again and rode back to a large retail area with big DIY-type supermarkets. I couldn't find a regular supermarket but found some bins outside a discount-type warehouse, where I found almost ten stubby dark green bottles of a cider-based pop; a packet of mini-meringues with about twenty inside; another six-pack of mousses, with one damaged; and a giant burst packet of crisps of some sort. Food just when I just needed it was so welcome. Well late in the day, I now filled in the map with 'Cahors 8.30 p.m. All uphill tomorrow' and searched for a bus stop for shelter out of the spitting rain. Tomorrow was going to be more of a test than I thought. And this place would confuse my memories. I found another town further on, very similar but a lot smaller, and the distance in between like 'Groundhog Day'. I remember envying the people who were enjoying the café culture along a steep wide street slightly darkened by leafy green old trees. The tables were full of civilised French people of all ages having wine and coffee, and very quietly socialising with family and friends. They were definitely posher than wot I is!

This street cum boulevard was full of French-style, busyness and money. I rode up and out of the main drag, along streets with traditional eighteenth century smart and typical terraces, and onto the N-20. Before I completely emerged on a high road, almost on the outskirts, it down poured again. I darted under a bus shelter, just to be out of the deluge for a few minutes. The light was fading pretty quickly by now. It was pissing down and I was wet, with nowhere to crash for the night. I looked up the road out of town. It was empty, with no buildings – just a steep winding climb up out of this river valley. For all I knew it could be like that all the way to Brive. I would have to find somewhere here for tonight. I looked back down the road into town, which was my only option for shelter... Hmmm! After cycling back a kilometre or two I stopped. To my right was a set of huge, painted, high, heavy cast-iron gates. I took a casual glance through the iron railings, which ran about ten metres along the front of a gravelled courtyard. There was a converted large building, set back. It looked like apartments had been fitted into a very old office or church-type building at least three storeys high. Across the courtyard, set back against a wall, was a large shelter to park cars under. It must have been some sort of building at one time judging by its slated roof. In the far corner, there was an old yellow fork-lift truck with a pallet lying across its forks. A curious place for a fork-lift, I thought. The fork-lift had a gap about a metre wide between it and the wall at its far end. Even though it was raining I could see that space was dry as well as being hidden, and it was going dark. I needed that little space, and no one would notice. I casually looked around the seemingly empty avenue and at the same time looked at the cast-iron gates, one of which was left open. Instant decision made, I walked in, taking the bike with me as though I were going home from work. Placing the bike against the wall next to the fork truck, I quickly got out my foam and my blanket and made a bed on the pallet in front of the fork-lift. I could lie almost flat but had to place my legs on the upright carriage of the truck. I was hidden by its mast and I covered myself with the grubby red blanket, wrapped myself in the neck of my bomber jacket and relaxed, listening to the sound of rain rattling away on the slate roof of this shelter.

I was out of the downpour. I had forgotten to write on the now dog-eared map. It was something I had to do. I only scribbled basic details but knew they would speak to me in the future, together with every grubby stain, wrinkle and tear. It was '7.30 p.m. on 30th April. Rained all day, bad journey'. I offered up my prayers unconditionally and disregarded every sceptic or anyone who thought they knew better. I slept.

A few hours later, I became aware of light shining over the shelter of the blanket and into my eyes, and the sound of an engine nearby. Thinking I was dreaming, I ignored it. I was too tired to lift up my head. I then heard a man's voice; he was conversing with a woman. They were very close by. I slightly opened one eye, and was blinded by the bright halogen headlamp of a Peugeot. I could tell it was a Peugeot by the distinct shape of the outline of the head-lamp. It was less than a foot away from my head. The driver had parked the car under the shelter, facing the wall. I first thought these people must have spotted me. They were still talking to each other in a purposeful manner. One of the car doors banged shut and the talking stopped. One of the people walked away across the gravel towards the apartments, whilst the other was still doing something inside the car. I tried to run through explanations in my head if they asked me why I was there, then realised I had no way of explaining to them. So I just stayed still. The other person returned to the car and the engine died. Both doors closed and after the sound of a few sentences and then a 'whirr, click' of central locking, the man and the woman both went back across the gravel into the apartments and never bothered me again, having been inches away from my corpse. I was soon off to a dry, sound kip.

Chapter Sixteen

Cloudy, Wet, Hilly and Green

Déjà vu and Downers

1ˢᵗ May 2007 Cahors to Brive – 100 Kilometres

I was up at the usual 7.45 and out on the N-20 (also called the D-820). I climbed out of Cahors up roads which rose to a maximum of four hundred-plus metres and then fell a hundred or more metres, for over ten or fifteen kilometres, whilst at the same time being lashed with rain again and again from thick dark clouds. The roads then dropped a similar amount, then rose another hundred or so metres, through leafy green, tree-lined, lush pasture. This process was repeated all day with almost no let-up bar a few minutes brief interlude, after which it lashed down again for the complete day – rain, rain and rain. Soaked through and a lot cooler than any time previously, I very occasionally stopped if I found a wooden bus shelter, once stopping at a wine tasting centre, which had a sheltered porch and empty car parks.

I had a morning of this where the scenery never changed: just hills, valleys and few places or breaks from anything but wet, rough, stone-chipped, grey roads. The few cars that passed had the regular rattle of the European common rail diesel engine that is so popular here. I thought of the faceless people driving them, in their dry warmth, with the radio on, going somewhere, home, maybe. They didn't realise how lucky they were.

This was like any countryside area in Britain except for the wine tasting places and the odd chateau here and there. It was so drab if only because of the incessant rain and dullness making the endless climbs a misery. With no sunshine to tell me what time it was, I realised exactly how much I personally depended on sunshine to maintain an upbeat mood. I had rain leading down into Cahors; during the night it rained; when I started the journey that morning it rained; and by now I was leaning against a wall in a tiny village on the crest of yet another sodden climb. There were no people around to be acknowledged by or given a nod from – or even one of those Gallic shrugs. It was completely depressing and miserable as well as cold. I didn't stop for more than a couple of minutes anywhere or I would lose the little heat I had built up climbing a hill. When I did stop, I snacked on anything I could find in the bag: the odd orange – well, my last one – then my last two bottles of that fizzy cider pop and the last few mini-meringues, which gave me a little burst of energy for yet another hill, long and dull to climb. My supplies ran out and I couldn't find any food: there were no supermarkets on this journey, just the odd little village or town, wet, and with nothing in the well-kept bins. This particular part of the journey was soul-destroying; in this green, rich and civilised country there was nothing to feed on and nowhere to rest. Just on and on. I had to get to Brive today and 'civilisation', where I might find food and some temporary shelter for tonight. It is difficult sleeping in cold and wet when there is no sunshine in the daytime to dry you out. I was so near to warmth and homes but so far away from comfort.

My pace today was poor, not just because of the rain and my mood but also because of the constant uphills then downhills, then uphills through lush farmland used for dairy cattle, though mainly with little food to be found. This was killing my enthusiasm for France in equal measure to the relief I felt a day earlier when tasting that sweet, cool clean water after drinking tepid, cloudy water in Spain – well, this stretch of it anyway.

I reached a place called Soullac in the afternoon, which seemed to be a smaller version of Cahors: it shared a similar position over a similar-sized river. I went over another stone bridge, then along a dark, leafy road alongside terraces of buildings and dwellings which looked as if they never received sunshine along their streets, being in a rain shadow from the surrounding green-covered cliffs deep in this river valley. I had a reccy around this small town, noticing that the road out was looking well steep. I needed some nourishment, but the only thing I could find was a large round loaf thrown out in a bakery bin. I ate most of this on the spot and used half a bottle of that lovely clean French water to wash it down with. According to the map, I wasn't far away from Brive so there was nothing else but to tackle that bastard of a climb up into the trees and get there. It had stopped raining whilst I was eating and looking around at this small river valley and its sunken town. The rain started again the second I resumed the journey, as though it was automatically waiting for me.

I rode alongside a wall for the first twelve metres or so, on this road rising steeply out of town, with a terrace of houses built with their front views across the valley. I had a brief look at this view. A brief lull in the low cloud let me almost light half a cig I had stashed hours earlier, but it was too damp to light.

No relief from my poisonous chemicals. Bugger it! Let's go.

I was grumbling and muttering to myself. For a complete night and most of the back end of yesterday it rained, and it didn't seem to fucking stop. For most of the 500-plus hours up till now that I had been on this journey, I was subject to the sun.

My mood dropped in direct proportion to the climb on these steep loops up and up around thick, tall deciduous trees, climbing around three hundred metres whilst being emptied on by leaves which would wait until I was directly underneath them before giving me another soaking, again and again and again. I thought dark thoughts again, like at that moment up on that dry thirsty road in Spain. Where was I going? Then the desperateness of exactly where I was and what I was doing dawned on me. Then I realised my food bag was empty.

My head dropped into a 'pity party' with every slosh of water from the deluge dripping down my neck and my sodden jeans: an endless lull with no happy endings in sight. I stopped, with the smell of damp woods amongst the steepness of this empty road, and leaned my head down, trying to think of something to give me some temporary relief out of this pit, but there was nothing to look forward to. I didn't know how far I needed to go to get out of the wet or get food or to change things in the future.

Last resort. Prayer. This was like my 'In case of a downer, break glass'.

"Please, God, give me something, anything. A thought. Some sunshine. I ain't a good example to anyone but I'm suffering enough to always be grateful for what you've given me for nowt. Give me something, anything, to get me back and get sorted! I guess we only need an umbrella when it's raining."

As I mounted the bike for the umpteenth time, the road had become not quite steep enough for me not to have to push. A melody slipped into my head. It slowly became more recognisable and gave me a rush of warmth and a lump in my throat, for absolutely no reason whatsoever.

Up through this damp landscape the effort became a little less and the rain subsided a little. What was that beautiful melody? It certainly wasn't Muse or Van Halen, or Razorlight. So what was it? It kept echoing through my head. Where did it come from? It must be a ballad of sorts. It was vaguely familiar, but not a song I would have listened to for any reason other than it accompanied something which I had seen and had an effect on me in the past. Was it a Killers song? Nah, they don't do stuff like that; it must be older than that. Journey? No. This song carried a massive emotional kick. It took my mind off my misery. It made me feel warm and gave me mental comfort. What was it? The line, which gradually slipped into my head side by side with the melody, over and over again, was just this line:

In the arms of an angel, you will find your way home.

It was a lady's voice. I stopped and went to bits on the spot! But it kept me going for a long time after that moment. It still does.

Was it the melody, or the words that appeared in my head after that particular moment? I couldn't explain. It was another one of those times where I had to do something, 'dared' to do something few people with their material comforts ever do. I prayed. It just worked for me.

Then I thought of the bad conditions which I loved so much up those muddy hills far away. My thoughts ran something along the lines of: I've seen worse than this. There was a hot bath for me at that time then, so why not treat each bit as though there is something good waiting at the end? There always is, eventually. There will be today.

So I dropped my pity party and got on with it, rain or not. The words and melody of that song kept fortifying me every time I thought of them from then on and every time my head dropped. I'd heard that one line in the film *City of Angels* and learned it was originally written about addiction. When a writer pens a lyric with feeling, I wonder if they know how far their feelings may travel. It was if I was never alone. Why that particular line?

It was like being carried.

The rain didn't stop and things were just as difficult, but less than twenty-seven kilometres later it did stop and I was in Brive, although to cap it off, as I reached the outskirts my back tyre went bang! This might be a problem as the repair outfit I had found in that bin in Sevilla had had to cope with so many punctures en route, I was having to cut the patches into halves, then quarters, then eighths, and there wasn't much left. Plus, I had caused a few more holes as the tyre went bang at speed whilst I was coming down into Brive. A good bonus from this day was spotting an Aldi somewhere along one of the roads heading slightly downhill towards the centre of Brive on the right-hand side of a built-up road with a fuel station, where I managed to harden the tyres, almost opposite the Aldi. I had to check it out. Around the back, there were two large bins but they were behind a ten-foot-tall heavy wire cage with a padlocked door. Why lock the bins up? They must have heard I was coming! I clambered over the top of the cage and fell onto the concrete and into one of the bins, using my ribcage for cushioning! This hurt a bit but it was worth the drop. Inside the bins were several yoghurts and three plastic-wrapped foot-long sponge cakes, a few decent oranges and apples, and some UHT milk. I ate ravenously, again until I was almost sick, and threw the remainder of the foodstuffs over the cage to fit into one of the bags. I then realised there was nothing to grip onto to climb out of the cage and I almost threw up having consumed two of the cakes, a pile of yoghurts, one UHT milk and two apples. I sat on the top of one of the bins until my guts settled a bit. My ribs were hurting and my foot blisters were stinging from me applying pressure on them from a different angle. My toes felt wet, as though some of the blisters were burst. I was in full view of the backs of many side street houses but no one looked or was concerned about some bloke raiding Aldi's bins so I sat and waited for a while before dragging one bin near to the fence and clambered over, good and ready.

After repairing this last puncture and raiding another bin, I had delayed myself again. I just couldn't make the same progress in France and the weather, the roads I chose and places to stop were less forgiving than those on my 'Tour de Costas'. I got lost in Brive and ended up feeling a bit sorry for myself in a park next to the river for a little while, before snapping out of it and then trying to find a way out. I cycled for a kilometre or two in one direction, then in another, before another study of the map made me venture back another kilometre before I found a huge hospital with a road exiting up a huge hill out of Brive towards Donzenac. After a slow climb in the spitting rain, I eventually crested this hill, where the road flattened out slightly. I wanted to call it a day by now: the alarm clock of too much pain was going off. Right, the first available bus stop or shelter will be my bed and I don't care where, I thought to myself. I then found a green, old-fashioned wooden bus stop sitting perpendicular to the road, facing back down the hill across Brive and the glum clouds. It was full of cobwebs, looked rarely used and was far too short for me to stretch my legs, and with a seat far too narrow to sleep on without falling off. It then rained a little heavier so the rain was bouncing in under the meagre shelter. This place was no good. As I crested the hill, I remembered noticing a large building on my left, which looked like a warehouse, about fifty by a hundred metres square, on a concrete slab but with only a roof and the framework of steel girders, though I did notice piles of cladding in stacks on the concrete slab. I had earlier discounted this place to sleep in because it had no sides, but I thought now that those stacks of cladding might make me a little shelter. I set off back towards the place. Why didn't I think like that earlier? It wasn't late but I was dog-tired and would benefit from a long sleep to catch up on the sleep deficit caused by the last few days' rain. I cycled to the construction site. I found several stacks placed next to each other, and they were held together with nylon strapping. I placed the bike between two of the stacks, then cut the bands on two others, turning one with its metal backing to the floor and using two more to block both ends, and one for the roof. I now had a little 'shed'. This was 7.00 p.m. on 1st May 2007.

Chapter Seventeen
Threatening Clouds, Ice Cold Toes and a Stolen Day

2nd May 2007 Brive to Limoges – 95 Kilometres.
3rd May 2007 and 4 May 2007 Poitiers and Angers

I was on the road again later than usual, having had a stop to sort tyres and fill my bag with more oranges, apples, bread and various detritus liberated from another Lidl bin. With a full bottle of water, I headed for Limoges. This was another day of black clouds and threatening skies. I made slower progress than I had done on the last couple of days because my feet hurt and stung all day, and the long flat distances were again replaced by more hills, bends and rain.

Today the rain clouds broke whilst I was climbing the longer but shallower valleys than the previous day, and I had frequent stops to rest my feet. Nowhere to sit though, or very rarely somewhere to sit. I just felt that even if I stopped and stood still for a bit, the movement of the pedals wouldn't irritate my fretting blisters. But starting off from a stop was agonising. I chanced a look at the soles of my feet at St Germain, where I found a wooden bench. They didn't look a pretty sight, with lots of burst blisters caused by my riding sockless for about a thousand kilometres but the burning on top of the stinging was being caused by red blood blisters, which seemed to be too deep under the skin to be burst. There was not a lot I could do to help them, apart from me feeling cheeky enough to walk across the road to a nearby shop and ask the fella if I could have one of his cigarettes, seeing as he was outside smoking one a few minutes previously. This cig didn't help my feet but it did some mental good from a relief point of view.

From the first glance of the map, before I hit the road I knew it was going to be an indirect route north. The main motorway north, marked as the A-20 on the map, was off limits to bikes, as I discovered by getting thrown off more than once. The only roads which gave me a northerly direction would disappear off to the west, then to the east, criss-crossing the motorway time after time throughout the day, frustrating me, especially when I ended up in tiny towns with nothing but more small roads out which seemed to go any direction but north. I first took the road not marked with any name, to Donzenac. This followed the nearby motorway, crossing over back and forth for a while. Then I went through Uzerche, after which, I thought, the road ended at the motorway (L' Occitanne), so I took a westerly road to Lubersac, and then headed in a northerly direction back across the A-20 on the little D-7b to a place called St Germain-les-Belles. The combination of intermittent rain, indirect route, and frequent stops to try and figure out exactly which direction I was headed in made this day a long one. At one point, a deluge of rain was so heavy it was like someone pouring buckets on my head. I mean like a waterfall! I stopped for a small while, only because I couldn't see in front of me, and watched lightning strikes big enough to split Europe in half. It stopped as quickly as it started though. Much of today was the same story. Eventually I seemed to be getting nearer to Limoges.

According to my scribbles on the map, I was in a place called Pierre Buffiere by half five that day. It didn't look like I had come far on the map but, boy, I felt like I had done a lot more.

For the last twenty or so kilometres I tried chancing the A-20. Being in a bloody-minded mood by now I stuck two fingers up at complaining traffic, especially to a group of bikers who complained at me whilst I was entering the A-20 motorway on a loop somewhere after Pierre Buffiere. They must have been the ones that alerted the gendarmerie because within about five kilometres or so a blue minibus with two officers checked me out then 'offered' to escort me to the next off ramp. Bastards – you would have thought they would have given me a lift!

Zig-zagging my way, I eventually came to the outskirts of Limoges, climbing an uphill dual carriageway with a hypermarket on my right and trees on my left, and clouds from the film *Poltergeist* above me, swirling and blackening., I just managed to reach somewhere near the city centre before the clouds emptied their entire load. I found shelter under the overhang of a closed discount shop near to a corner, where the main street seemed to lead down into the city centre and huge river.

Trolley buses glided by silently as I laid out my grubby foam and got out my dirty red blanket. I contemplated my loudly complaining 'plates of meat', which were very sore. Mentally and physically worn out today, I wanted sleep earlier than usual. Even though I was wet through and soggy, there was that wonderful feeling of drifting off into a dark world where conditions didn't matter if you were completely tired. You just hibernated through the hours, asleep. My tiredness even overcame my hunger. I jealously looked over the road to a fella leaving a pizza parlour with a large box. I then dismissed the thought but definitely filled in the map though, knowing I wouldn't remember in the morning or care to do it. The scribble on the map said 'Bastard of a journey – gendarmes threw me off again – shelter – shop doorway – big black clouds again. 7.30 p.m. 2nd May'.

It was never a problem going to sleep when completely and utterly knack-ered at the end of a long distance, as anyone can testify at any time in their lives. You forget 'issues' and worries and problems you just can't deal with; when you just fade into black, nothing matters. But those of us with underlying issues have, sometimes, only sleep to escape. I never realised just how much junk we had that we don't need to be thinking about and wasting our brains fretting over. In the past, I loved sinking into bed after a long hard day and drifting off in minutes, especially with someone you love.

At this time, I pushed myself to the brink of utter tiredness because I had a goal to get somewhere. As a result, I became so dog-tired that I would forget what was at the end of this journey, and the past, the future, the cold and the damp; but just die into true escape for a few hours. There was no going to bed bored, but just to rest a weary set of legs and body. This is a therapy that works, although I wouldn't recommend doing what pre-empted this journey. It just gave me immense mental strength that would later blind me to the life I previously had, and change the values I had forever.

I realised that people are basically good, but there are many with mental issues and the majority of people believe in the bullshit of the modern popular media which fills their heads with aspirations which 99.9 per cent of them will never achieve. It's like they are looking in a dark room for a black cat that isn't there. All things relative to where we are in life or what we can afford, whatever possessions we buy, become either out of date, rust, or are stolen. Where is it all going? I used to think that life in the UK was 'normal'.

I woke shivering. It was still dark. Glancing at the radio, I saw it was four-something in the morning. I tried to reposition myself for some extra warmth but this didn't work. About two hours later, I decided to get on the road before I froze where I slept. The blanket was stiff with the cold. It was definitely freezing or not far off it. I strapped my stuff on and headed over the mist-covered river just down the street. My feet were that cold I couldn't tell which way my ankles were pivoting, I had to actually look at them, for there was no feeling in them. On the other side of the river, I found a post illuminating a map of the city. I remember 'dithering' whilst studying a way out of Limoges, at 6.30 a.m. I found half a cig, which I couldn't light because I was shivering so much, then asking a bloke to light it for me. Half an hour later, I was on the northern outskirts of the city and as the sun broke through I had another bang! – Flat tyre. Not having a lot of the puncture outfit left, I emptied out my bag to look for other things I could use. I found a foot-long, plastic-wrapped sponge cake which I didn't know I had: fuel for today's journey. I eventually used the tiniest piece of rubber to mend this puncture, with cold fingers, on a side street next to the N-147 out towards Poitiers. I was eventually on my way, and with the sunshine and early-morning freshness cheering me on, I headed on. I found a petrol station to blow the tyres rock hard again, which caused my next problems.

Out in farming country the road was straight and out came the heat of the day. I made it past a place called Bellac and then about midday, north of this place, I had another puncture on a long straight. And another problem: the back tyre had split and the tube was sticking through in a bulge. Shit! Miles from anywhere. It never actually went bang but it made me fret good style. I managed to get enough pressure into the tyre with that foot-pump I had 'acquired' somewhere near Aguadulce in Spain. I didn't pump too hard in case the tube popped, plus the pump rod bent and then broke in half and was now scrap. I was at a lay-by on a long hot straight by now, with nothing in sight away up ahead. The map showed nothing until Poitiers. What can I do now? I looked at the bike for a while. How can I fix this? What can I use? I used a little plastic wrapped as tight as I could around the tube, and I cut off a piece of the rucksack with my small blunt knife. Right, I will give that repair some help,

I thought to myself, so I dumped as much weight as I could. The saddlebags I had found in the rain in Almeria went. I ate what I could find in the depths of the bags: an orange and two apples and that cake wrapped in plastic, threw my grubby grey woollen jumper, the now useless pump, and then my Benfica tracky top, which I was later to regret throwing. I had only the lashed-on rack, the rolled-up piece of sponge and my bottle of diminishing water, less than half-full. With all that weight ditched to give the tyre a chance, I could possibly reach the next civilisation.

On I went, hoping to reach Poitiers, food, and to 'score' a tyre and tube. About ten kilometres further on and the tyre was making a 'squeak squeak' noise as the bulge had popped through the tearing tyre wall and was rubbing on the frame. I stopped and tried to rectify it with bits and pieces but the tyre was 'wedi marw', or dead! I could up my pace easier than before, realising that even in light headwind those saddlebags had cost me hours and distance due to the weight of them and the way they caught the wind. I should have ditched them ages ago – I only seemed to carry junk in them anyway. Now I was in a spot of bother and expected to be pushing for the remaining thirty kilometres or so. There was nothing on these roads: just straight with huge fields all around. I pedalled slowly over a slight rise and freewheeled downhill on my brakes, expecting to hear a loud 'pop' any second. I came up to another lay-by with an artic lorry parked up. The driver was probably having his tachograph break. The truck trailer was a flatback carrying two huge rectangular concrete culverts, or bridge sections, all chained down. I leaned against the back of the trailer, had a good look at the bulge which was stopping the tyre from turning now – without effort. I then looked up at the first culvert on the back of the truck. It was about six feet high. In a split second, I threw the bike up on the back of the flatbed and used the bungees to strap the bike down, then peered over the first culvert and recognised the rear of the egg-box cab as a white Renault Magnum. It was facing north and for all I knew it could be going to Paris and not stopping, but I had to take that chance. Anyway, I could always jump off at some traffic lights. I sat with my back against the first culvert, enjoying sitting there in the warmth of the sun with my arse being rested. I would be going somewhere, anywhere – north, I hoped.

In less than ten minutes the driver fired his rig up and was accelerating away up through the gears. I could hear as he went up into high range and could tell exactly when he used the 'splitter' on the top four gears when approaching hills and rises so as to keep the engine in its narrow turbo boost. I watched the road narrowing away behind me. This truck was a 480-horsepower Magnum, making light work of its load, the driver pressing on with an urgency, never missing a gear, and using the exhaust brake exactly and efficiently. He drove professionally, getting across roundabouts and up grades, and through tight villages, with ease. I was treated to the sound of the twelve-litre turbo engine doing its job with gusto. Not much traffic followed this lorry, and it was keeping up a good average speed on these French roads. I decided to climb over the first culvert and rest against the next one in order to hide from the sight of, and avoid unwanted attention of, the gendarmes. As I jumped up, the wind almost sent me back again, but I eventually got over the culvert and pulled my cap tighter over my head to avoid losing it. I settled between the second and third culvert in the middle, to keep well out of the wind. Sitting dead in the middle, I stuck my hands in the pockets of the now zipped-up bomber jacket, and pulled the straps on the neck tight as the wind made the journey a bit chilly.

I had a brief thought with pictures, A scene of carnage flitted through my mind. It was of me being blown off that culvert by the blast of wind sending me off the back of the trailer, and then me being squashed by following traffic. This made me shrug and straightaway discount the negative thought; it was just a brief 'worst case scenario' that the sensible (?) part of my brain would probably store, to remind me not to climb over a concrete culvert, fifteen feet up, on the back of a vehicle doing ninety kilometres per hour. It's not a natural act, but I usually thought about that sort of danger last.

The driver went over a series of roundabouts, then onto a motorway. Truck drivers we passed on the stretch of motorway would occasionally notice me but no one else did. I got cold towards the end of this journey and looked forward to stopping in the last of the daytime sunshine. I couldn't quite figure out where I was going now, couldn't see signs, but we seemed to travel for an hour or so, before the driver pulled off the motorway and back onto ordinary carriageway. He then pulled up at a little roadside service area with some toilets and a little picnic area. I jumped off the side of the trailer and undid my bike, pulling it to the ground. Another lorry pulled up behind and gave me a glance. I wandered over to the toilet, looking over at my chauffeur's mirrors, just to catch sight of my unsuspecting driver. A bespectacled chap of about fifty tanned years glanced back, with no idea he had had a passenger for a while. He had taken me onto the D-347 and then onto a motorway to just south of Angers, and had saved me maybe seventy kilometres or so.

I filled my water bottle up and had a wash at this rest area. I had warmed up after that wind blast off the back of that lorry. Then my ears returned to normal and it seemed really quiet all around apart from the odd car or lorry flying by on the nearby road. I looked at the rear tyre, which still had the bulge popping through one side of the tyre wall. The city wasn't far away now even if I had to walk it. Just then I was hit with a giant feeling of guilt?! This sounds strange now. I had saved maybe a day's riding and lots of energy, but lost the feeling I had begun to enjoy – the struggle and another day's adventuring. The feeling of 'What's around the next corner?' had been wiped off for this particular day and the feeling of accomplishing something had gone. The coming future ordeal would not allow me the choice of doing things like this for a while and I had just lost hours of freedom and struggle. I had 'sold out', and this left me feeling empty and guilty – the same sort of feeling of being a traitor to myself, like the feeling I had whilst looking out across Carcassonne from David Mussecca's top-floor flat window after being fed, getting clean, then drunk, with the sounds of rock and punk music blaring out behind me. It was what I loved for years: the excesses after a day's work. It was 'work hard, play hard', for years, with me eventually becoming 'tired always'. I guess this journey reminded me of 'work hard, play hard' but this was 'ride hard, rest hard'. Today the 'ride hard' was missing.

I was very slowly riding towards Angers, trying to ignore the 'squeak squeak' of the bulge rubbing on the bike's frame. By now I thought, 'Bugger it; if it goes, it goes.' Every metre it doesn't go pop is a metre nearer to that city. It lasted a remarkable distance along a five-kilometre stretch, with the late-afternoon sun away to my left. I crested a shallow long rise before a village where the road narrowed and wound through and became a little tight. As I rode on through this place I was overtaken by my lift as he took those huge concrete culverts to some destination. Maybe I should have stayed on the back, I thought to myself, then reasoned that I couldn't have sat on the back any longer: too impatient. Plus, it could have been hours until the driver stopped again, east, west or wherever. That was enough justification.

I reached a place which had a hypermarket on the opposite side of the road, similar to one I had found further south. It had a huge steel fence all around it with a door, which slid open for large vehicles to enter a big, concreted unloading area large enough for artics to swing their trailers around. These places left palletised boxes of goods outside sometimes, which I had exploited a couple of times for the odd bottle of pop or some fruit if there was a pallet with easily-cut shrink-wrap. I only did this if there wasn't access to the bins of thrown-out food or produce. Strange to think that some places had better security around their giant wheelie bins than for their fresh produce. This place was easy: a lorry was exiting out of the giant sliding door and I just walked right in and over to a box about ten metres inside, near the loading bay. It had Asian pears inside and some oranges. They looked damaged but there were a few good ones. These must have been set aside for disposal. I blatantly filled my rucksack with about half a dozen of the best I could find and then stood next to the exit door, waiting for it to open as a lorry was manoeuvring outside to reverse in. As I stood eating one of these Asian pears – which I didn't know the name of at the time – I was amazed at the soft, huge and juicy fruit which reminded me of a pear but looked like a giant apple. It was completely 'boss' – really succulent and sweet, and filling my palm with its huge size. I took great thirst-quenching gulps. It was one of the best fruits I had tasted on this journey, along with a few huge red apples, which I thought were the 'best' somewhere down along the Costa Dorada, and the gigantic sweet oranges eaten just when I would appreciate them most. The huge door began to slide clear for the lorry, revealing this tramp engrossed in this huge fruit to a pair of tall, smartly dressed French management-type fellas in suits. This brought me out of the daydream of this new fruit discovery. The fellas looked at me with frowns over the clipboards they were both comparing whilst talking. I smiled and offered 'em a Gallic shrug with a *Ca va* (Hi): the best greeting I could offer 'em at the time.

"You must not be in here!" the more senior-looking one told me.

I duly obliged with a smile. I'd got what I needed and as I rode off on the squeaky bike I wondered how he knew I couldn't speak French. I had only said one word. It was like that moment the park keeper told me I couldn't sleep on his park bench in Perpignan. Whatever, at least I had some fuel now; let's get this bike sorted. The sunlight was dying and low in the sky. I'd better get into that city. I rode on slowly, then stopped at several bus stops and sheltered seating areas, not sure whether to ride on, call it a day, or hunt for a 'donor' wheel. I was out of sync and not sure what to do. As I slowly wheeled into Angers the tube inevitably gave up the ghost with a loud pop, which snapped me into focus mode and made me feel instantly better for some twisted reason. Now to find a replacement or a bike shop that may have some tubes in their bins. Within half a kilometre of walking with the bike, my feet became like walking on needles despite the rest I had had today. It was probably those blood-type blisters, deep under the skin, I saw a few days earlier. They obviously were nowhere near getting better yet.

One bonus was pushing the bike straight in front of a supermarket, where I checked out the skips and found more fruit. I walked almost to the centre of the city along a long straight boulevard, then asked a fireman outside a fire station if he knew of a bike shop. I didn't know the words for 'skip yard'. He directed me to a bike shop, where I might blag a second-hand tube next morning. It was shut by now.

I practised asking for an old tyre whilst laying out my bed on a thin piece of rolled-up sponge I had found earlier on the trip. I was sheltered from the rain, which had resumed – it was spitting by now – with help from the overhang of the shop front, just about. I filled in my map, and then eyed up the brand-new carbon-fibre-framed race bikes with ultra-thin wheels, tyres and frames. I bet they were as light as a feather. Imagine the mileage I could do with one of those, I thought to myself, with brief thoughts of throwing my bike through the plate glass window and cycling off into the distance with one of those racing bikes. But besides the fact I felt I was making peace with my maker now and karma would deal me back another blow somewhere along the line – it always does! – I felt some kind of repentance for years of abusing my body with years of madness.

If I stole one of those bikes, I could be a hundred kilometres away by tomorrow morning and double the amount by the next day or more – easily. But that was too easy. Across Spain, I could have stolen a dozen motorbikes, cars and lorries over the past two thousand kilometres but that would never have replaced the beauty of this struggle that I wouldn't have swapped for the world. There was nothing like it. Although I would nick a wheel if I had to...

I kipped until the owner opened the shop the next day. I did my best to explain to him that I needed a second-hand tube as mine had gone bang; no money etc, etc. I then got the impression that if I returned later on, there may be a second-hand one he had removed from a customer's bike.

Sound, I thought. So off I went in search of food, with my bike upside down with no wheel on outside of the shop. I was basically wasting time too. A circuit to the centre of the city had me a soggy cake with plenty of sugary icing on it outside of a cake shop. And there was a bike chained to a nearby lamppost; it had quick-release wheels. My need was greater than theirs...

Off came the wheel in seconds. *Voila!* – A new tyre and tube. I separated the tyre from the tube so the bike shop owner wouldn't suspect I had just taken a wheel. This I would pay for in the future. And I did.

I now began the return to the bike shop, and got lost. My feet couldn't stand more than a kilometre of walking: my blisters were agonising. I ended up back at the cake shop before finally finding the bike shop. With the bike still outside of the shop, upside down on the pavement, I borrowed a spanner from the little side workshop, used the air line, and was off. Within an hour I had to fix this tyre: being in a hurry, I had nipped the new tube.

This caused me to blag a patch off a Kwik Fit-type place next to a super-market on the road out of this city on the way to Le Mans. The boys there even let me use their tyre bath, air line and spanners. Now I was ready to rock, again.

I had lost a lot of time this morning and that is how I treated it – wasted downtime. Nothing like a goal to give you focus. I needed to make some progress but my feet were a problem. They were so sore I was forced to stop and take many breaks today, just to give them rest. It was a case of ride a kilometre or two, stop and sit or just stand, then ride a little more, then repeat the process again and again. As a result, I did very little mileage but having had the comfort of travelling at least seventy kilometres without pedalling, I felt I could have an 'early' rest. So the day was used for riding slowly – rest and ride very slowly. A wasted day, 4 May.

About thirty or maybe forty kilometres out of Angers, I hit more of the long tree-lined straights common to France along the distances between large towns. They were quite helpful, especially when encountering the wind, which is more prevalent in the north. If the wind was side on and strong, the trees would give me temporary mercy for a split second, and then a blast, then temporary shelter as I passed the lee of each tree. It reminded me of dragging a stick across railings as a little kid, with the light flashing on then off then on then off as it fell through the gaps in the railings, except this was for well over a hundred kilometres and on a grander scale. Not far from Angers I found an Aldi on its own to the left of the N-323, which I investigated and in the bin I found a couple of apples and oranges and a few bananas, not quite as big as the fruit found in Spain or southern France but this would be tonight's supper. But, more importantly, I needed somewhere to rest my feet, which were now seriously sore. I had disturbed my daily rhythm after jumping on the back of that truck and then leaving Angers late and making rubbish progress along the straight roads today. My feet were howling too. This day was very poor as far as distance was concerned, but at least I was a little further up the road than I would have been, courtesy of my French chauffeur.

Le Mans was just under seventy kilometres away according to a sign I had just passed. It was about 8.00 p.m. as I rode through a small hamlet along this dead straight road. The sign had told me that Le Mans was too far to attempt, and seeing as the straight carried on outside this hamlet and looked featureless for as far as the eye could see, surrounded by flat fields, I wasn't likely to find anywhere to sleep along that road for a long time. So I stopped and rode back to the little place. Its few houses were set back behind tall trees surrounding a large green with wooden picnic tables. There was a WC with running water at its far end. I sat at one of the tables and ate the fruit I had found. It was great, actually sitting at a table eating for a change, with something wide and flat for my bum. I cooled down from today's journey and enjoyed the lovely apples and some bananas, which I saved until last. Crazy French kids from nearby houses chased each other around this green as I sized up this bench as my bed, but got put off by the numerous ants roaming across it. Also, as it began spitting with rain and the wind grew chilly and gusty, I would need a hidey-hole for tonight. There was nothing on the southbound side of this road. The houses and a few more buildings set back behind the trees around me might be hiding something. I could see a road going behind the nearby houses. I got up and back on the bike, and slowly rode around the houses to see if there was anything. I found an abandoned repair garage with a few old Citroen and Renault cars parked around, most of which were partially submerged in sun-baked long dry grass. There was a field behind this garage, with a house. The houses had conifers hiding me from their view and there was no one around. There was an old Renault Traffic camper van in the deep grass so I made my way towards it and checked the doors. The driver's door was open, and this was a bonus. I dumped the bike in the thick deep grass, took my bag inside the van with me, and decided to kip across the seats. Hang on, what am I doing? This is a camper van. I clambered over the knackered engine and transmission, which a mechanic had removed then dumped on the floor space behind the front seats, and plonked myself in the corner seats at the back. There was even an old white duvet. Great! I was out of the cold and with a blanket as the windows received the diagonally-spitting rain. I even had curtains to draw. I was now out of sight, and out of the rain and the draught for the night. I got comfy, with my feet resting on my 1600 cc bed partner. This was my first out-of-the-wind sleep since that little alcove on the corner of the old shop near Barcelona, apart from in David Mussecca's flat.

Chapter Eighteen

Echoes from Past Riders

5th May 2007 Angers to Le Mans, to Alençon – 105 Kilometres

I slept reasonably well that night. I even woke late: at 8.30 a.m. according to the radio display. This made a change from 7.45 for most of the last twenty or so days. I loaded up and pulled the bike from the deep grass. Refreshed from a longish kip, I went for it along the straight tree-lined road with flat landscape occasionally broken up by a copse of trees here and there, or very slight hills across vast areas, with a huge sky above. I thought about the lack of shelter in the Second World War for troops to fight their battles in this country: it seemed miles of flatness up north. Occasionally there would be monuments to the French Resistance, many times with a Sherman tank in stone to credit the help from the Americans, but never anything to credit the British. I thought this was maybe due to historical or political reasons.

The French, on the whole, seemed to be a conservative, civilised, tidy, well-dressed bunch. The townies and city dwellers mostly always looked tidy and well-dressed, cool and polite. I assumed that this conservatism was the reason for their choice of president, who was elected a few days later, albeit with a less than a five-per-cent majority. This choice of president didn't seem to sit well with the young student from Limoges I had met further up north, or David from Carcassonne, and the Moroccans I was later to meet. But the young who had drawn Hitler moustaches on the posters of the new president, from Narbonne to Le Mans and on, were obviously in the minority.

The road to Le Mans – the N-323 – was, apart from small neat villages, almost dead straight with very gradual rises. The wind slowed my effort down dramatically except when I rode in the lee of the occasional copse of trees, which would give my legs and sore feet a little rest from the effort. The long sections had many kilometres of poplar trees lining the roadside, which helped stem the wind and caused intermittent blasts of sun, wind, lull, shade, sun, wind, lull, and shade, which was mesmerising sometimes. The scenery didn't change much for most of the day.

I reached a little town called La Fleche and desperately needed a rest. This was a very smart French town next to a river. I couldn't find any supermarkets; it had a distinctly 'posh' feel to it with traditional specialist shops and the look of a small, well-off community. I found a tourist office, where I looked at a map, being confused by my own map. As I studied the tourist office map a lady asked me first in French then in English if I needed any help. I told her where I had come from and where I was headed. This started a conversation which inevitably led to her wondering how I ate. She then told me I could obtain some food vouchers from the town hall, and directed me towards it. The town hall was near the river in a tidy modern building, part of which was built across water adjoining the river. I was introduced to a lovely receptionist who had been phoned by the lady in the tourist office. She arranged to provide me with some food to take. I was so grateful at this point of a happy, chance find. Whilst the lady dispatched a colleague to seek out these vouchers I chatted with the receptionist about the journey and where I was from. We even talked about our kids as if everything was OK and I was equally happy with my life and looking forward to seeing them again soon. Her son supported Lyon and I told her my girls are Liverpool supporters. I was talking absolute shite. I don't know why I did this. It was as if I wanted to fit in and find common ground with a fellow parent. About the only thing true was I had children; the rest was empty conversation. I only thought about this whilst waiting outside the main doors, and picked two cigarette stubs out of a sandbox, as I waited for her colleague to return. I smoked one and then the other as smart people passed me on their way through the doors to the reception and gave me their smiles, together with a *bonjour*, which made me feel happy. To be greeted by polite people is a class thing and I have so much respect for people who do this. It doesn't cost anything and goes a long way. It certainly did for me on that day.

The lady's colleague returned with a small carrier bag, which was given to me after the receptionist had inspected it. I thanked the ladies for their efforts and told them I wouldn't forget. I made my way back towards the road through town, and stopped next to the tourist office. There was a paved area which ran for about two hundred metres, with squares of neatly tilled beds with roses and flowers every five metres or so. There was a large area of calm water, of which I didn't take enough notice to tell if it was part of a river or just an ornamental large long pond. I was too excited, wanting to find what was in the bag. I sat on a black metal bench, parked the bike next to it, got the radio out, and took out the contents of the bag. I was determined to enjoy this 'engineered' windfall. I pulled out a litre of fresh milk in a plastic bottle and savoured creamy gulps. It was fresh, *fresh*! It was beautiful: the best milk I had ever tasted – as good as that UHT milk I had found in that bin in Tarifa near Gibraltar after trekking from Puerto in southern Spain in the heat. It quenched my thirst and my hunger, me being mentally aware it was like a liquid food. Next, there was a tin of a kind of solid moist food with barley, rice and vegetables minced up – a kind of heavy, cold, solidified soup. I was eager to get at it and scrambled around my bag until I found something suitable to open it with, eventually using my little wooden-handled knife I had found during a long climb on the *autovia* just outside Sevilla. This reminded me of an incredible sight I had seen after bending down and picking up the knife off the road: the heliostat. This contributed to Sevilla's massive demand for electricity by using a system of hundreds of gigantic mirrors, all reflecting the abundant sun's rays onto one collector. From miles away, it looked like a ten-mile-wide spider's web of thick gossamer around a central hub. I couldn't tell whether it was solid or not; it was at least ten kilometres away, down on a plain. It looked incredible and I thought about what it might be. I didn't find out until years later. That moment of reminiscing caused me to almost cut myself stabbing the lid of the can to open it.

I let my mind wander randomly back along the journey as I tucked into duck pate. Only in France would a tramp blag this luxury. I spread it on the best-tasting fresh French stick I had ever eaten, and only spoilt my class lunch by tipping all four sachets of Nescafe straight down my caffeine-starved neck, for a hit of stimulation on the rest of the journey to Le Mans. I was going to keep a sachet of powdered soup, the last item in the bag. I could mix it with some water later on. But I then reasoned that I am bound to find food in Le

Mans and would need the calories for fuel for now, so I finished the meal with this powder, which I thickly mixed with water in its sachet, and washed it down with a drink from my bottle of water. I now had energy, which lifted my mood, and I was ready to go. I had a long stump to smoke as I sat, completely fulfilled, in pleasant, well-to-do surroundings, feeling like some kind of vagabond 'king' with a full gut. Surely a tramp with a full gut in the sunshine has achieved Nirvana!

I was soon back on the tree-lined straights, with a slight side wind blowing at me between the poplar trunks, then long stretches of fields, then more trees along this dead straight road. The food I had consumed was being broken down inside of me and giving me plenty of onward progress, like coal in a steam train. The better I ate, the more miles I covered and faster, instead of plodding for hours and using fat reserves, like I had done for the greatest part of this journey. I had a sweat on my forehead and constant energy, or so it felt like, to get across the distant rises. I was at my happiest going somewhere in the sun; not cold, not hungry, and not unhappy or stressed, but just going somewhere, with endorphins giving me a natural high, which overcame any physical pain – almost.

Getting nearer to the city, the traffic became more manic, with each passing group of cars being sucked faster and faster, like water going over the edge of a waterfall, as though the drivers were being reminded of their urgent appointments and destinations. Rush, rush, as they flew by. The roadside homes and small businesses were becoming more frequent and built up. The nearer to Le Mans I got the further away it seemed. I even rode on part of the motorway without hassle from the gendarmes. I got nearer to the centre, past huge retail parks, spaced out and bearing no resemblance to the British retail parks, which looked claustrophobic in comparison. The French retail parks had only occasional brand names bearing any similarity to the ones back in the UK.

Nearer to the centre, Le Mans became more historical; with stone castle walls. I stopped next to the river, north of the main city, and found a couple of benches in the sunshine, where I needed to check out my stinging feet after that fast push from La Fleche. They had a new pain, which hurt far worse than the 'standard' pain, not helped by the fresh 'fuel' that had just punished them along the last fifty kilometres. I collapsed on one of these benches in the strong warm sun and removed my boots, letting the air cool the ferocious stinging of blisters and bright red areas of skin with blood trying to get to the surface. I thought I could almost see my pulse through these areas of red. I was going nowhere for an hour or so: it was just too painful, my right foot being by far the worst. I tried to stand and put weight on it… OUCH!! No way! It was only a few hours of riding but my appetite had already returned as I thought about that food I was given and then thought I could eat it all again now, this minute. The drain of calories by my muscles was never-ending and my scruffy and worn black jeans were slack around the waist where previously they were slightly tight. I inspected my belly and it was devoid of any extra flesh, most of it eaten away by work in Portugal combined with good balanced meals with the total absence of the fatty diet and snacks; the rest eaten away by the past two and a half thousand kilometres of distance, effort and time. I would have loved to have a well-fed belly again, like the people walking along the path next to this city's stone walls. They looked smart and well-fed, many hand in hand, strolling along the grass which separates the Sarthe River from the centre of old Le Mans. I was on the solitary bench next to the Pont Voltaire, the large bridge I would be shortly going over. I didn't fancy venturing up the hill on my right into old Le Mans, only because it was too steep to spare the effort. I sat here and people-watched for about an hour, before noticing the sun had started to drop in the sky a little. It was time to move. I put my boots back on painfully and plodded very slowly across the bridge, looking for signs to Alençon, the next place I had just seen on the second dog-eared map. I was now right up north in France, not less than a couple of hundred miles from le Havre, and wondered if my feet would get me there or whether I would be lying at the roadside with burst veins on the soles of my feet.

I had to stop on the road across the bridge as traffic impeded my progress. As I dismounted in agony, limping on both feet as I crossed the road to the far side of the river, people overtook me as they sauntered by. I moved at convalescence speed. Getting back on the bike, I very slowly rode up the straight and narrowing street looking slightly similar to the street in a similar position out of Limoges on that ice-cold morning, the buildings full of history and Gallic style. Being aware of the burning pain reminded me that I had done my 'score' for today. As I crested a slight hill, where the streets got narrower and more downhill, I came to a junction where the road I was on entered the next road out of the city at a forked angle, with a busy little newsagents on my right at its end. Outside, with her back against the front of the newsagents, was a young hippy-looking girl of about twenty or so, with braids in her hair and wearing cami-trousers, her knees up in front of her, with her arms between them, looking carefree as she smoked a rollie. Next to her, she had a can of cider or beer.

"Excusez moi, Mademoiselle," I started, and then with difficulty saying 'can I have', managed to obtain a roll-up off her as I explained I can only speak Portuguese and English.

The young girl explained in English that it was no problem as her boss was an Irish fella who ran a restaurant, so she spoke good English. As we chatted she told me her name was Evo, and offered me her can of cider, which I refused, and I necked some more water. She was waiting for her mobilet moped to be repaired nearby. She asked me where was I from and I said Pays de Galles without pronouncing the 's', just as a French person wouldn't, and told her my usual story. I thanked her for my cigarette again and again, and she must have realised how much I was enjoying this occasional pleasure. Evo got up, went inside the shop and returned with half an ounce of tobacco with a box of matches and some papers.

"Merci beaucoup, Evo!" I said thanking her for her spontaneous kindness with the gratefulness only another smoker smitten with this addiction to nicotine would be able to show. Evo was moving to the Cote du Rhone with her fella and gave me her phone number in case I ran into trouble. I hoped I didn't run into any more trouble than I already had done, but didn't explain this. I got up from my kerbside seat and bid Evo farewell and good luck for the future, telling her that all favours are returned in life. Evo was cool, seemingly without a care in the world. She said, "See you, Shortie." This reminded me that I had a name, and made me feel good.

I made my way out of the city along a busy dual carriageway with retail parks mixed with houses and large roadside buildings looking like they were built in the past forty years and well used. I made my way over to the middle of the road as the carriageway stopped at a junction. As I rode across the junction to explore a retail park area with a supermarket, I heard a croaky 'beep beep'. It was Evo winding her way through the traffic on her moped, with her helmet not actually on her head but perched on top of it, with her braided long locks blowing behind her as she waved. What a cool character!

I scavenged around this retail park but the supermarket bins had been emptied for the day or weekend, though I did find some things I needed in a skip next to a clothing supermarket. There was a woollen yellow-and-turquoise striped jumper, clean and perfect, together with a pair of stonewashed black jeans which looked roughly my size. These were 'keepers' and I stuffed 'em into my bag. On my way across the road and up the carriageway I stopped to fill my water bottle at a fuel station, and then decided to try my 'new' clothes on. I went around to the side of the building, only because I had no 'drawers' on under my black worn-out jeans. The old pair had no crotch or arse in them, being completely worn away through saddle chafing. The new jeans fitted perfectly, if a little tight. I would have these for a year or so. The jumper was clean and warm so I rolled up the sleeves and put my bomber jacket back on. I stopped at a McDonald's just as the motorways and main roads left the city, and found three bags of cold fries with half a burger. It was about six or seven o'clock by now. The sun was in retreat and I had made a very slow journey across Le Mans, due to my feet mainly. Stopping just short of the main route into the countryside, I tried to figure out a route using no large roads. Doubting my ability to do the distance tonight, I looked back towards the city, where there would be food and some shelter for tonight. Curiosity got the better of me and I went a little further until I sat next to a roundabout. There was nothing but fields alongside the N-138 to Alençon disappearing off into the early-evening sunset. A sign said forty-five kilometres. I sat on the kerbside and let my feelings guide me to a decision.

My head said, "It will be dark soon and there is nothing but fields. It's getting a little colder and there is no shelter. You have binned most of your warm stuff and seventy-odd kilometres is enough for those wrecked feet today!"

I then rolled a cig and asked what I felt I wanted to do.

My heart said, "It's forty-five kilometres, twenty-eight miles – not that far. You will be further up the road and there might be food there. The arse is protesting but ain't going to be much worse. The feet have reached their peak of pain, I hope. Let's try the feet in a different position on the pedals."

I got astride the bike and placed my left foot with the arch right on the pedal. It didn't feel that bad, so I rode a little and did the same with the right. That hurt more but was just about bearable so I went for it, plodding on slowly, using the insteps of my feet, which made a smaller circle as I pedalled and the jeans I had found rubbed my thighs a bit, but I reckoned that in about two hours and a bit I could make it to Alençon.

The sun was fading away to my left, with a beautiful sunset in progress, a huge sky ahead and miles of straight road peaking and dipping. With the first frost-damaged rough tarmac I had encountered since Spain: not worn rough but cracked and uneven, with pebbles that were enough to give my bum and feet grief by now no matter how small the pebbles were.

I had not quite covered twenty kilometres about an hour later. Sweating a little by now, I could feel the conditions cool on my face as steep valleys slowed me further. Another hour and according to the signs I had only added another twelve more kilometres and still had twenty-two to go. The light was now fading fast into a horizon which, despite my pain and tiredness, couldn't have been more breathtaking if it was painted by a classical artist. The road seemed to be on a kind of plateau with deep narrow valleys, running across my path every few kilometres or so. I thought I could see the channel by now, it was that elevated and flat, but this was just wishful thinking. There were miles of this agricultural land, looking like fields of shining gold, off to the west. As I rode on I passed through a sleepy backwater village twinned with a similar English village with a 'marsh' in the title, after which the road climbed steeply up out onto another plateau, where I stopped to look at the last of the sun going down over the west horizon. I was next to a lay-by with a bin. The chilly night air and all-round pain of a body of forty-three years and not properly nourished sent me on a little downer as I lost the sunlight, feeling as though I was failing today. But I had to get to Alençon, as though there was something I needed there. Sore enough for one day, I had reached Le Mans. That was seventy kilometres. Then add another twenty-five kilometres and I still had at least another twenty-plus to go. I thought that when I was in better nick I would have eaten up these miles but I was really beginning to regret my decision to leave Le Mans a few hours earlier as the cold sent shivers around my arthritic shoulder carrying an arm with the scars of nine separate bone breakages over a decade or so. My two outside fingers were numb with cold, to add to the arse ache and stinging foot and rumbles from my belly. I rolled a ciggie to take away the discomfort but sucked the smoke in that deep it made me feel a little sick.

I went on, losing more light after having a crafty prayer asking for the strength to get to Alençon, and food if I did. I free-wheeled the bike down another steep valley and then rode it almost to the top of the next crest – more flat area. The wind was slightly into me as I passed alongside a large maize field on my right, the road still straight ahead, rising slightly through a tiny hamlet with a hill over to the east, with a copse of trees upon it. There was a small rock or a monument or something at the edge of the road where it met the field. I couldn't afford to pay it much attention in the fading cold light until I was almost past it, as I was trying to keep the momentum to crest the rise up ahead. Then something caught my eye on that strange upright rock standing out on this flat desolateness of field and road. I'm sure I saw a picture of a bike or bikes as I passed it. It made me stop and I turned around to look at what this upright piece of granite had to say to me. The monument was about three feet tall and roughly diamond shaped, and on the polished front was engraved the picture of three race bike riders who had been killed on this spot on their racing bikes a few years back. This was a monument to them. Just then the cold stillness had meaning. The most strange feeling came over me, together with a strange breeze from behind me which disappeared eastwards over the maize field, as though an invisible shape like a giant hand had flattened the top five or six inches of the maize. This then gradually petered out as quickly as it had begun, leaving the field about fifty or sixty metres away until everything was as it was a few seconds ago – cold, calm, perfectly still and totally silent. All the hairs on the back of my neck moved. All the hairs on my body moved. A strange but warm feeling came over me in this lonely spot, which I felt a total affinity with. These lads' lives had come to an end whilst they were striving to meet their goal. They were Tour riders – a small peloton. It lifted my spirits and made me feel warm all over, empathetic – the most strange sensation. This urged me on.

I could have been overwhelmed by the pain I was feeling, or it could have been coincidence with the wind, or I was looking for some kind of sign, but I wasn't. It was a truly warming feeling I felt here, which I wouldn't have been in touch with or maybe wouldn't have wanted to understand a year earlier. I was too much of a 'nuts and bolts arsehole' to even acknowledge anything other than my own small, misinformed opinion on anything I couldn't understand. But this had just happened: very memorable. I went on up the rise after doffing my cap to the monument, and couldn't stop thinking of those riders as I crested the shallow long rise towards the little hamlet.

Almost at the top of the crest there were a few houses along its length, together with another monument of a Sherman tank in stone. It had writing in French and in English explaining how a battle had been fought here near the end of the Second World War and the French-named Sherman tanks had successfully taken out German artillery hidden in the trees nearby, though not before the Germans had taken out a few tanks first. This monument told of the day when this little hamlet was liberated. Later I tried to find a record of this in books and various sources, with no success. I think the hamlet may be called Fye – between Beaumont and Alençon – but I can't find it on a map. It is one of the hundreds of places I hope to return to one day.

Having crested the rise, there were a few more up ahead. It was now dark and I felt as if I was covering a lot of distance. This was just the cold and quiet dark giving me that impression. The road was at one point like a matt black belt crossing the valleys and fields. They weren't going to stop me now. I upped the pace, and felt warm against the cold of this night, as though I was being helped to rotate the wheels easier. The hills and the soreness didn't seem to matter now I was getting to Alençon and hopefully finding some much-needed food tonight. I could see distant lights, which I presumed were of the town I wanted to reach. They looked five or six kilometres away. Some mental arithmetic said about seven kilometres or so. No matter – I pushed on as though this was the last couple of miles of the whole journey. By now, it was black and a little cloud was blocking the moonlight. There were no stars and no lights on this bike or on the road. The occasional vehicle would light the way for a few seconds but, being another weekend, this was only very occasionally. Not being able to distinguish the roadside dirt and stones from the clean tarmac, I would now and again hit lumps and bumps whilst pedalling on and on. It felt really late and I could have stopped at a couple of villages in the dips and called it a day, but no – I had to get to Alençon. After what seemed like an eternity, the lights on the outskirts could be seen about five kilometres away and I'm sure I could see that familiar square yellow of a Lidl signpost amongst the faraway lights, or was it more wishful thinking? Either way, it spurred me on. That distant yellow blob would be my food if I was right. Another downhill was followed by a long slow uphill, at least a kilometre long, to where the lights were. I wobbled up this dark hill, pushing myself to crest the rise and find out if that sign was a Lidl… Yes, it was! I hoped my crafty prayer had worked. I badly need food and rest. Cresting that last hill was harder than usual; I put this down to mega tired legs. I didn't care now my prayers had been answered. The first place on the right was a Lidl with full bins behind the back, which I headed straight for. It even had a security light to help. I found two skips ready for the binmen, packed with oranges still in their nets; bananas, nearly all perfect; two six-packs of chocolate mousse with ten complete portions; a Dolmio jar; biscuits; cheese; crisps; and some apple juice. The waste of France was my gold, and after a couple of days of sparse eating and a lot of painful miles, sights like this caused my legs to buckle and give thanks.

There was a pile of blue plastic sheeting in one bin, which I used to nestle between the bins on a clean concrete floor out of the slight but cutting wind. I set out my thin foam 'bed' and had my 'feast' placed on a piece of cardboard, whilst lying with the plastic on top of the thin red blanket which not quite covered my boots. All I had to do until I finished this supper was to keep activating the motion-sensor bedside lamp. I checked out the time; it had just gone 10.00 p.m. I went to bed completely full of food. What a great feeling after struggling for miles with unbelievably sore feet. That last forty-five kilometres from Le Mans *really* hurt, but after getting that strange warmth and strength from the place where the riders' monument was, I knew I would be OK, like there was some invisible impulse egging me on through the pain.

The next day I was up at 7.45 – back to normal. It was very cold. I had pulled the plastic over my entire body the night before and this crunched with frost and pieces of ice as I threw it back and rose from the foam and concrete. After a call of nature I found my rear tyre flat: that must have happened in the dark, running into the roadside debris. My fingers froze as I stripped the tyre off and removed a metal prick. This explained why that last hill was so difficult to climb. I haven't totalled the punctures on this journey – sometimes I had more than three a day – but it must have been somewhere between twenty and less than forty. This one was the coldest to repair.

Chapter Nineteen

Long Way Round to Le Havre, the End of Freedom

and the Greatest Memories

6th May 2007 Alençon to Lisieux – 119 Kilometres

I crossed quiet and deserted Alençon and found the road towards Lisieux – the D-438 – and even found another supermarket on the edge of town, which provided me with two packets of processed cheese and some good bananas for fuel. The roads were straight and mostly flat, heading north-easterly, with tree-lined fields, fields and more fields a little smaller than those of the previous three days. The scenery became more like back in the UK. The weather was overcast and windy with occasional drizzle, but it became brighter every hour. Maybe the wind was blowing the greyness away, giving me a last reminder of the sun, which lifted the mood for my last hundred or so kilometres to Le Havre, not a day away now. Every now and again, I would see a sign for Le Havre, which gave me mixed feelings of elation at having completed a journey I had never done or considered at any other time in my life. I wasn't a cyclist before, apart from on muddy tracks, and I had not been on any great distance before. To me this journey, with its discomfort and pain, feelings, huge skies and awesome sunsets and sights, people and places, was the most beautiful thing I had ever done, which contrasted to what I would have to do when I reached Portsmouth. Although the thought of being clean and fed was a big draw and would certainly become a novelty I would be grateful for, together with warmth at night. I had missed these things for a long time, it seemed.

I had great feeling of accomplishment now I had managed the three thousand kilometres on a succession of heaps, sleeping rough and eating rougher; but keeping going every day I had transport, sometimes doing well over a hundred miles in a day, and sometimes as little as forty or so. I think I averaged about a hundred and thirty kilometres most days, not including the riding around the majority of places on the search for supermarket bins. That was hitting the ninety-mile-per-day barrier. For twenty-two days I was riding, not including a couple of days stuck roughing it in one Spanish city near to the border with Portugal after wrecking another bike. So, three thousand kilometres divided by twenty-two is just over a hundred and thirty-six kilometres. With no proper food, money, comforts or shelter. And most of the journey done on a bike that had only two selectable gears, half a back brake, and an orange squeaky chain, a seat rock hard because age had stripped it of its padding, and a pile of punctures with no tools, just my fingers or the odd borrowed spanner here and there. The journey did wonders for my brain, and it all began on a whim.

It also definitely made me realise exactly how little I need to actually exist, and how ordinary little things like food, warmth and health are so taken for granted. How distant I wanted to be from my previous self. It also put the past in perspective. I would no longer hold on to the past: it was dead and gone. I would deal with what's up ahead and move on. I will be doing more biking in the future even though I had lost almost two stone on this journey through an almost total lack of protein. But physically I felt great – just fatigued and obviously sore where feet and bum met the bike. This fitness would soon pay me dividends. And my body would recover.

I got off the D-438 and found a road heading north-west cross-country on the D-819 in order to avoid a detour and about twenty kilometres, which needlessly arced away from Lisieux. I had a water break after midday on the outskirts of Orbec: a small quaint town with retired folk wandering around looking at period buildings and tiny shops. I tried to figure out which direction to take, before finding another signpost to Le Havre almost next to me. I was now on the D-519, heading straight for the city on 'feel-good' straights, with sunshine and a distinct sea freshness in the air. In my mind, the coast was just over the horizon, but it wasn't. The faster I tried to ride, the further the coast seemed to be away from me, but I was enjoying this journey totally now. The usual pains didn't matter now because of where I was and how far I had come, almost on an impulsive whim, five hundred hours ago. I was now loving every mile of sun, wind and pedalling. I tried to fix in my head the outdoor sights, the sky, the roads and the beauty of being free. I would keep these inside my head for the future and then live from day to day until I could live again, instead of being tied to a 'five year plan' as I had been in the past. This had robbed me of my previous freedoms and jailed me with the responsibility of paying a four-grand diesel bill. I had dozens of bills for shit which I never saw the benefit of, and being a convenient 'man' who could be replaced in a weekend by people who really didn't give a toss about sacrificed years of graft and going without holidays for a decade.

I had forgotten the original reason I followed my ambitions, and had dragged out a better living than a job gave me. The hard-won thousands of pounds each month were sucked away faster and wasted; without a thought about giving any to someone who would really need it. I had become a wastrel, blowing what I had left on alcohol, drugs and absolute shite because I lost the reasons why I had wanted to earn it: a family who was proud of me.

My dad, 'Shortie' Senior, turned up after twenty-two years, only wanting my skills and abilities to further his ambitions and please his family, who were strangers to me. He still had a great work ethic, but he seemed torn and shallow. We parted company indefinitely for the second time after a windswept dock road confrontation over money and business priorities, late in 2006. My choice this time. He didn't look too happy about it.

My mam had never been close since I was eleven. She reminded me of the boxer's mother in the film *Million Dollar Baby*. The few conversations I had with her revolved around how disappointing I was thirty years ago, about the time when my biological father ran off with a neighbour.

The various mams I had three daughters and one son with were not prepared to stick it out with a tired and grouchy arsehole and before I had made any sort of decent money I lost 'em one after another over the past fifteen years, multitudes of jobs and businesses, and drinking.

My Nain and Taid were dead. The genuine people were gone. There was nobody for me to gain any credit or recognition from, so why carry on thrashing myself? Getting rid of one business also got rid of the burden of people fighting over how to spend the money I earned. This instantly lost me access to two more reasons – my youngest daughters. What else does one do? I got pissed and stoned, and lost my desire to get on in life.

This journey took me right back to basics, away from the nonsense of living a life with loads of money but no fulfilment whatsoever. It helped me to appreciate the absolute basics: food, rest and shelter. The sights, sounds and people I met are irreplaceable and priceless. I can visit my friends in Portugal again one day and they will be happy to see me for me, and not for what I can buy them, because we were all in the same boat – skint.

This journey is not to advise serious touring cyclists, unless they want to do a trip the same length as the Tour de France over almost the same amount of days riding (although in my case a lot slower), with no tools, medical equipment or decent food. So this doesn't compete as a 'real' cycling adventure book, because it isn't meant to do. It's also not a religious book, despite how I learned to pray in desperate times along the route, 'cos I had no other way, and specific things I asked for I got.

Some of the things I found just after a crafty prayer would make me look around to see if someone was watching me, there were that many moments a greater unknown force seemed to be there when I needed it most. This something we all think about sometimes in our lives, and this intangible thing the world has various names for wouldn't be obsessed with ceremony and hierarchy and bullshit. The strange inexplicable warm feelings I found after those long wet days in constant rain, feeling cold and hungry. With that melody echoing through my head, that most strange warm feeling I found on that cold night after being compelled to stop next to that riders' monument, which stayed with me until I reached that bin full of food, might seem inconsequential, but to me these happenings, and many others, changed my values about life. There were hundreds of 'you had to be there' moments which I purposely think about now if I feel myself forgetting where 'normal' life had got me, and sometimes feel myself being sucked into again like a kid with no one to tell him "that's wrong!" I look for different things now. I've lost the desire to buy things I 'think' I need, apart from a bike to re-ride that journey, and also to replace the three I have had nicked since. Karma?

I eventually got into Lisieux about five o'clock, I think, with the tiredness in my legs from the trip from the night's riding yesterday catching up with me. I found the centre of this smart French city and sat in front of a large square in front of a huge cathedral-type place, resting my legs and watching people for a while. No one seemed in a hurry, and the people were dressed smartly in their clothes, some hand in hand – young dudes and 'dudesses' hanging around this square. The people here were rich looking, and there weren't many poor people around. I went to the window of a nearby cake shop and lusted at the chocolate and cream cakes, thinking out loud, "One day!" and being stared at by a few people passing by.

Time to find somewhere to sleep. I reckoned I could easily get a good sleep early tonight, but not on this empty stomach. If I was to find anywhere to sleep I would find it en route to Le Havre. As I found the route from Lisieux to Le Havre I was on the lookout for food. It was not quite a hundred kilometres from Alençon to Lisieux and I had consumed those calories from last night by now. I was desperate for energy from anything so the bin-finder ariel was on again. I came across a closed cake shop with a convenient alleyway around the back. It was a sort of bakery as well and the two bins outside which I rifled through, pulling out empty paper flour sacks, to reveal two huge glazed latticed tarts with apricots and half a dozen or so squashed choux pastry cakes, all of which went down my throat without touching the sides, until I felt sick. I put the rubbish back inside the bin and wiped my sticky hands; and then I was back on the wide street out from the city.

Fortified by a rush of sugar, I decided I would ride on until my batteries died again. This boost took me along the D-579 for another twenty kilometres, where I found the road going steeply up between trees out of a maze of flyovers from the main motorway towards Hornfleur. I think the place was called Blangy-le-Chau. Not having the energy to ride any further up the steep hill, I stopped next to a little row of houses on the right and found a concrete ledge joined to a small, old shop or chapel-type building. I unloaded my roll of grotty foam and found the packets of cheese I had forgotten about from the bin outside Alençon, and a few bananas. I was worn out again – my favourite feeling. I sat and thought about the day for a while as the sunset and darkness came. This place was lit by the orange sodium lights lining the road going up towards the dark tree-lined hill as I positioned myself and lay almost flat on the narrow ledge, thinking how I would actually be in Le Havre tomorrow at the end of this journey. Then I drifted off, pulling the grubby red blanket over my now sideways-facing body, dead to the world. A couple of hours later I was disturbed by lights, engines and voices of people talking in a concerned tone just in front of where I was sleeping. I was far too tired to open my eyes and get into a conversation explaining why I was here, and didn't care what they thought or did. I just knew that if I slept they would eventually go, and they did. It was silent once again.

Up at 7.45, I slowly loaded the bike up. Instead of getting straight on the bike as per normal, I took five minutes to get my head around the impending hill and the fact that I would be in Le Havre by the end of the day. The early-morning sun was warming me as I leaned against the concrete ledge with one foot balancing the bike upright, and looked up the hill, trying to make it smaller in my brain.

"*Bonjour*," came a lady's voice. She came from one of the houses next to the little ledge. She stood in front of me, and offered me a cup of coffee in her French tone, to which I replied, "*Merci beaucoup, Madame*" then proceeded to explain to her I only spoke Portuguese and a little Spanish and needed to learn more French. She could speak a little of both Spanish and Portuguese and some English: enough to ask me where I was going and to understand where I had been. As we limped through an international conversation, I told her this was my first decent hot cup of coffee since Gibraltar, in that Methodist chapel, on that Sunday night, on the 16th, I think.

"*Portugal com cyleta?*" she enquired, wide-eyed.

"*Si*," I proudly replied instead of *Oui*. I then went into a trance for a split second, as though someone else saying it gave some validation to where I had been a few weeks ago. It seemed as though I was in a different year now, not just in a different country.

We chatted for a short time and then she told me she must be off to work, the French word for work sounding very similar to the Portuguese word for work: *travail/trabalho*. This was a great start to my final day and the coffee gave me a tremendous burst of caffeine. I waved *au revoir* to the blonde middle-aged lady, who was still in her dressing gown. I was so grateful too, and attacked that hill. It was steep but no bother now, even though it felt about five kilometres up to the top.

Eventually finding the D-144 road through farming country, with no wind against me, I ignored the spitting rain towards Hornfleur. Bends and long straights eventually gave way to downhills with the smell of the sea. I eventually glimpsed the channel: can't be far now. But it was still a little further than I thought. Eventually riding along a dual carriageway to the Pont de Normandie, the bridge twelve hundred metres over the estuary to Le Havre, I studied the map and couldn't see a way over for bikes. There was a path over both ways but it wasn't very clear to me at the time. I wish I had found it because the rest of this journey was hard work. On the east side of the roundabout under the bridge road, I was studying the last piece of my France map, now as dog-eared as the Spanish map. A fella on a British-registered BMW K100 motorcycle was stopped at the side of the road just further on. I asked him if I could inspect his map, which was no better detailed than mine was. I small talked with him for a bit and asked him for any spare change he had got, but he couldn't find any. I wanted to celebrate with a sit-down brew when finally reaching Le Havre. No bother, I bade him farewell and rode on up to a junction next to a corner, about a kilometre away, where the D-180 bends south, and I was looking for this little road called the D-312. The fella on the BMW pulled up next to me, telling me I had rode along that straight quick enough! He then handed me about five Euros in change. Cheers, Pal! He rode off and I realised there was a strong wind following me, coming straight off the sea over the nearby marshes. That would be fun when I got across to the other side. On the map, I had to ride about fifteen kilometres or so to Tancarville, where there was a slightly smaller bridge with probable access for me and no charge, I hoped. The road twisted and turned along the estuary marshes, running roughly parallel with the river. I made this distance quite fast, having the wind with me. It ran along the mudflats through a small village. A change of direction through some trees, then around some cliffs and a straight, and I was up to the second bridge – an old steel affair. I made my way onto it. This was an experience! I realised just how strong that wind was coming directly from the sea, easterly. I tried to ride on the path across but it was impossible, no chance. After two or three attempts at riding across, I kept being blown into the metal railing by the prevailing easterly wind. Then passing artics would block the wind off and almost suck me onto the road, and then once each truck had passed by, I would be blown back into the metal railings by the naked windblast. Ouch! I dismounted and walked with the bike. This was almost as dangerous, the wind being that strong. I felt like a steel ball being bounced around a pinball machine!

My feet couldn't stand much walking, with terminal blisters. There was a ship passing under the bridge which looked to be battling the 'white horses' pounding its bow. I eventually got over the bridge through the toll area and climbed out onto the road, which wound through the top of Tancarville – the A-131. I kept on smaller roads as much as I could, away from the traffic. These roads took me through a small village, where I found some apples in a bin, before hitting straights, with the wind right at my face. This road ran parallel with the A-131 but through hamlets and shopping areas. I went along empty straights for about fifteen kilometres until I found the well-worn tarmac-and-concrete roads which entered Grande Le Havre, and then Le Havre. What a hard last few kilometres in second or, if I was lucky, third gear against a dead-on headwind which destroyed the last of my energy and my feet.

I was so glad to get to Le Havre but got completely lost with the shelter of flyovers and buildings which I rode around and around before eventually going down into the centre. I even ended up at Grande Le Havre hospital and went through its building site, where one part of it was being built on, so I could access a flyover going towards the centre. After an hour of getting lost I rode along the road, with railways and docks on my left, and hundreds of tall grey flats and houses on my right, getting the impression that this place was huge, but it would do after days of small towns and villages. I went in circles for almost an hour then. Being totally drenched by a downpour, I took shelter under a road bridge for a while and climbed to the top of its inside. I sat on a dry paving slab; thinking of sleeping there for the night, but after an hour of rest curiosity got the better of me so I headed along and then turned left down the main boulevard towards the centre and the dock area. I found LD Ferries and learned I needed fifteen Euros to get on board for the next sailing. Right: I would find the money somehow tomorrow. Until then it was back to town for a rest.

Rain pouring down by now, I splashed through the huge puddles and went back to look for some food first. I found some squashed cake in a skip behind a supermarket off the high street, then went to a café, bought some cheap baccy, plonked the bike outside and sat in a little shelter just outside the main part of the café with a well-earned coffee, and savoured today's progress. Moreover, I thought about how I would get that fare for tomorrow. I could sell the bike for the fare? I would then be in the UK the next day. I smiled to myself about the journey, then sat and watched the rain on the boulevard outside, not sure where I was going to sleep tonight.

Just then two lads came into the café, got their coffees and sat at a table to my right. One of them was very tall – way over six foot five – and was wearing a skullcap with blue-and-white patterns on it. His friend had a trendy leather jacket with a peaked cap, which didn't draw attention away from his protruding ears. He was the younger of the two. The tall fella was about thirtyish. I listened to them chatting for a while. Then a guy came in to greet them. I thought the three were Spanish at first after hearing words that sounded familiar to me. After their friend had gone I asked their names. The tall fella was called Abdul and the other fella Haji. Abdul spoke Portuguese with lots of Spanish thrown in and after a while I found he could speak pidgin English. The lads were tanned and looked slightly North African. I found out that they were Moroccan lads. Being in no need of the bike anymore, I asked them if they would give me some Euros for it, or if any of their friends would buy it. Haji's car – a BMW – had gone kaput, its cam belt having snapped, so he needed transport. I explained that I needed the money to get across the channel.

"Where have you been?" The conversation ran across Europe again. Abdul immediately offered to let me stay overnight at their flat until the morning, without me asking for their hospitality. I was prepared to rough it for one last night but Abdul insisted. After another coffee we headed back behind the main street to a side street. I had to ask them both to slow down because my feet, which I had forgotten about, couldn't stand the pace. I felt fit except for my arse and my feet. Eventually we went into a doorway behind some tenement-style older French building down a narrow alleyway and up some black-painted corkscrew, concrete stairs which seemed to go round for ever. Haji helped me carry the bike up three stories, which felt like thirty-three, and so dark that at one point we got out lighters to feel our way and to help Abdul find the lock to his front door, it was that black.

Inside, Abdul brewed up Moroccan tea, in a thin and tall brass pot, with a green plant left brewing in the water for some time. This drink he offered me was sweet and spearminty. They then offered me a meal and told me I could use their shower. Within forty minutes, I was clean and shaven, and I almost tripped over Abdul as he prayed on his prayer mat aloud. After he gave me some clean clothes I offered them the rest of my money but he refused.

They cooked and offered me 'lubiens' with rice and sauce. Lubiens? Lubiens? I asked him what they were but he said, "You will see; it's difficult to explain." Our conversations were in a mixture of three languages. Haji couldn't speak any English, Spanish or Portuguese. I limped with the French I had learned here and there. He was polite and smiled. Abdul explained that Haji was a good student and a hard worker as he gave me a plate of tasty rice with a spicy gravy-type thin sauce and large beans. Lubiens – le beans! This hot food was so satisfying. After dinner they asked if I wanted to smoke, and I answered yes as I got out my small pouch of tobacco and began rolling up.

"Estas aqui!" (This here!) Showing me a small block of resin.

Oh, that sort of smoke, as I crumbled the soft resin offering into my half-built cig and had a slight hesitation, with an attack of conscience. Since leaving behind that sort of thing on this cathartic trip, stubs off the highway and that cup of coffee the lady in Lisieux gave me were the only stimulants I had taken for a long time. I thought I had no need to do this but then reasoned that it may be a long time before I will have the chance to ease away pain for a while, after tomorrow. I smoked and chatted. Abdul picked up his guitar and played Led Zeppelin's 'Stairway to Heaven', 'Hey Joe' by Jimmy Hendrix and 'Hotel California' by the Eagles. In fact, any classic rock tune I could name, he could play. Even Haji strummed a few tunes. It seemed surreal lying on a comfortable soft chair, very low to the floor and glancing out across the roofs of Le Havre's tenements towards the sea, slightly stoned, listening to this well-played sound, totally relaxed, clean and painless. My back stopped aching and my feet stopped stinging. My outside fingers were still numb but comfortable. Then the lads gave me the guitar. All I could manage was a blues riff I always played when confronted with a guitar, playing with the guitar facing the opposite way around and upside down – thanks, Johnny Mac! It was too complicated to explain why it was the only way I could play, which puzzled them and made them both laugh. They invited me to come and meet some of their friends.

We went in an old red diesel Merc to a small place, where we sat in a brightly lit bar as Abdul was greeted by his friends. Abdul insisted on buying me a beer. We talked at length about the journey and how I had prayed for things which 'came' my way, and for health to get home and sort things out. He told me he found work easily enough in construction and how he always gave thanks for all the things he had. We both agreed that prayers work. He had been in plenty of difficult situations in countries far from home. It was quite a deep conversation.

Back at the flat well after dark, I was provided with a mattress and blankets, which were overkill for this night's comfort. Abdul, it turned out, was a national high jumper for Morocco in his twenties, having jumped one metre and ninety centimetres on a regular basis. That's over six feet! But being such a skint country, the Olympic budget was almost non-existent at the time so he never got to realise his dream of competing on the world stage.

Next morning they fed me and I gave them the bike although later on I felt it was misplaced payment: it wasn't mine to give. Abdul gave me some change. I thanked them for looking after me and promised to revisit them one day. I walked back to the docks into the terminal and waiting area, found a gaggle of people crowding the departure lounge, and remember standing in the middle of 'em all and shouting, "Any English, Irish, Scottish or Welsh here? I need another seven Euros to get home. Can anyone spare any loose change please?"

Within about a minute, I had my fare plus a few extra Euros. I shouted a loud thank you.

I asked the French lady, whom I bought my tickets off, if she had any Sellotape to fix my maps, with which she obliged. I then went upstairs to the waiting room with my ticket. There was a large group of French schoolkids being seen off by their mams and dads, and being organised by their teachers. Their mams kissed them goodbye or *au revoir*. I wondered and hoped that all of them never end up like I had done in their later years.

Everyone went through the check-in area with little fuss, until it was my turn. I was thoroughly searched by the port gendarmes, with suspicion because I had very little luggage apart from a little rucksack/bag Abdul had given me, a dog-eared map of France, and an even 'doggier'-eared one of Spain, with dates and writing all over them. I suppose this long-haired hippy type had to remove his boots and turn every item of clothing inside and out in case he was smuggling contraband out of France. What were they going to do? Lock me up for being in possession of long hair, blisters and non-conformity? I suppose it must have wound 'em all up, as I laughed to myself as I was getting dressed again. One of them even searched my bomber jacket twice.

Eventually I was let on the ship, last person of all. I leaned against the stern railings and watched Le Havre slowly disappear as I smoked a succession of rollies until the wind, out on the open sea drove me inside like it used to on the *Innisfree*, the *Innismor* and the *Ulysses*. When en route from Holyhead to Ireland for years of hard work in various truck garages – which killed off at least one of my common-law relationships. I made my way to the ship's café and ordered a cup of tea. Having lost two Euros somewhere, I struggled to find enough change to pay for this overpriced tiny cup of tea – welcome back to UK prices! A Scouse lady in her fifties offered to pay as she heard me enthusiasti-cally telling the bar lady it was my first cup of tea in nearly half a year. Cheers, Pet! Another bonus was that the serving lady was Portuguese, so after a chat I got another cup *por gratis*. A bit later, she was outside having a fag and I told her my story. She then told it to her mate who came to join us. This lady looked after the luxury seats at the front. We all chatted in Portuguese for five or six minutes. This proved to be another bonus. The lady beckoned me through to the front seats, which were expensive because they reclined flat in a comfy quiet area, with a marble bathroom to shower in. I kipped for a while in perfect peace and quiet, like my body was trying to catch up on months of deprivation. I also took a roll-up on the aft deck with a couple of bikers whilst watching the container ships go by in one of the world's busiest shipping lanes.

Returning to the comfy seat I had 'blagged' with Potuguese banter and tuning my tiny palito radio into Radio One's Scott Mills. Listening to 'Chappers', with their daft laid-back sense of humour mixed with the up-to-date sounds instead of the eighties crap music which the Brit stations play in the Algarve, as though they are trapped in the cheesiest decade of last century. I had to get my mall thinking over ready for what I must do, I had to give myself in to the dock authorities and get ready for the next chapter and ordeal. This crossing takes a little over six hours, with plenty of time to think, and it was almost dark by the time Portsmouth Harbour lights were drawing near. We drew in slowly past the lit-up warships and the lights of dockside pubs, where people were dressed in their weekend gear for what would be the bank holiday booze up. It seemed such a different world to the one I had lived in; and it would be a while before I ever did that sort of thing again. The thought of how much I used to drink made me feel queasy.

As the ship manoeuvred into port, I chatted with another Portuguese staff member for a while. He told me there were previously Italian staff on this ship but they were replaced with Portuguese staff because they are cheaper. It made me feel like his employers looked at him and his colleagues like some twat of a dog enthusiast would look at the separate merits of different breeds of dogs to choose one suitable to go with a new home or car. The fella also told me about Maddie McCann, the little girl who had gone missing from the Algarve five days previously.

As I travelled on the bus on the way to the port building, I talked with a French student backpacker from Limoges, who told me about how the French president had been elected with less than a five-per-cent majority, which had caused riots on the streets. One of his agendas was his strict immigration policy, which didn't sit well with anyone I spoke to considering his immigrant heritage. People like Abdul had voiced their worries about this. Racism and paranoia have no place in Europe or anywhere in the world today. It was about half nine or ten-ish as I queued up for the customs lady to inspect my passport and ask me if I had anything to declare.

"Yeah, a ride to the police station!" I answered as I handed my passport to her.

She asked me to stand next to one of the dock security fellas so I stood outside, rolling a last cig.

Two bemused-looking coppers arrived and couldn't believe I was in good spirits as one of the security ladies said, inappropriately, "Are you sure about this?" bending her head forward and widening her eyes as though she was talking to a schoolkid. So I glanced up to the ceiling as though pondering her question.

"Nah, I've changed my mind." As if I had a choice…! And there was a long sort of silence for a few seconds.

"Nah, I'm only joking!"

The two coppers actually laughed and so did the other staff.

Chapter Twenty

'Normal'...

What's Normal?

I guess this short book could be longer or more profound in the hands of a 'real' author or someone with proper writing skills. But it was copied off roughly-scribbled notes using a dog-eared map as a guide, and then written in block capitals by a truck mechanic. It's just a true story about a fella who went on a bike ride – long by my standards but nothing special by serious tourer standards. Many people do these distances for pleasure. Bins, benches and broken bikes was over almost the same distance as the Tour de France, in virtually the same timeframe but with a lot more saddle-sore hours per day to complete the same distances.

There are plenty of incidents I remember but cannot recall exactly where or when they happened... Like the *autovia* I rode on for about two hours, which was brand-new and unopened, and I never saw a soul on it. One hot afternoon somewhere in Murcia, I think, I was on the wrong side of mountains separating me from the coast. I don't recall getting off this *autovia*, only climbing up another embankment and across a shiny new Armco, across the central reservation, whilst workers about a kilometre away completed an on-ramp. There were plenty of incidents like that but nowhere I can pin 'em to.

I discovered things I had never taken the time to appreciate before; the things that are free to us like health, sunsets, a succulent fresh apple or a giant sweet orange. Smells, sunshine, warmth and water are all beautiful in my eyes.

I no longer want a new XR 600, a Ninja, a new £90,000 lorry and a house – been there, done that. Things like that are all childish ambitions. I do enjoy music with candlelight, and warmth outside four walls, which all soothe the pain of arthritis from the multiple broken bones around my frame, but if I never get these things, it doesn't matter. The most basic things made me very happy.

Apart from the map of Spain that I found in a bin in Huelva, a city near the bottom end of Spain and next to the border with Portugal, I had never looked at a map of Europe for any length of time, or realised the distance involved when I decided to ride to the French border. It was just a little map about twelve inches square. It could have been no bigger than Wales from north to south as far as I was concerned. So many people I have since had conversations with about this journey have said, "I've done that" or "I've been there" as though they know the distance doing fifteen miles an hour. This frustrates me because they just don't get the point. Modern conveniences get things done quicker and vehicles get us from place to place quickly but so much beauty and interest is then totally lost to us. Speed has desensitized us like kids become desensitized by the blood and gore in computer games.

The size of Scotland used to frighten me.

If I had known the total distance I rode was three times the length of the UK, I probably would have been a lot more intimidated by it. Especially after the first couple of hundred kilometres of hunger, bad weather and that night-mare after midnight in the Sevillan downpour on Friday the 12th, and then that 'mishap' the next day after dodgy bin food. But not long after then, I began to enjoy the struggles on a daily basis for food, covering the daily 'score' of city to city, and the achievement of not giving in to pain, heat, rain, hills and wind or the numerous punctures and problems, together with no cash. It became a challenge to survive. I could have easily made a phone call to one of my good friends and done it the easy way. Not a fucking chance! If I can't do this I'm letting me down forever.

I then found things and rewards which are just priceless to me now, which I can never properly put into words and no one else could see unless they did it for themselves, with no money, heaps of junk or any decent clothes; no sleeping bag, tent, food, phone, tools, medical equipment or credit cards. I doubt many but the hardiest souls could do it. If you think you're up to it then do it, and I would love to sit down with you afterwards and see if you have the same feelings as you did before the trip. It was in countries full of the conveniences everyone lives by today but at the time such conveniences seemed so far away from the bloke on the bike with only enough ability of the languages to limp around with. About the closest thing to being on a desert island – emotionally.

I wasn't going home either.

The adventure also helped me deal with plenty of demons and I began to understand why things were as they were. It let me see almost straight through people I had met, have met since, and people I have yet to meet. Like a 'Shallow Hal' sort of view.

I don't resent anyone; we do what we learn. Today's thinking – or lack of it – is producing a large, selfish, material-based society of people who won't be able to improvise or get on if hard times come. The consumer boom won't last forever. Along the way I spent many hours thinking of how I would rebuild my life after I eventually got it straightened out again; where I would live and work; what *things* I might buy with what I would earn… But those *things* just don't light me up like I had previously been programmed to allow them to do. Lads and girls I've met since show me with a swaggering pride their possessions, as though they are wanting to be liked for what they have; and I am not talking teenagers: these are fully grown men and women brainwashed by western modern culture. The Third World and people in poverty are of absolutely no consequence or consideration to us any more; we're all too busy, busy, and busy, wrapped up in our own lives.

I remember seeing an advert once, can't remember what it was for, but it was a cartoon which showed a foot 'strumming' the floor in the open air and humming to itself, fresh and free. Then its owner suddenly drags a sock over it and the foot begins a muffled complaint, trying to free itself, and becoming more frantic in the process. Then the sock-clad foot is bundled into a shoe, further muffling its complaints. The owner of the foot then walks off. That's what I feel like about routine now. I just don't want to conform, but then I don't think I ever could. I am jealous of the real heroes in life who struggle on but keep together a job supporting a family and partner through the financial and personal setbacks. They are the real people: the ordinary dad or mam having the guts to bring kids into the world and stay together, for better or worse. I failed at that many times over, with money and without. Whether I earned £150 per week for forty hours work or £11,000 in one month running two businesses, I failed as a real bloke, and after a time I realised I was no happier with money than without money. Money caused me headaches and surrounded me with 'keeping up appearances' people who had totally seen me coming, with my pockets full of spare cash and carefree, dope-smoking party head firmly fixed on and facing my arse like an ostrich trying to escape, not waving but drowning.

I just want to ride a bike the opposite way around to the original trip, back to the struggle and lack of comforts, and this time benefit someone along the way. It puts things into perspective for me. I would then appreciate maybe a warm bed and a shower after roughing it. If not, I'll wash my arse in the sea and kip on a bench or in a box, and survive.

Selfish is what I used to do – buying Bollinger at forty quid a bottle from the supermarket, or in a night club, with two glasses in the other hand, sending out the wrong signals. Great idea at the time but what a misinformed arse!

Selfish is walking past people collecting for a good cause; we've all got change in our pockets if we have a job. Or walking past the genuine beggar usually sat shivering with a blanket, with no thought or time or money to spare. Many I've met are addicts trapped in the hell of addiction, begging for money for their next 'fix'. I've met some so spaced out they couldn't remember me the next time I spoke to them. But even today I can't walk past 'em without rolling up a fag for them, or giving them a pie. Thinking of some words might redeem them, rather than just giving them cash (although many times I do), just in case they *might* use the money to buy drugs from the same sort of arseholes who I've had tools, motorcycles and bikes stolen by in the recent past.

I doubt whether words would redeem those addicted to various substances; words never helped me until I had time to think about them with a clear head somewhere between Faro and Le Havre. Who knows what their demons may be? Who are we to judge? But it won't stop me sparing the time to ask 'em their name and tell 'em mine. I bet there are people who think they are good Christians or Muslims who don't do this but just walk on by; which just illustrates the hypocrisy of organised religion, along with its added hierarchy. A person with real faith doesn't have to tell you: you just see it in them and in what they do.

The bad stuff that happens around the world is because we all have free will, but the good that happens goes unnoticed because bad makes news. The people that gave me the most while I was on my arse up until this year were the ones who had the least. Some were Muslims, some were just good people, and some were Christian, all from various nationalities. I am not religious. I pray and I hope, *but* I wouldn't like to live in a godless world, and I know there is something we don't understand that is greater than us all. I've felt it around me, and you can't buy it or earn it or get it out of privilege or status. How did creation happen by chance if the laws that govern it are ordered? Ask a scientist to explain love.

Of course, maybe you don't agree. Maybe you've never been on your arse and never will be. Maybe you can't think of a time in your life where you have been so hungry that the sight of a bin gets you excited; or slept under plastic sheets; or been desperate for help. I hope you don't: it's not the best place to be. It stopped me complaining and griping about stupid little things that won't be important six months or a year from now. It would be interesting to know the thoughts of dying atheists, by percentage, and see how many have a desperate crafty prayer.

This trip cleansed me of my vices, if only for a while. It just worked for me. I've since been asked, "Why don't you do *normal* things *normal* people do?"

Normal, what's normal? I felt normal eatin' from bins, sleepin' on benches, and ridin' broken bikes.